Social Work and
Social Control

PETER R. DAY

Social Work and
Social Control

TAVISTOCK PUBLICATIONS
LONDON AND NEW YORK

First published in 1981 by
Tavistock Publications Ltd
11 New Fetter Lane, London EC4P 4EE
Published in the USA by
Tavistock Publications
in association with Methuen, Inc.
733 Third Avenue, New York, NY 10017

© 1981 Peter R. Day

Printed in Great Britain by
Richard Clay (The Chaucer Press) Ltd, Bungay, Suffolk

British Library Cataloguing in Publication Data

Day, Peter R
    Social work and social control.
    1. Social service — Great Britain
    2. Social control
    I. Title
    361'.941   HV245   80-41676

    ISBN 0-422-77520-7
    ISBN 0-422-77530-4 Pbk

Contents

Preface

My sincere thanks are due to colleagues in social work including my teachers and students for the encouragement and constructive criticism they have given me. Individuals have a singular responsibility for the books they write but exploring difficult territory is often made easier by the suggestions and guidance of earlier and contemporary explorers whether or not you observe all the directions they have provided. Thus I am indebted to others who will not necessarily agree with the aims and route I have chosen. My partners in this enterprise, the clients and social workers in Probation and After Care and Social Service Departments, have been generous in sharing their ideas and experience with me, and I am grateful to them for discussions which were often illuminating and always interesting. I have taken care to respect their anonymity and I trust that they will find that their views have not been misrepresented. Finally I thank those friends and members of my family for the encouragement they have given consistently over the lengthy period when I have been preoccupied with the controversial topics which are dealt with in this book.

Peter R. Day

1 Introduction

It has been said that the political, social, and ideological place of social work has never been satisfactorily discussed, nor has its possible exploitation as an agent of social control been taken seriously (Bailey and Brake 1975:1). I do not pretend that this book will provide a satisfactory discussion in response to this challenge but the question of social control will certainly be taken seriously. The general question which is the subject of the book is how social workers balance their concern for the welfare of the individual and the welfare of the community, and how their clients see this dual commitment of social work. How do caseworkers perceive the possible conflict between, on the one hand, the development or self-realization of the individual and his or her social adjustment on the other? Do they see, and do their clients see, the 'caring' and 'control' functions as compatible or not, and, if they perceive ambiguity or conflict how do they deal with this? These questions raise moral and political issues and are not susceptible to exclusive empirical invest-igation, although this contributes to an understanding of the problems. This chapter introduces the main themes and terms used later and provides a context in which they will be set. First, the question of the nature of social work will be introduced briefly. The next part of the chapter will deal at greater length with the nature of political activities (social work, I assume, is a political activity) and government. From discussion of social order as a central function of government I take up the problems of deviance and social control. At the end of the chapter I follow up an earlier point about the im-portance of historical perspective in a brief discussion of problems in studying the welfare state and contemporary social work.

The Nature of Social Work

An important aspect of social work which has been consistently expressed in the course of its history is the supreme value placed on individual men or women. their personal development and their contribution to community development. Their importance is stressed within the social context of human interdependence and social solidarity. Among the implications of this problematic dual emphasis — both upon the individual and the social context — is the paramount need for the social worker to cultivate deep sensitivity and the ability to respond to individual and communal needs and the subtleties of communication and control. There is, of course, a political dimension to all this. Totalitarian inhuman societies (and institutions) deny basic human rights and in the present century millions of people have been destroyed for expressing their personal and dissenting views. In a world that is increasingly interdependent sensitivity to individual needs is necessary because of the impact that the words and actions of individuals or small groups may have. It is necessary because of the consequences that the decisions of politicians and policy makers (including social workers) have, sometimes with devastating effect, on the lives of individuals. The emphasis placed on personal development by social workers (who can claim no monopoly in relation to this broad and ill-defined principle) involves them in stressing the dignity of the individual and personal freedom. These principles will be examined and qualified later; a comment made by Schumacher (1977: 39-40) is helpful in underlining the last one. He wrote that:

> 'close observation discloses that most of us, most of the time behave and act mechanically, like a machine. The specifically human power of self-awareness is asleep, and the human being like an animal acts — more or less intelligently — solely in response to outside influences. Only when a man makes use of his power of self-awareness does he attain to the level of a person, to the level of freedom. At that moment he is living, not being lived. There are still numerous forces of necessity, accumulated in the past, which determine his actions; but a small dent is being made, a tiny change of direction is being introduced. It may be virtually unnoticeable, but many moments of self-awareness can produce many such changes and even turn a given movement into the opposite of its previous direction.'

The British Association of Social Workers attempted in 1973 (Discussion Paper No. Three) to 'identify the quintessence of social work ... and what contribution it makes to the life of the community'. Social work was an evolutionary phenomenon with its roots in social philosophies and ethical values. During the previous one hundred years it had developed dramatically in response to profound social changes which had both benefited and burdened the individual. Professional social work could be regarded 'as a spontaneous development, a manifestation of awareness of the need to create a means of protecting and helping those individuals adversely affected by changes which are reshaping society'. Social work exists for the good of individuals and must influence and seek to adjust the social care structure as well as carry out agency policy and function. This dual responsibility, to the individual and to the agencies which have been established to serve him or her, may draw social work into situations of conflict. Its special function is to protect and promote the interests of clients: the community's concern to safeguard and promote the welfare of the individual within society manifests itself in part through social work.

Haines (1975: 1-3) wrote that:

'social work is a human activity in which certain members of society, paid or voluntary, intervene in the lives of others in order to produce change... The aims of men in society are also the aims of social work insofar as its central concerns are basic necessities of life and the regulation of behaviour, but the means employed by its practitioners are influenced by their values and beliefs, which tend to place limits on the methods they use, excluding, for example, warfare and repression. Social work may be said to spring from those means of interaction between human beings designed to bring about change through caring and concern although many of its practitioners do not entirely rule out certain forms of conflict...'

Haines goes on to discuss problems in social life and in relationships with others — remarking that however permissive or repressive the social structure man still finds difficulties in relationships with others, and that the history of the last hundred years has shown that there is a role in society for various experts in human relations.

This account of two approaches to the nature of social work contains a number of points for discussion. They include reference to social work in historical perspective, to its underlying ideologies and values, and to social work as a response to, as well as an agency of, change in society. Of particular importance in the present context there are references to social workers' dual concern for individual and community welfare and to social work being involved in the regulation of behaviour. These points will be taken up again but I will now discuss the roles of government and social institutions in maintaining social order and promoting social change.

Politics, Government, and the State

If one asks what is meant by activities such as politics and social work one obtains a range of answers, from descriptions of what people think social workers and politicians *do* to more abstract definitions. Social work is not alone in being difficult to define. It is something to do with welfare and with helping people. Politics is about what political parties try to do but people also talk about politics in the context of managing or directing organizations or moving people towards particular aims. Sometimes these activities are described as if they involve rather suspect or manipulative behaviour: they are rather dirty words. In discussing social work and politics together I am assuming that they are associated in real life, that social work is a political activity or that social work acts have political implications. This is too general a statement but it is not easy to qualify it and make it more precise, and both in everyday life and in literature we often allow such generalizations to pass and thus avoid the need for further analysis. For the moment I propose to look more closely at the meaning of politics, leaving the nature of social work until later. What is politics about? Political activity is specifically about the way that an organization or group is run, and therefore about who has the power to get things done. Politics is to do with the way that social life is regulated, ordered, or changed: it is about government, although not everything to do with government is regarded as being the concern of politicians. A strictly political act is something more than the performance of an agreed routine task. It is to do with disagreement.

The analysis of social order in sociological theory depends on terms like power, authority, and control. The relationship between legitimacy and control is fundamental: in general, legitimacy refers to the rules, beliefs, and practices in a society or community which form its basic order, and the concept may also be used in discussing smaller social units, for example an occupational group. The legitimacy of a particular set of beliefs and practices depends on the support of a dominant group but there are invariably competing accounts of legitimate methods of dealing with certain events or problems. Power is usually identified with the possibility of coercion by military or police forces or with administrative bureaucracy. Unlike the authority which arises directly from social function and association, it raises the problem of legitimacy. Some actions once regarded as threats to the authority of the state, for example the right to take industrial action, which was a punishable offence, became legitimate as workers gained acceptance for their views. The use of coercive measures such as military or police force is usually unnecessary in most areas of social life. Less dramatic forces of social legitimation found in major institutions like the church, education, the mass media, and the law are sufficient to protect the interests of dominant groups (Berger 1971:51). Authority refers to the social power that an individual or group believes to be legitimate. Those who recognize the authority believe that it is justified and the exercise of authority is then likely to be effective in achieving its aims. The nature and extent of authority exercised in a society has important consequences for the kind of social order existing in that society (Nisbet 1967:6).

A song which was Top of the Pops in 1979 gave expression to the view of social control as a sinister and dirty word for a wholly unacceptable aspect of education as an instrument of public policy. 'We don't need no education' (although grammatically an affirmation of establishment or right-wing ideology the lyric was plainly intended to point to its opposite) continued 'we don't need no thought control', and 'teacher, leave them kids alone'. The film accompanying the song was rich in imagery, large hammers descending on groups of children, and a high brick wall encircling them as the lyric continued. The most powerful sequences though were shots of the school children who were singing the doleful words to an appropriately menacing tune. It was a particularly interesting example of a protest song about the manipulation of school children – and it aimed to manipulate children. It thus raised ethical questions about influence and control. For example, is it desirable that song-writers or other mass communicators should encourage children to believe that they 'don't need no education' because it is solely an instrument of repression and that teachers' social control function is to induce unreflective conformity to the status quo? My reaction is reflected in the question and in my answer which is that this form of manipulation seemed to me to be wrong in principle. More concretely it seemed a crude and cynical misreading or misrepresentation of the social function of education, and represented a partial view of a politically extreme kind. I felt sympathy for the teaching profession because of the way it was denigrated and, again, crudely misrepresented. This is not to assert that teachers are all benevolent or that they all see their role(s) in a naive way, or that all teachers reflect on them in depth. However, the roles of teachers and social workers have points of similarity and this was one reason for attending to the message of the song. Second, it serves to introduce discussion of such concepts as influence, control, and legitimation.

It is a platitude that government obtains its justification from its capacity to keep order. There is a lack of capacity for agreement and cooperation in modern society (and this becomes clearer the more developed society is). This requires the maintenance of institutions which will keep the peace between different interests and provide for sharing of resources. Government is also the means whereby interests compete for the satisfaction of their demands and is the source of recognition of their diversity: this is a further justification for its indispensability. Fortes and Evans-Pritchard (1940) in defining the study of political organization wrote that 'we have to deal with the maintenance or establishment of social order, within a territorial framework, by the organized exercise of coercive authority through the use or the possibility of use, of physical force.' Their definition thus comprehends the extreme sanction of coercive authority and its role in social order. From the point of view of external observation a society can be seen to consist of a framework of associations, groups, and institutions. Here the emphasis is on society as essentially a regulated (or moral) order. Underlying this are the values and sanctions which are simultaneously (a) the core of regulations in the framework of social institutions itself and (b) the core of regulation in the experience and behaviour of individuals. These values and sanctions are easily seen as parts of the pattern of social control. But this is not to say that social order and society are entirely synonymous. Political dissent is said to be tolerated in Britain but a strong argument can be made out for regarding tolerance as very unstable. The open discussion of dissident views is tolerated while the dominant groups in society feel that their material interests are secure and while they feel that these views carry little weight. But when established norms are seriously threatened freedom of expression is quickly sacrificed to the demands of order (Arblaster 1974:24).

As well as being aided by the agencies of force control in society is maintained through the production of ideas which embody and project the social structure. This aspect of legitimation is referred to as ideology. The term ideology has been used in a variety of ways by social scientists and has been given a number of meanings: clarification is difficult. Zijderweld (1974:143) wrote:

'Emotions are not kept under rational control exclusively. They may also rationalise themselves into symbolic systems. Rationalised emotions are usually called ideologies. An ideology is a rational defence of certain interests that are based on emotionally and irrationally adhered to positions. Asked for his logical rationale the ideologist, pressed hard enough, can only point at some emotionally held 'convictions', 'beliefs', or 'dreams'. This point is quite important, since ideologies are often institutionally disguised, functioning as semi-rational but fundamentally irrational legitimations of the actions undertaken by certain interest groups. Institutions are ... models of rationality, but they often hide an ideological and thus irrational content. For that reason, an age of institutional crisis in which man turns inward to his irrational subjectivity has to be an age of flourishing ideologies.'

Berger, Berger, and Kellner (1974:143) discussed ideologies in their analysis of modernization and its institutions. They analysed how modernization, particularly technology, far from liberating human beings, had increased their feelings of helplessness, frustration, and alienation. One level of deliberate and systematic reflection they referred to as ideology, noting the number of meanings given to it in the social sciences referred to above. They distinguished three different types of ideological response to modernization.

'First there are ideologies that directly endorse or legitimate modernization. Next there are ideologies developed in opposition or resistance to modernization: these might be called counter-modernization ideologies. Third, and most important of all today, there are ideologies that seek to control or contain modernization in the name of values that are conceived to be independent of that process.'

The quotations given illustrate points made by Nisbet (1967:16 and 22) who sees ideologies as 'seedbeds of doctrinal and conceptual issues'. Nisbet also notes that 'the relation between events and ideas is never direct: it is always mediated by *conceptions* of the events. The role of moral evaluation of political ideology, is therefore crucial'. It will also be seen that the content of ideologies may be varied but they are often religious or political; they may be conservative or revolutionary in character and concerned to maintain or change the status quo.

Ideology was important in Marx's analysis of capitalist social organization; it implied a distortion in beliefs, a separation of so-called 'real' and actual interests. It represented one distorted form of class consciousness and was part of the 'superstructure' of society. Aron (1968:177) wrote that: 'In general Marx understood by "ideology" the false consciousness or the false image a social class has of its own situation and of society as a whole. To a large extent, he regarded the theories of the bourgeois economists as a class ideology.' Writing on the process of alienation Bottomore and Rubel (1963:21) referred to ideology as a system of beliefs: 'Marx's concept of "false consciousness" and "ideology" are related to the concept of "alienation". False consciousness is the consciousness of individuals in a condition of alienation, and ideology is the system of beliefs produced by such a false consciousness.' Geertz (in Apter 1964:47-76) discussed how the contents of ideologies are formulated and wrote: 'the form ideologies take cannot be explained simply in terms of the functions they perform...the link between the causes of an ideology and its consequences too often seems adventitious because the connecting element, the autonomous process of symbolic formulation is neglected.' He analysed two main approaches to the study of the social determinants of ideology which he referred to as the 'interest theory' which regarded ideology as a mask and a weapon and the 'strain theory' which regarded ideology as a symptom and a remedy.

In times of economic and social crisis or considerable change there are strong pressures on government to exercise discipline and regulations so that freedom of action is more constrained. Those in power are likely to make greater use of the communication media in relating to the public in order to shape public opinion towards supporting the 'law and order' ideology. This may be illustrated by considering the relationship between the government and the police during the late 1970s. Examples of regulation by other bodies could be found of course but the police force clearly has a role in law enforcement, itself a controversial topic. Demands for 'more law and order' and the move towards more discipline and stronger authority are reflected in the increase in relevant legislation during 1978-80. The factors in the return of this ideology are complex but it is partly rooted in the increased power and intervention by the state and it finds its rationale in a return to a traditionalist morality and an unqualified respect for authority as ways of resolving social tensions. For the police it is increasingly the 'public order' role which receives publicity and most clearly aligns them with the interests of the state and the status quo. A distinction is not always made between the functions of government in law making and the functions of organizations responsible for implementing legislation and carrying out duties placed on them by society. The police, of course, are inevitably implicated in debates about law and order but their contribution needs to be clearly defined. They have views about how to carry out their responsibilities and government ministers consult them about their work. But the police are one example of a potentially powerful ideological force. In taking part in public debate about law and order, senior policemen have the opportunity to influence the legislators and public opinion.

The distinction to which I referred above can then become blurred. As establishment figures it is expected and understandable that policemen have conservative views on issues that arise concerning law and order such as methods of policing and methods of dealing with offenders. Senior police officers rightly have views about sentencing policies as well as police practices. What is questionable is whether it is altogether right that their personal, often conservative opinions, and their views as professionals, should be blurred. The problem then is whether it is desirable for the police to be an active law and order lobby, or an ideological force which mobilizes public opinion. This role seems to have been assumed by the Police Federation which functions as a professional body giving expert help on policing problems but in addition acts as a militant law and order

campaigning force. It is in exercising this influence that the distinction between social and political impartiality in law enforcement and
public involvement in shaping opinion becomes ill defined, and it is
not entirely clear to whom the police are accountable. The function
of the Special Patrol Group for example seems to have changed
considerably since they were reorganized in 1972, from being an
anti-crime squad to being a highly equipped force to maintain public
order. This is the point made by Miller (1965:14) who wrote:

> 'The essence of a political situation, as opposed to one of agree-
> ment and routine, is that someone is trying to do something
> about which there is not agreement, and is trying to use some
> form of government as a means and as protection. Political
> situations arise out of disagreement ... Government is routine up
> to the point where someone questions it and tries to change it;
> then it ceases to be routine and becomes a political situation. The
> questioner may be silenced or he may prevail, or some way may
> be found of satisfying him by a change in procedure. Whatever
> happens, political activity will have begun at the point where he
> objected and ceased when quiet is resumed. Politics is about
> policy, first and foremost, and policy is a matter of either the
> desire for change or the desire to protect something against
> change. But it need not be ... the policy of some party or set
> of ministers or mass movement; it may be the policy of a small
> group in or out of the government or even of a single man... Nor
> need it be some policy which embraces the whole life of the
> country; it can be the wish for the smallest change in a regulation
> or even in the administration of a regulation.'

Although attempts to define the term 'State' or to discover a
theory which can comprehend the obscure and mysterious processes
of government appear rather unfruitful (Poulantzas in Blackburn
1976:238-41) it is possible to describe some of their features. One is
obviously the mystique of authority: the assumption that the citizen
cannot understand how public affairs are ordered, since they are so
complex. But Miller (1965:131-34) points out some of the opportunities open to the state which 'is less limited in the exercise of
power than any other institution'. It can make war and peace with
other states, it can levy taxes on its citizens, make laws to regulate
their lives, educate them; it has more power over persons and groups
than any other body. In society you find a plurality of opinions and

a range of interests which he describes as a kaleidoscope of shifting purposes which may fall into recognizable patterns for a time but which are subject to change as the basic inequalities in society alter. He continues:

> 'it seems to me irrefutable that governments by virtue of their special position as the preservers of public order and the only authorities which can make binding laws, are besieged by a variety of interests, all demanding more than, in total, the government can provide. It is inevitable, in these conditions, that governments will try to find, at the very least, principles of rationing what there is to go round.'

The question of provision and rationing of resources will be referred to again but first there are further points to be discussed in relation to maintaining public order.

Deviance and Social Control

Social control is a term which will be used and discussed at several points later in this book. It was first used by Ross, an American sociologist, in a book first published in 1901 (Ross 1969). It has come to mean any social mechanism by which individuals are compelled to keep to the rules of society or their part of society. Basically, then, it refers to concern with the way order and stability in a society are possible and what conditions may facilitate or affect social change. Two perspectives on social control are important in the present work. (a) The view that emphasizes the integrative and consensual nature of much of social behaviour. It places less emphasis on coercion or deliberate influence and it should be noted that these two kinds of processes will be explored later in more detail. (b) The view that social life is not harmonious particularly in modern capitalist societies. In common with other terms considered in this book, deviance is not susceptible to easy definition. The extent to which deviant behaviour is disruptive of social organization and how far it can make important contributions to the vitality and efficiency of organized social life is only beginning to be explored, for example. Provisionally, however, deviant behaviour can be regarded as behaviour that violates normative rules, although this statement is not free of ambiguity (Cohen 1966:24). However it enables us to proceed to an analysis of conceptions of deviance.

One conception of deviant behaviour is known as the welfare model. According to this such behaviour is seen as a public social problem for which some remedial, correctional, or therapeutic intervention is required to alter, modify, or control the deviant and his behaviour. Although there may be disagreements about its cause (such as heredity, social environment, or childhood experience) the basic assumption is unequivocal. Deviant behaviour is bad and it is a public responsibility to do something about it and the individuals involved. Another basic assumption is that the deviant is seen as being different and it is his or her behaviour which needs to be explained and not taken for granted like normal behaviour. By finding explanations and thus accounting for the difference and 'normalizing' the deviant behaviour it is defined as abnormal. The main aim of this kind of account is to translate the deviant behaviour into an indicator or manifestation of the person's essential self. The deviant is thus regarded as having a defective self. To summarize, the welfare model has three main features. First, it sees deviant behaviour as a public problem existing outside the framework of normal social life; second, it considers this behaviour to be an expression of a deviant self different from that of the normal person; third, it promotes efforts to account for and correct this difference. Deviants are approached from an individualistic, psychological, and rehabilitative framework (Horowitz and Liebowitz 1968).

Another conception of deviant behaviour originated with the work of Durkheim. It says that the conditions for the emergence of deviant behaviour are inherent in the social structure. A typology developed by Merton (1968) emphasized the structural inconsistencies between cultural goals and institutional means. Cohen (1955) attempted to explain working-class delinquency using the concepts of class structure, status frustration, and subculture. Cloward and Ohlin (1960) introduced the notion of opportunity structures and like Cohen attempted to integrate psychological concepts in the social structure framework. Like the welfare model the structural model regards deviant behaviour as an easy problem to locate and describe. In addition it sometimes depends on psychological factors, for example individual frustration and reaction formation. It differs from the welfare model in viewing deviant behaviour as an expression of a faulty social structure and not a defective self. The model consequently promotes structural and policy changes rather than individual and psychological ones. Another model first developed by Durkheim was the functionalist. Durkheim (Wolfgang, Savitz, and Johnston 1962:10) said that crime, the most well-known form of deviant behaviour, presented all the symptoms of normality since it appeared closely connected with the conditions of all collective life. He said that the existence of criminality was normal provided it did not exceed a certain level. He continued: 'Crime is then necessary; it is bound up with the fundamental conditions of all social life and by that very fact it is useful because these conditions of which it is part are themselves indispensable to the normal evolution of morality and law.' Later expositions of the functionalist approach elaborated on deviance as activity 'which is generally thought to require the attention of social control agencies'. Erikson (Becker 1964:13-15) referred to the importance of boundary maintenance in the social system and the way people relate their behaviour to those boundaries. 'The only material found in a system for marking boundaries ... is the behaviour of its participants; and the kinds of behaviour which best perform this function are often deviant ... In this sense transactions taking place between deviant persons on the one side and agencies of control on the other are boundary maintaining mechanisms.' Deviance cannot be dismissed simply as behaviour which disrupts stability in society, but may itself be, in controlled quantities, an important condition for preserving stability. The functionalist model is a radical departure from the welfare model in its assumption that deviant behaviour may lend stability to a system rather than just be an expression of a defective self or a sick society.

The societal reaction model regarded deviant behaviour as a social category created by responses to certain kinds of behaviour. From the point of view of this model those attempting to change behaviour they saw as undesirable might play a significant part in maintaining the behaviour they try to eradicate. Becker (1963:9) said that:

'social groups create deviance by making the rules whose infraction constitutes deviance and by applying those rules to particular people and labelling them as outsiders. From this point of view, deviance is not a quality of the act the person commits, but rather a consequence of the application by others of rules and sanctions to an "offender". The deviant is one to whom that label has successfully been applied: deviant behaviour is behaviour that people so label.'

Cohen (1966:11-12) said that 'the label ... does more than signify one who has committed such and such a deviant act. Each label evokes a characteristic imagery. It suggests someone who is normally or habitually given to certain kinds of deviance; who may be expected to behave in this way; who is literally a bundle of odious or sinister qualities.' The deviant label comes to be used as a status that solves major problems of interaction by providing an overriding or salient definition of the person that can organize or structure interaction. Rule-breaking behaviour is taken for granted; the model focuses on what society makes of rule breaking and under what circumstances it reacts to it. In addition the model analyses the transformation that occurs of deviant act into deviant actor (Becker 1963:9).

A number of views of deviant behaviour and its relationship to control have been outlined and again terms used later in the book have been mentioned, for example social structure and the self. I will return to the relationship between the individual and society shortly and the two perspectives on social control described briefly here will also be developed later in the book.

The Welfare State and Social Work

In order to understand the problems of the Welfare State today and the state of social work theory and practice we should take account of their historical development. Without some understanding of the historical background, implications of contemporary policies and practices may not be perceived, or may be seen in a partial way, thus leading to prescriptions that have little regard for an analytical and factual basis. Parry, Rustin, and Satyamurti (1979:161) wrote that practical stances 'which disregard deeply entrenched cultural and structural formations are not likely to amount to very much. Programmes deriving from fashionably theoretical systems (the way the Seebohm changes were implemented is a case in point) formulated with scant interest in the facts of social work practice, are unlikely to realise their objectives.' These writers provide a volume of essays aimed at providing a structural and historical framework within which to situate modern social work and a variety of political viewpoints is represented. The essays indicate how the state mediates and conditions the relationship between social workers and clients and controls the role of the former in contemporary society. They are, therefore, an important source for the present writer. Saville (in Butterworth and Holman 1975:57-70) wrote:

> 'The Welfare State ... has come about as a result of the inter-action of three main factors: (1) the struggle of the working class against their exploitation, (2) the requirements of industrial capi-talism (a convenient abstraction) for a more efficient environ-ment in which to operate and in particular the need for a highly productive labour force, (3) recognition by the property owners of the price that has to be paid for political security.'

He concluded: 'The Welfare State is the twentieth century version of the Victorian ideal of self help ... The State now "saves" for the working class and translates the savings into social services.'

Marshall (1972) pointed out that:

> 'from the point of view of the consumer of welfare services there are two main ways in which it may be thought that the authori-tarian or paternal character of welfare must do him injury, namely by limiting his scope for the exercise of choice and by weakening his initiative and self reliance. Obviously there are values at stake here, the values of freedom and independence, both of which have a crucial role to play in the democratic and the "capitalist" components of the composite society. So there is bound to be conflict but at what level? It is not, as I see it, in the nature of a head-on clash between irreconcilable beliefs or of a contest seen by each side as a battle between good and evil. Welfare recognises the values of freedom and independence, not only in the abstract but in its daily work, and the champions of these values know that without some curtailment of them, welfare could not meet its responsibilities. You cannot make the optimum use of scarce skills and resources in a nation wide service open to all if you allow every applicant for its help to pick and choose where he pleases. In some cases like primary schools choice is geographically limited; in others the knowledge on which a rational choice can be made is lacking. So the issue is one of balance and proportion, of deciding how much freedom of choice can be provided for...'

Major issues of value are involved. Quantitative change inevitably leads to qualitative change as could be seen in discussions about cuts in educational services in 1979. Medical care and education are obvi-ously areas in which differences of opportunity do more to create and sustain class distinctions than any other.

Debates and conflicts about the administration of the personal social services, and their aims and methods, are continuous, and of course, they are not morally or politically neutral. This can be seen for example in debates about social security systems which could make the 'best' use of available resources but are rejected because means tests are involved and offend the idea of human dignity. Similarly an economic policy which at first seemed acceptable might be rejected because it would cause an unpalatably high level of unemployment. Care and control can be seen as complementary aspects of public policy towards the poor and deviant. It is argued that these two elements, originally separately institutionalized, have converged in the role of local authority social workers. The implications for local authority social workers, it is suggested, are that it is difficult to reconcile care and control, humane objectives and statutory duties, and this has been partly responsible for the 'crisis in social work' and social workers have to find ways to survive (Satyamurti 1979:90-6). In his book on the moral and social presuppositions of casework, Plant (1970:1) argued that caseworkers, because they are involved with the welfare of the individual and with the welfare of society, need to be very clear about the relationship between the individual and society. As he points out the elucidation of this relationship is far from easy, and it raises questions about problems which may arise if the welfare of the individual and the interests of the community conflict, and whether care and control are equally important in social work.

The experience of these questions of care and control by clients and the dilemmas raised for social workers and how they deal with them are the concern of this book, but it is clear that they need to be analysed further with a view to making them more manageable and less vague. Statements about helping activities, which include social work, and their relation to social control require consideration: as Halmos (1965:177-78) suggested the myth of non-directiveness is exploded because therapists and social workers influence patients and other citizens. Directiveness is one kind of influence among many at the level of face-to-face interaction and different kinds of influence and control operate at different levels of society and are communicated in different ways in the social system. Although different caseworkers have different views on trying to develop their client's understanding of their situations and the bringing about of emotional and cognitive changes in clients (and/or in the client's environment and situation) one suggestion that can be examined is that the client comes to perceive the caseworker as a benign figure (or benign parent figure) who can be trusted and to see the relationship as compounded of mutual respect. Just as the parent continues to be loved when the child's idealization of him or her is modified so the effective teacher or caseworker who is directive and sets limits to the client's behaviour continues to be liked and trusted. Another problem to be examined is the idea that caseworkers do not resolve the apparent contradictions involved in providing caring relationships and in explicitly or implicitly giving moral guidance or providing a model of desirable or appropriate behaviour. If they cannot how do they come to terms with it? The third set of problems, associated with the other two, are those concerned with the political and wider implications of caseworkers' roles. Is it possible to identify different casework or social work ideologies? If it is what are their implications for practice? In his vivid study of client-social worker relationships Rees (1978:1) asked some social workers and clients to explain what they thought was occurring in their face-to-face exchanges and what significance they attached to them in relation to other events in their lives. In attempting to identify the meaning of social work on both sides, and of clients' assessments of social work help, he was exploring largely undocumented aspects of social work. This does not entirely apply to the present book which, while it has points in similarity with Rees' work, deals with rather different questions about social work activity. But, like Rees, I claim that the interpretations made here have significance beyond the details of a single encounter.

Society, Community, and the Individual

Since the main focus of this work is the relationship between individuals and their society it may be helpful to recapitulate and develop some ideas discussed in earlier sections. In considering influences on human behaviour we often refer to the society into which individuals are born or the social framework within which they grow and develop. This has its own sets of beliefs, values, attitudes, and ways of thinking and behaving. It contains a variety of social groups such as families, schools, work places, and so on; it is thus an idea involving complex relationships but it stands for a definite distinct set of constituents. The social framework consists of components which serve to regulate behaviour, and affect the ways meanings and values are experienced and conceived by individuals. Society comes into being over a period of time and as it changes new ways of describing experience and social life have to be found: this historical perspective needs to be borne in mind in analysing the influence of social change on individuals and social institutions, although reference to history will be brief in this work. The term society, then, refers to large scale, impersonal, contractual bonds between people; it is an abstract term and connotes structure or mechanism. The whole of society is large and complex and beyond the individual's knowledge but he or she comes to terms with it and discovers some very specific aspects of it in his or her family and school and the economic system. They are all definite organizations (or consist of definite organizations) and the individual finds that as well as offering channels for relationships with others they have rules or traditions which constrain behaviour. The term community is also an important one: it includes the local community and also comprehends religion, work, family, and culture. It refers to social bonds characterized by emotional cohesion, depth, and continuity. The idea of community indicates closer personal relationships than society which, as indicated above, is more impersonal. The uses of the terms are distinct but they overlap in that the social units which they contain are described under both headings but in different ways. Community can be taken to refer to 'real' and organic life and society as imaginary and mechanical structure. (This is how Tonnies distinguished them. See Abraham 1977:244-45.)

Durkheim (Brown and Stevens 1975:133) wrote:

'There is in every society a certain group of phenomena which may be differentiated from those studied by the other natural sciences. When I fulfil my obligations as brother, husband or citizen, when I execute my contracts, I perform duties which are defined externally to myself and my acts in law and custom. Even if they conform to my own sentiments and I feel their value subjectively, such reality is still objective for I did not create them; I merely inherited them through my education.'

The social system is perceived subjectively and symbolically by those who live in it. The individual experiences and accommodates him- or herself to the elements of social structure in developing from birth to adulthood. It is not necessarily assumed that the personality is determined by them but that the individual is affected in one way or another. A social institution is an observed regularity in behaviour which the outside observer may perceive as useful or necessary to social survival. It is also a regularity which is perceived by those who conform to it and which they can discuss in terms of its purpose in their society. The institutions of society are in process because in and through them sequences of events occur and because institutions, and the regularities of behaviour entailed, alter and involve different parts of society in complex ways. One reason for the complexity of these subjects is found in the way elements of social structure are interconnected although often they are spoken of separately. Some aspects of society are referred to as 'economic' and some as 'educational', yet the organization of government for example is clearly a politically constituted system in which the legislature, the civil service, the judiciary, and so on are all related. This applies also to the legal system and the economic system, while marriage is a religious, legal, familial, economic, and political institution. Society, then, is a total framework of experience and behaviour and possesses some qualities which are pervasive. The extent to which parts of the whole are separated out is largely a matter of conceptual, theoretical, and ideological convenience for description, analysis, and explanation.

Accounts of the development of individuals including their personalities are usually found to refer to and incorporate elements of experience of society. It is necessary to conceive of the gradual structured awareness of society which is essential for the process of the creation of the individual's self. 'The self is essentially a social structure and it arises in social experience. After a self has arisen it, in a certain sense, provides for itself its social experiences and so we can conceive of an absolutely solitary self. But it is impossible to conceive of a self arising outside of social experience' (Mead, in Strauss 1964:204). For the purpose of the present work it is particularly important to recognize the seemingly simple idea that human beings respond to the actions of one another in ways based on the meaning they give to their actions. Human interaction then is facilitated by the communication of verbal and non-verbal symbols, by interpreting them and by trying to understand the meaning of one another's actions. It is important to recognize too that the human being is conscious of self-hood and can be the object of his own actions. He can act towards himself as he might act towards others. Conscious life is a continuous stream of interpretations of signals and symbols and their meanings for the self. The problem of the meaning of meaning has a long history in philosophy and it has central importance in interactionist theory. What may have meaning for an actor may be a situation, act, idea, or object; meaning is established only where the response elicited by a symbol is the 'same' for the one who receives it. Meanings form part of the structure of a society as they exist before and apart from any individual actor. They derive from society, its language and its institutions, and through interaction men modify, change, and transform social meanings (Rose 1962:129 and 590).

The subject of this book requires examination of different theoretical and philosophical approaches relevant to behaviour regarded as deviant, and social work practice. There are various views on the nature of social work practice and a range of theories can be applied to it. The theoretical basis of social work consists of knowledge of social structure and institutions, social policy and social services as well as information about individual and group behaviour. It is not at all easy to link these components in a coherent way nor is it always possible to see how they complement each other. Social workers face uncertainty in trying to help other people in situations or with problems which are not going to be 'solved' but which care, concern, and understanding might make more bearable; being physically or mentally handicapped, or being related to a handicapped person or coping with a range of other deficiences are examples. Involvement with people in need of material help or needing psychological help because of emotional and relationship problems sometimes leads social workers into situations that are controversial. Social work is carried on in a social and political context and the worker may be required to seek compromises when 'ideal solutions' are not available. This is another source of difficulty. It may not be possible for the social worker to assume the role of arbitrator although self-awareness may lead the worker to an understanding of others' roles and attitudes as well as his or her own reactions. Political skills may be needed and some social workers are more effective in this field than others. Further, they adopt a variety of political stances but they share awareness of the complexity of contemporary social and political problems.

The aims of social work are often ill-defined or at least difficult to articulate as many attempts at definition illustrate. If the task in general is one of interaction, in being involved with people needing material resources, or requiring psychological help because of emotional and relationship problems, it needs to be seen in relation to the political and social context of practice. If practice is aimed at changing balances between individuals and social institutions static or closed systems of ideas will not be relevant. They need to relate to individuals' life styles which change over time and differ among cultures. Social work involves processes of influence. The social sciences themselves are at an early stage of development and unfortunately one of the least developed areas is the analysis of interpersonal influence. Since social work often involves attempts to change relationships between individuals and social institutions, and may also attempt to facilitate changes in individuals and institutions a degree of openness and dynamism is required of ideas and theories to apply in practice. They need to be relevant to changes in individuals' life styles and the different social institutions and their cultural bases, which are also changing. Although there have been changes of emphasis in the history of social work one configuration, the 'person in the situation', has consistently been a unit for attention. Again there can be no total and final explanation of this notion. Personality theory has made its contribution. To understand the social situation it is necessary to draw on fragmented theories of social role, social class, social problems, and systems theory. Systems theory, it is sometimes claimed, has provided the framework for a reconceptualization of knowledge in reciprocal terms. This seems questionable since personality and social theories are at different stages of development and levels of abstraction; to speak of a unifying theory is debatable to say the least and social work is not to me a unified profession.

Some aspects of theories are thus more highly valued or seem more relevant to practice than others. An obvious test of relevance is whether a theory assists social workers in understanding how most people develop and cope with their lives. Social pressures, environmental limitations, and emotional problems place limits on people's development and their capacity to realize their potential. To gain some understanding of failure to adapt successfully theory needs to account for the continuum from health to illness and from ability to cope to inability and demoralization. An important aspect of methods of study of social interaction has been the tendency to focus on behaviour, influence, and other variables on the level of common experience with them. Empirical research uses observations from a selected part of 'everyday life'. It thus tends towards observation in some form rather than experimentation. A second well-known characteristic is the assumption that behaviour and social life are constantly changing. Third it is assumed that social phenomena are interpreted by the individual and have social meaning. The associated assumption is that man lives in a symbolic environment. It is reprehensible to ignore a range of relevant perspectives on human social behaviour and it is very naive to deny that it can be avoided altogether. Social psychology is a helpful discipline, possibly insufficiently exploited by social workers, which aims at integration of knowledge of the psychological functioning of individuals in the large and small social settings in which they live. Analysis has to comprehend individual behaviour as it derives from the social context and as it acts on that context.

Two major themes are discernible in interactionist theory. One is through the study of the socialization of the individual and is social psychological in focus. This is sometimes called 'symbolic interaction theory'. The second is through the study of social organizations and social processes and may be seen as mainly a sociological study. The two themes are interrelated so that distinguishing them is not always easy. While it is a central concern of sociology social control may be studied at a variety of levels from socialization in the family to larger reference groups and institutions such as the legal system. This approach to the study of reciprocal relationships between individuals has not developed as a separate school but has remained an open system of ideas in sociology and social psychology, and it thus satisfies the requirement of dynamism stated above, at least to some degree. By the time this book reaches readers there will no doubt have been shifts in perspectives on the uncertainties and problems sketched here. In sharing some of the current difficulties, we may hope to make a contribution to the continuing debate while reviewing the different perspectives which will be contributed by others.

This book has two features.

(1) Evidence about the views of clients and social workers on care and control and what the social work relationship means to them.

(2) Discussion and analysis of wider questions concerning ideological

perspectives and controversies which appear to affect social work practice.

Studies on consumers' views are reviewed (Chapter Two) and results of a study of the views of probationers and probation officers are reported (Chapters Three and Five). Social work in Social Service Departments and the relationship between the organzational context and social work practice is studied (in part of Chapter Four). Under the second main heading above wider questions have been raised in this chapter and they are developed in later discussion of social work practice and processes of influence and coercion (in part of Chapter Four). Clients' and social workers' views on the directive aspect of social work and its constructive and unconstructive uses are analysed. The problem of the use of deterministic theories and the question of client self-determination are difficult problems which are also dealt with (Chapter Five). Analysis of the concepts of social order, social interaction, and social work (Chapter Six) is a step towards further discussion of the care and control dilemma (in the last chapter) and arguments for supporting a modified form of the consensus view of social life and personal and social problems, in contrast with the conflict view, as a philosophical base for social work.

2 Consumers' Views
on Social Agencies

This chapter reviews some assumptions about the client's situation and related attitudes which have influenced social work practice. It reviews some consumer attitudes from the United States and Britain and deals with client's expectations of probation. I outline a project on how probationers and probation officers perceived the purposes of probation and their views of and attitudes to 'care' in the light of their experience. Findings from this study will be reported and discussed in more detail later.

Assumptions about Clients of Social Agencies

The purpose of this section is to review some assumptions made about social workers' clients to be found in the literature. This provides both descriptions ('people coming to an agency are under stress') and explanations ('because of cultural and psychological factors'). The researchers have not tested a number of similar assertions although they could be tested, but work on consumers' expectations and views has gradually increased, as the account in this chapter shows. The assumptions that have been made about clients seem to be plausible and therefore worth re-interpreting here. I want to examine the idea that being a recipient of service (or a potential recipient) or being in a subordinate position raises psychological difficulties for most people. There is a danger that roles will be misperceived in the initial contact between worker and client. The social worker may see his role as exploratory while the client expects 'help' from the beginning, in the course of the initial interviews. Towle (1957:60-1), in a publication for public assistance workers in the USA which had great interest for social workers generally, discussed the subject in detail. Towle said that for the most part the services for which people seek help in public assistance represent a failure in their expectations of themselves and in the community's expectation of them. Help is taken with more humiliation, fear of social consequences, resentment, and resistance than ordinarily occurs in other professional services. Applicants feel a potentially demoralizing degree of humiliation and obligation. In trying to diminish such feelings it is known that the individual is motivated to self-dependence through the maintenance and restoration of his or her feelings of self-respect and in trying to cope with stresses out of hope and confidence rather than out of despair and self-depreciation. To feel excessively and shamefully dependent is to feel helpless, worthless and resentful. Resentment may lead a person to become dependent out of fear or of retaliation against the helper, while feelings of inadequacy may lead to inability or unwillingness to cope.

The assumption by the client that he has to accept a dependent role often leads to ambivalent feelings. He wishes to be autonomous and self-dependent but at the same time he wants help. So his self-image is called in question. This conflict is illustrated by the refusal of sick people to seek treatment and by the way old people refuse help, sometimes literally to the point of death. Adults often have great difficulty in accepting a dependent role. When a client comes to perceive his role more clearly and sees that the social worker wishes to encourage independence his ambivalence may be reduced. This also applies to clients who want a dependent role and try to project all responsibility on to the worker. A number of casework theorists have discussed this subject and Butrym (1976:95) points out its importance:

'the preoccupation with the meaning of experience inherent in social work which emphasizes the importance of the "how" as well as the "what" makes it imperative to pay serious attention to the effects that "being helped" have on the individual. It is not only whether or not a social worker has succeeded in securing a badly needed "commodity" for his client which counts. Equally important is whether the acquisition of what was needed and desired has been a positive personal experience, enhancing his sense of self respect and worth and giving added confidence for future living, or whether it has had the opposite effect of undermining him further, making him feel barely tolerated or pitied, a social liability carried grudgingly but inevitably by a "responsible society" through its social work agent.'

Discussing the nature of the difficulties, Butrym refers to the nature of the need and the threat it constitutes to a person's well being as a major factor which influences the degree of vulnerability. Social values with regard to different kinds of problem are of major importance. On the whole being in need of medical care is more socially acceptable in our society than needing help with an unruly child. Previous experience of dependency also influences how a person views and approaches his or her current need for help. Developing these points in a discussion of the way emotions operate in determining responses to helping efforts Towle explored the concept of ambivalence in relation to social services and human needs. She said that it would be much easier to understand and help people if they always felt decidedly in favour of or definitely against a situation, a person, or a course of action. It is probable that they more often simultaneously feel two ways. Consequently, love and hate, attraction and repulsion, daring and fear, go hand in hand. As a result of this two-way pull, individuals may shift back and forth in their actions and decisions. Or at times, when both sets of feelings are equally strong, they may be indecisive or blocked in action. As we focus on understanding emotions we soon realize that both positive and negative feelings occur in close interplay. It is not uncommon for applicants for public assistance to have two-way feelings about their experience.

On the one hand the individual may feel relieved, even gratified that there is an agency to which he can turn in time of need and an understanding worker upon whom he can depend for competent guidance. On the other hand he may resent and fear this agency. He may be fearful that his need will not be met or that, if it is met, he will be unduly obligated so that he will have to pay the exorbitant price of having the management of his affairs taken out of his hands. He may resent his predicament and feel hostile towards those with whom he must share it. His initial response may be one of dislike for the worker, in whose eyes he feels ashamed because he himself finds his situation humiliating. It is because of these complex feelings which public assistance recipients commonly bring to application experience that helping each individual establish his eligibility is not a routine clerical task if it is helpfully performed. At such a time, when a worker fails to understand, feelings of humiliation and anxiety over status may be readily reinforced, thus contributing further to the person's sense of inadequacy. When the applicant feels inadequate, he is prone to become more dependent. Therefore, if we are to strengthen individuals at this decisive moment when commonly even the adequate person may feel somewhat helpless, it is important that the negative feelings about the experience be dissipated so that the positive ones may emerge. Only as the individual feels secure, has little resentment, and maintains or regains his self-respect will he be able to make constructive use of the agency.

Towle (1957:29-30) quotes the following as a distillation of the views of experienced social workers:

'In times of trouble when people are emotionally disturbed, they tend to be more sensitive to the reactions of others, and consequently they may assign great meaning to what we say and do in helping them. We have found that just ordinary kindness and seemingly casual relationships with a client to whom we have given only a bit of service at time of need, is commented upon long afterward in glowing terms. At such times we have been surprised to learn that what we did meant so much to the person. Likewise, a brusque manner, a hurried and inattentive response, abrupt questions timed to our pressure rather than to the applicant's readiness to answer them, may take on values irrelevant or out of proportion to their intent. In such an instance, the individual may personalise our response and charge us with having been rejecting, indifferent, or suspicious when we were only busy and fatigued. When this occurs, his feelings of mistrust and resentment may well be strengthened. Insofar as he must have the assistance with little feeling of right to it, he may build up a strong sense of obligation with a resultant sense of inferiority. This, is turn, may lead to a dependent response in which he looks to us to manage his affairs. Placing his affairs in our hands may have dual gratification: he reassures himself thereby that he is accepted here, and he has an outlet thereby for his resentment. Demanding attitudes may mount as an expression of his continued need for reassurance and of his increasing hostility. Or, some applicants may express their mistrust and resentment through remaining singularly unfree to make known their needs and to use their right to all forms of assistance available to them.'

Individuals tend to resist change. Sudden change, anxiety, resistance, is a sequence which almost inevitably people have themselves experienced and have observed in others. New customs, new ideas, new demands, new situations which call for different thinking and acting are commonly decried and struggled against. We repeatedly encounter people during catastrophes which bring sudden and sometimes great change in the individual's whole way of life. Some of the anxiety and some of the resistance to our helping efforts may, therefore, stem from the element of change in the person's life and may not mean that he literally does not want, or gradually may not be able, to use the help which he momentarily rejects. He may have to adapt to new conditions slowly and in the process may revolt against the hand that would help him make this adaptation.

This tendency to resist change is an energy-saving principle which, although creating problems for people and particularly for social workers as they try to help people, has been a useful principle by and large throughout the individual's life. Rooted in our early automatic behaviour, the persistence of this tendency to live by habit has meant that 'when the best behaviour in a given situation has been determined by experiment, and through repetition has become automatic, the mind is no longer required to function in that type of situation'. The advantage of automatic behaviour is that it is effortless. Its disadvantage is that it is adapted to definite situations and is not easily modified when changed conditions require it. As the individual masters his environment, as he gains maturity and independence to function on his own both physically and psychologically, automatic behaviour plays a less important role and he meets changing circumstances more readily. Dependence on others and fear of new situations go hand in hand. Therefore, the factors and forces of life which can be marshalled to give the individual basic emotional security will lead to less dependence on habitual ways of life and should increase the individual's capacity for greater flexibility in meeting new situations. In this connection, we have learned that sometimes a person cannot use his changed life situation in a responsible, resourceful fashion until certain basic dependency needs have met through supportive help of one kind or another.

Expectations on the Part of Probationers

In my study of a group of 100 probationers and their probation officers I found a similar vagueness in expectations as has been indicated in other studies of social agencies' consumers. Sixty-nine probationers said that they did not have any definite ideas about what they expected of their probation officers, but eighty-three men said that they thought probation was intended to help them. Fourteen men said they expected the probation officer to be firm but kind while sixteen expected him to be severe and authoritarian. One probationer who already knew his probation officer said that he expected him to be easy going.

In the early stages of probation the probationer's perception of the probation officer is probably influenced by salient features of the situation. It is probably largely defined for the majority of probationers by having the Order served. Being a mandatory relationship the officer is, to a certain extent at least, perceived as holding the probationer (or parolee) to the requirements of probation. The basic pattern for the relationship is defined and status positions and role expectations will have their influences on the perceptions of probationers and probation officers. While the probationer in coming to meet the probation officer may often be vague about his expectations he may also be apprehensive about the encounter. Some probationers expressed fear about possibly being blamed or treated punitively by their probation officers. Probationers having personal problems also have hopeful expectations of their officers. They express the wish that they may in some way rid themselves of uncomfortable feelings or impulses. In discussing the kind of person they see as the probation officer, or as they wish him to be, they mention such things as someone to rely on, someone who accepts you, and someone with whom you can share your problems. These ideas and feelings may be discussed with particular reference to psychoanalytic theory. In everyone, there are some hopes which are unfulfilled, and every new venture tends to arouse our ideal expectations. It is as if we were saying 'This time it is going to be different: this person will give me all I ever longed for'. In as far as our expectations are ideal they are unattainable; in as far as they are reasonable, they have a chance of being met. Basically, the ideal the client hopes for is that the caseworker will take away all pain. To this end the client may tell the worker what she should do: for example, 'Get me a house, then my wife will look after the kids properly, and I won't go to the pub any more.' Alternatively, he may treat the caseworker as if she was an oracle: 'Tell us what to do.' 'Tell me who's right.' 'I'll do anything you say.' 'You know what's best.' These attitudes are met with again and again, both in individual work and in groups. The pressure to get the caseworker to give answers and to make decisions arises from the avoidance of emotional pain connected with not-knowing, uncertainty, and self-hate and guilt when things go wrong. If the caseworker does not fall in with such demands, she may be told that she gives nothing worth-while and become the object of hostility.

Another way the client may rid himself of his troubles is to pour them out, with no effort to try and understand them. A social worker will say: 'He told me too much in the first interview, he won't come back.' Such intuition implies that the client has used the caseworker as a dustbin, has massively evacuated his problems into her and is likely to become frightened in case the worker will put it all back, reproach him, or make him feel ashamed. If the client is looking for someone temporarily to carry his anxieties, to share his burden and to help him towards finding a solution, this can become the basis of a realistically helpful relationship. 'You are the first person who has taken the trouble to listen to me, who is really interested, who cares,' are expressions of gratitude and show how great is the human need to find someone who is a good listener, capable of carrying anxiety — and how rarely this need is met.

To be cared about is every human being's deepest desire. At the very deepest level this means being loved as we are, with all our faults and shortcomings. This requires that someone should under-stand us in the widest sense of the term and yet not reject us. It is such understanding that the more mature part of the client is striving for. Yet there is always the doubt whether it is possible to be loved if the truth were known, and hence the worker may find herself being seduced into a relationship based on mutual admiration of each other's nice qualities. If this happens she must ask herself what has happened to the bad aspects of the client and herself. If, because of her own need to be loved and admired, the caseworker allows herself to be idealized, she is not helping the client to face the inevi-table frustrations and disappointments of reality. On the contrary, the client will all the more concentrate his anger on someone out-side, for example, the marriage partner.

As the client comes for help because there has been a failure in dealing with himself, his family, or the outer world, the notion that he will be criticized is near at hand. He may be full of self-reproaches, 'It's all my fault' (which is unlikely to be the case) or adopt a belligerent attitude. 'It's no good investigating me, you will find nothing in my family that accounts for Janet's behaviour' was the opening remark of a mother to a psychiatric social worker. Implicit in this statement is the client's assumption that the purpose of the interview was to attach blame and that it would end in a moral indictment. Feelings of guilt may lead to the withholding of important information or blaming someone else: 'I am sure it is the school'; 'It all started since she has been going out with that boy.' The client tends to pick on some simple external reason to explain what he dare not or cannot understand. There is a positive aspect to this, however, namely the belief that if the true cause can be discovered some answer might be found (Salzberger-Wittenberg 1970).

There are other perspectives on the different attitudes and feelings probationers may have about probation and the officer. This is important because, in practice, a variety of approaches to 'treating' or 'helping' clients are needed. The psycho-social therapy model described above may be helpful in working with some clients: others may be reached through a different kind of relationship or a different probation officer. Similarly probation officers have different ways of working. A different orientation (Pearce 1976) to those already described illustrates this. It had been suggested that client strategy in the probation interview may be to withdraw. This withdrawn and uncommunicative response may be effective in helping the client to maintain distance from the probation officer. Or the withdrawal may be a function of the probationer's inability to make the probation officers' questions and approach intelligible in terms of his understanding of the punitive purpose of the interview. The probation officer's friendliness may be suspect. From the probation officer's standpoint the client's suspicion may be seen as indicating hostility to authority (a negative transference) rather than a purposive adaptation to the situation in which he finds himself. The probation officer is led to maintain his focus on the client's personality by the latter's management of the interview as opposed to disruption of it. On the other hand the client may attempt to maintain ambiguity about his delinquency and will deny the probation officer access to his own perceptions of his world. From the probation officer's viewpoint the client's apparent inability to comprehend the probation officer's meaning may be understood in terms of low intelligence and/or educational deprivation, or difference between his language and that of the client. The probation officer is concerned to locate a 'cause' for a person's delinquent behaviour and he makes use of the ideas that the delinquent has been the passive victim of 'sick' families, 'delinquent' subcultures and bad environments as causative factors. The delinquent's sickness is seen to be grounded in his inability to exercise control over his own life. But the probation officer's search for a 'cause', it is argued, frequently prompts a defensive withdrawal, although the probationer may come to accept the sick role and view himself as powerless to influence his own future.

The next point in Pearce's argument is that to overcome the communication barrier the probation officer should relinquish his focus on individual causation and attempt to discuss delinquency in a general way. This kind of discussion is likely to be felt to be 'safer' by the client in that it does not directly threaten him. Also, it is likely that accounts about 'us', 'others' and socially shared meanings are more familiar modes of communication. The client does not then have to directly acknowledge the relevance of generalized material to himself but at the same time makes appropriate cues available to the probation officer. The client's power to introduce his own framework of meaning into communication with the probation officer can be facilitated, for example, by the probation officer's willingness to meet the client with his friends and not necessarily at the probation office but on the client's home ground. The probation officer needs to be prepared to suspend his assumptions about what is meaningful communication and to try to 'reach' his client in terms of the client's language, and social context. The probation officer does not move towards a role with his client that denies his role as a probation officer. But he ought to have sufficient confidence in his role to enable him to sustain communication with his client in situations where the client has some control over the content and context of communication.

This article by Pearce (1976) seems useful in pointing to some factors which could contribute to misunderstanding by probation officers and their clients. Over-concern with the 'causes' of the delinquent act, as seen by clients, the office environment, and social work 'theory' could all lead to misunderstanding. The kinds of strategy used by clients are probably seen quite often in practice. The article makes a useful link between theory and practice, but as with all work of this kind there are difficulties in generalizing. Pearce's approach seems to be relevant and valid in relation to some clients. The possibilities of different kinds of interaction are greater than he suggests, but to attempt to describe them all would, in the context of current thinking, be foolhardy. By focusing on exchange and games models he appears to share some of Jordan's (1970) ideas, but the latter writer carried them further, and Pearce does not refer to his work. The comments on Bernstein's (1973) work are also helpful, although the question of authority is not discussed in Pearce's article in relation to modes of control. I share his view of the client being enabled to assume control (Day 1972) but have developed the idea of a contrasting role for the probation officer as an authority in an article on social skills learning (Day 1976). Pearce reminds us of the social skills many probationers already possess and this is salutary.

Studies of Consumers' Views on Social Work

Studies which have been made of peoples' expectations and knowledge of social work organizations show a high degree of variation. It has been said that the social worker's image is not as clear as that of some other workers. He tends to be associated with income maintenance and with general ideas about authority figures. Glastonbury, Burdett, and Austen (1973), found that social security staff and doctors' roles were better understood. Similar accounts of the imprecise image of social workers and their roles were found in a study in the USA (Bolton and Kammeyer 1968).

In the minds of some prospective clients social work is associated with officialdom. In one case where social workers were housed in an office block with other local authority departments clients assumed that they were council officials. Old people thought they would see that the elderly were cared for and mothers that they would ensure children were not ill-treated. People with housing difficulties were reluctant to approach them ('the welfare') because they thought that they worked with the housing department, an authority to be avoided if possible (Rees 1973). In this sample of sixty-five clients referred to a voluntary and local authority agency in Scotland no-one knew about the formation of a single department out of the previously separate health and welfare, and probation and children's departments. There was similar ignorance about re-organization in England and Wales according to Glastonbury, Burdett and Austen (1973). In their random survey of 385 families in South Wales respondents were more often correct about the functions of the probation service, the NSPCC, and the Citizens' Advice Bureaux; less than half seemed to understand the work of the new Social Service Departments. It was also found that young people have a tendency to group the functions of various agencies indiscriminately — such as the police, health visitors, probation officers — and each official is thought to be likely to tell all the others whatever he knows about clients. In an earlier study it was found that the best known social worker was the probation officer. Only 2 per cent of the sample had not heard of his work but over 75 per cent knew nothing of psychiatric social work and little more than 50 per cent had heard of a child care officer (Timms 1962).

One deterrent to seeking help is unpleasant previous experience of receiving aid, particularly financial entitlements, which seems to carry a stigma, because of the values of independence and success (Gould and Kenyon 1972; Marsden 1969; Land 1969). Studies of attitudes to social work show an underlying theme of distinguishing between the deserving and undeserving (Glastonbury, Burdett, and Austen 1973). Until they receive different treatment from social workers some clients believe they risk being regarded as undeserving. In one study the only people who denied feeling some sense of shame on being referred to a social worker were social security clients of long standing, adoption applicants, and disabled people requiring aids (Rees 1973). Previous treatment by officials perceived as having influence and power colour future expectations. A characteristic response to authority is submissiveness and this may be particularly true of people who are poor, dependent, and who feel subservient. The majority seem to have no broad social expectations almost as though they had learned that the gap between expectation and reality would be considerable (Coates and Silburn 1970).

A more recent survey in the United Kingdom showed continued vagueness about what social workers do. It was carried out for London Weekend Television and was of a sample of 1018 people. 24 per cent thought social workers allocated council houses, 29 per cent that they dealt with unemployed people, and 44 per cent that they dealt with people claiming social security. Widespread publicity had made people well aware that social workers dealt with battered babies but lonely old people were the client group most often mentioned. The mentally ill did not even appear in the responses to the questionnaire. 17 per cent of the sample thought social workers essential for solving problems, 14 per cent thought they were a waste of public money. 15 per cent of those who had had contact with them regarded them as useless. The survey was commissioned for a series of programmes called 'The Do Gooders' (*New Society* 49

(878): 2 August 1979).

One purpose of the reorganization of British social work services was to reflect the interdependence of family and community needs and resources. But feelings of stigma associated with social work seem to have remained an obstacle. Whether or not people have had experience making them feel humiliated, such feelings seem more likely to influence their actions than official definitions of social services' aims.

In a study based on the views of clients who had been in contact with the Family Welfare Association in London it was clear that people would not go to social work agencies unless their problems were very great and they felt under great pressure (Mayer and Timms 1970). A study of consumers' attitudes to one local authority Social Services Department was carried out in Southampton. 305 people were interviewed. An attempt was made to ensure that they understood that the interviewers were not connected with the Social Services Department. But there may have been confusion in the clients' minds about the interviewers' connection with the social workers and this could have influenced the replies. The main aims of the study were to discover how clients had initially come into contact with the service and what expectations they had of it, and how their views corresponded with those of their social workers. As has been indicated earlier it is likely that expectations are affected by previous experience and the images and perceptions held of a person's social worker. In this study less than a third of the clients said they did not know what to expect or that they did not expect any help. There seemed to be a link between lack of expectations and lack of knowledge about the department. One third of those who expected help had not heard of the department compared with two-thirds of those with no expectations. Any kind of prior knowledge seemed to be the important factor rather than what they had heard about the quality of the department. This seemed to suggest that if the department had been better known people would have been clearer about what to expect from it. This was also mentioned by the department's social workers. Several of them considered that clients came with unrealistic expectations and that more public education would lead to a clearer and more realistic idea of the services offered. Lack of expectations was also related to being contacted by the department. Age made a difference to whether or not the clients had expectations. Over half of those who did not know what to expect were aged over sixty. Whereas the majority of the social workers thought clients expected most of all to be able to discuss personal problems and to receive advice, sympathy, and information, less than 10 per cent of the clients said they expected help of this nature (McKay, Goldberg, and Fruin 1973). This confirms Mayer and Timms' (1970) findings to some extent. Clients mostly expected practical help such as aids, services, clothing, and bedding. Their expectations coincided with what they actually received, practical help being among the most frequently mentioned. Practical help is more tangible and might be more easily remembered than advice and sympathy. Another discrepancy between the clients' and social workers' perceptions was found in the 15 per cent of clients who said they expected help with housing difficulties and just over 10 per cent who said they wanted financial help. The social workers on the whole thought clients did not expect this kind of help. The emphasis placed on practical help did not mean that clients did not appreciate help in the form of listening and sympathy. One third said that they had experienced some relief of emotional stress, had become less anxious or depressed, more confident or stable. Clients' perceptions of the qualities needed to be a good social worker reflected their appreciation of the non-material aspects of help. They laid the greatest stress on such personality characteristics as understanding and sympathy, a pleasing personality, and such social skills as the ability to put people at their ease.

Two-thirds of the clients said they were satisfied and less than one fifth expressed dissatisfaction. Over 80 per cent found their social worker understanding, sympathetic, and easy to talk to. Nearly all thought they were good listeners and many made appreciative comments about their personalities and the help they received. Clients who said they had received no help were the least satisfied and the proportion of satisfied clients increased with the amount of help they had received. Age was related to satisfaction. The elderly seemed to be slightly more satisfied, particularly those over the age of 75. This might be linked to their low expectations and possibly also to a feeling of dependency on the goodwill of the services. It was reassuring that the elderly seemed satisfied because the social workers were more interested in work with younger age groups. On the whole clients were satisfied with the frequency of visiting. But out of nine clients who saw their social worker less than every three months, eight said they were satisfied. It emerged that all but two considered that their problems were solved and that they were being visited infrequently as a routine follow-up measure. The remaining two were foster mothers who received statutory six monthly visits. Another finding which was consistent with other research was that clients who did not return to the service were not necessarily dissatisfied; they may well have got what they required.

We have now moved from looking at clients' expectations to their experience with social work agencies. Attempts to investigate consumers' reactions began in the mid-1960s in the United Kingdom (Younghusband 1978, Vol. 2:129), rather later than in the United States. An example is the work by Kogan, Hunt and Bartelme (1953) where it was found that clients who were judged to have shown 'no improvement' as a result of social work intervention were just as likely to place a high value on the help they received from the social worker and the agency as were clients who were judged to show 'great improvement'. In 1973, in the UK, Cheshire Social Services Department carried out a consumer survey from an area office. A postal questionnaire was sent to 118 clients and 83 responded. 48 per cent expected to receive information and advice. 33 per cent said that they felt their problem had been understood and 74 per cent said that they felt satisfied as a result of their contact with the department (Gravett 1973). Butrym (1968), in a study of medical social work, asked a small number of patients their views on the social work service. The great majority were positive: more patients than social workers rated the service as successful. Medical social workers were regarded as people 'who have an interest in patients and do all they can for you' and who are helpful at a time 'when you are desperate with worry'. Among their more positive attributes were kindness, sympathy, a desire to help, ability to listen, warmth, and a capacity to understand.

Views on Direct Influence

There is evidence that some members of the public (in particular lower working-class groups) tend to expect social workers to be authoritarian and directive and sometimes consider such direction as appropriate and useful (Lipset 1963:87-126). (This view was expressed by a high percentage of the probationers interviewed in the course of my investigation in Probation Departments.)

Clients of probation departments and family service agencies both in the USA and Britain who have wanted to be given direct advice and have been frustrated have seen this as the aspect of services they most disliked. (Reid and Shapiro 1969; Mayer and Timms 1970.) Sainsbury (1975) studied twenty-seven families referred to a Family Service Unit (five of whom were 'second generation' FSU families) who were representative of those known to Family Service Units nationally. In relation to other families in the community they were noticeable for the greater number and lesser intelligence (and other special needs) of the children, the high unemployment rate of the fathers, the prevalence of serious debts, and frequent contact with the courts. The families and their caseworkers were asked about their recollections of the casework process.

With one exception, all the families received material help. A high degree of congruence was found between the needs presented and the initial modes of helping. The clients remembered the helpful nature of material aid, emotional support, and social workers' reliability in crisis. Attributes of social workers valued by clients also included being easy to talk to, honesty in discussions, patience, equal caring for everyone in the family, and politeness. Support through directive help fitted in with the families' views about their needs. Social workers exercised firmness and set limits in their work with twenty-three of the families. This did not seem to be incompatible with friendship. This quality of friendship seemed to make both firmness and the exercise of authority and power, and direct advice about certain social obligations acceptable, for example. Long-term resentment was not increased through the exercise of authority. Clients did not expect social workers to permit total freedom of behaviour. Sainsbury said that the capacity of the social workers to take control of people (as well as events), to be firm, and to limit personal destructiveness, was widely referred to as a valuable attribute. Success, as assessed by the social workers, was most apparent in areas the workers had previously designated as the most pressing material and emotional needs. The areas most changed were those relating to a client's performance as parent or spouse, coping with inner feelings of distress, and responding to the stress of unexpected external events. One task seemed to be that of overcoming the cognitive and emotional distances between workers and clients. Reciprocity in relationships was often seen by clients and workers as fundamental to effective casework. Workers were often active as friends would be; this quality of friendship is referred to above. The social workers also exercised power in clients' lives, and this was perceived as consistent in the context of friendship and professional caring and not as arbitrary and unpredictable. It was suggested that the expression of authority in relationships is not in itself incompatible with warm feelings between client and social worker or with the client's identification with the worker.

Forty men probationers were given intensive casework treatment by a special unit in London (Folkard, Smith, and Smith 1974). Of this group almost three-quarters thought their probation officer was least like a policeman and most like a teacher or welfare officer. More than half thought of him as most like a friend and least like a busybody. Almost all of the probationers liked their probation officers, felt they were treated fairly by him, and believed he wanted to help them. Three-quarters thought that probation would help them to keep out of trouble. The majority of the probationers said that they were given support, encouragement, and practical help and that they were helped to understand themselves and their behaviour. Twenty-five per cent thought that their probation officers ought to exercise more control and less than one third thought that their probation officers were strict. Overall attitude scores indicated that the majority of the probationers had very favourable attitudes. But the probation officers were less likely to think that clients thought well of them and thought they would more often be seen as busybodies; sometimes they predicted incorrectly that clients would think they were not understood.

Problems in Using Consumer Research

This chapter ranges quite widely over consumers' views and experience of social agencies. It raises questions about the interpretation of clients' views, whether they are understood and, if so, how they may be used by policy makers. Shaw (1976) discussed these problems and observed that it is possible for consumers' and service providers' views to become muddled. This was seen in a study of patients referred to medical social workers (Butrym 1968). Cohen (1971) said that one serious problem was the difficulty experienced by clients in finding a language to use in discussing and evaluating services and he illustrated their feelings that social workers' actions were either arbitrary or absurd! For some clients the idea of evaluating services they have received is alien and it is all the more difficult if the service is represented by someone who is likeable and well meaning. Clients may feel disloyal or unfair to him if they criticize the service he represents. McKay, Goldberg, and Fruin (1973) referred to the difficulty of differentiating between clients' attitudes towards the department, the services received, and the individual worker. In a study of how the parents of boys appearing in a juvenile court understood the procedures Voelcker found that parents had a favourable picture of individual probation officers but little liking for probation as a method of treatment. This analysis is supported and developed by other researchers but while it is necessary to recognize the problems involved it has become progressively more acceptable to weigh the views of clients as well as other interested people. In conclusion it seems that the earlier views and hypotheses put forward by Towle and used by the earlier caseworkers are coherent within the framework of psycho-social therapy and receive support from more recent consumer studies. Some of these studies also indicate that in certain situations consumers expect direct influence and find it helpful. It is necessary to exercise caution, however, in drawing these conclusions, partly because of the problems inherent in consumer studies and also because of the variations found in relatively sparse evidence.

Probationers' and Probation Officers' Perceptions of Probation

With these warnings about the problems of consumer and practitioner studies in mind I now give an outline of a project which I completed with the help of the Probation and After Care Services in several English counties. It may be possible to generalize to some extent and to suggest that there are implications for social work in other settings. Problems of control and influence in local authority Social Service Departments will be discussed separately later since for social workers in that setting experience of the care-control dilemma is frequent and often very taxing. I studied the views of probationers and probation officers on the purposes of probation and their attitudes to and experience of the exercise of authority and its relationship to help with probationers' needs and problems. Interviews were carried out with one hundred male probationers over the age of seventeen using a semi-structured questionnaire as a guide. The views of the thirty probation officers responsible for supervising the probationers were obtained by using structured written questionnaires similar to those I used in interviewing the probationers.

On the whole it was found that there was a substantial level of agreement between the two groups in such key areas as the purposes of probation. Eighty-three men said that they saw the purpose as having the dual function of helping with personal and social problems and giving advice and direction about their behaviour. They did not regard these aims as incompatible and recognized the unequal nature of their relationships with their officers which did not prevent the development of friendliness between them. A separate postal questionnaire was sent to thirty other probation officers and twenty-six replied. They were not in the same services as the probation officers referred to above but their views were sought to supplement and add to the information obtained from local sources. (The questionnaires used are described in the Appendix.) Fifteen of the postal respondents perceived a conflict between their court duties and their professional ideology. One of the main ways they reacted to this was by open discussion with their probationers. Some long-serving officers emphasized their role in serving the court and said that for them conflict did not arise. Taking all of the probation officers as a single group it was found that more of the long-serving officers appeared to have narrower views of the purposes of probation. More officers nearer their training seemed to be more questioning of their role and were more flexible in their approach and ways of working. Forty of the probationers had been on probation for one year at the time they were interviewed and their views and those of their officers are described later. In the next chapter probationers' and probation officers' views on the purposes of probation will be reported and processes of influence and control will be discussed.

3 Orientations to Social Work
and Social Control in
Probation and After Care

This chapter is concerned with the views of probation officers supervising the probationers who were interviewed and gave their views on probation. It also includes the views of probation officers from other areas who returned a postal questionnaire. (Schedules relating to the questionnaires are to be found in the Appendix.)

Dimensions of Casework Help

Probation officers do not necessarily confine their activities to one method of social work but in this book the focus is mainly on their activities as caseworkers. There are many definitions of social casework but a useful provisional one is that it is a personal service provided by qualified workers for individuals who require skilled help in resolving some personal or family problem. Its aim is to relieve stress, both material and emotional, and to help the client to achieve his maximum well being. The caseworker seeks to do this by means of a careful study of the client in his family and social setting, and of his problem, by the establishment of a cooperative relationship with him in which his own capacity for dealing with his problem is increased, and by the mobilization of such other resources or professional aid as may be appropriate (Davison 1965:126).

In an attempt to identify dimensions of probation treatment the following concepts have been used.

(1) 'Support', refers to anything which is said or done to help the offender solve or mitigate his personal or social problems. This may take the form of material, psychological, or social help.

(2) 'Control', refers to activities directed towards regulation of the offender's behaviour. This may take the form of disciplinary measures, or anything which is said or done to induce the

offender to conform to socially acceptable standards of behaviour.

(3) 'Individual Treatment', refers to activities focused primarily on the individual offender, usually in the form of personal interviews with him.

(4) 'Situational Treatment', refers to activities which are focused primarily on the social environment of the offender, and which make active use of his relationships with other people.

It has been pointed out that in probation practice these categories 'are not mutually exclusive and a probation officer may use any one of them or various combinations of them in his treatment of individual probationers' (Folkard *et al.* 1967:16). Also he may vary his approach, treatment may have different emphases, and the value of the above categorization has been in helping to identify the main forms of treatment (Moffett 1972:57-75). Folkard and his colleagues pointed out that some authorities stressed both support and control. Dawtry (1957:180-87) said that the probation officer saw his task as helping the individual to lead a happy and socially acceptable life, while the Morison Report (1962) discussed the functions of probation as being to seek the well being of the individual and to protect society.

One of the main aims of IMPACT (an experiment on Intensive Matched Probation and After Care Treatment) (Folkard *et al.* 1974: 16) was to divert the major emphasis of probation casework away from the office interview between client and probation officer towards a greater situational involvement in the areas of family, work, and leisure. Presumably a greater situational emphasis will lead to proportionately fewer office interviews and at the same time bring the probation officer into increased contact with the client's family and associates. The experiment was carried out in four probation and after care areas to evaluate the provision of more intensive and matched treatment for relatively 'high risk' offenders. It was found that the type of offender with moderate or high criminal tendencies and average or few personal problems did significantly worse (in terms of one-year reconviction rates) under intensive situational treatment than under normal probation supervision. The type of offender with low criminal tendencies and many personal problems appeared to have a more successful outcome under the experimental treatment although this was not statistically significant. Thus there were some very tentative indications that the latter group might benefit from intensive treatment and that those with high criminal tendencies but not a lot of personal problems would not benefit. The more extroverted and stable did worse if anything on intensive treatment whereas neurotics did better. It is possible that extroverts found the close contact with the probation officer irritating, frustrating, and meaningless and so they reacted provocatively.

It seems that continuing criminality and reconviction are not affected by the sentence and treatment. There is no simple cause and effect relationship. Reconviction is a crude indication of an offender's response to sentence or treatment. Although intensive treatment may be of considerable help to a probationer this type of outcome is difficult to demonstrate (or even to ascertain). Reconviction may be seen as an indication, given the social context and influences on a probationer, of possible personality defect leading to failure in social adjustment. In attempting to assess how much control and how much support an offender needs the probation officer's perception of his personality, needs, and social situation will be an important influence. The control element which seems to be more important in respect of offenders with high criminal tendencies, may be better provided through community service orders, day training centres, and through ancillary workers. The support element which seems to be more important in respect of probationers with many personal problems may be better provided in traditional or 'routine' probation through the one-to-one relationship. It was found that generally the treatment categories where there was higher control were associated with cooler, regulated, directive, and disciplinary relationships. There were tendencies for individual treatment to be seen both by probationers and probation officers as supportive and situational treatment as controlling. It was found that there was more individual treatment (office interviews) than situational treatment (home visits). When high control was given it was unusually with high support. Generally there were no significant differences between expected and actual failure rates following particular types of treatment. Particularly where there was a delinquent and stressful situation there were tendencies for more treatment in the form of greater support and greater control especially to be associated with a higher failure rate (Folkard *et al.* 1974:16).

Supportiveness is regarded as a fundamental casework method which involves interested, sympathetic listening and the communication to the client of the probation officer's concern and desire to help him, and his acceptance of him as a person worthy of respect (even when his behaviour is not approved). Included in sustaining techniques are recognition of the client's strengths and the provision of material and practical help. The emotional support offered to the client is sometimes referred to as the 'good parent' aspect of the probation officer's role (this is a vague general notion although it may be defined more tightly in individual cases).

The Use of Control

As a treatment method the use of control and direction has frequently been disapproved of by the helping professions. This may be because of associations (assumed or realistic) with damage suffered by clients or helpers. This has tended to divert the attention of social workers from the personal and social controls operating in the process of treatment. There has also been a tendency to see treatment and control measures as opposed. The possible usefulness of controls for some clients may have gone unrecognized as a result. It has been argued that to protect people's dignity social casework should deal only with the voluntary client and social workers still sometimes dislike the idea that they are to produce social competence in clients for the good of society. But whenever anyone − parent, teacher, or social worker − is involved in setting limits on behaviour according to social norms, that person is involved in social control. Control is implicit in such goals as strengthening family life, improving interpersonal relationships, and building community life. Verbs such as 'better', 'relieve', 'develop', 'assist', 'help', and 'encourage' are repeatedly used in social reports. The social agency is an institution which is evaluative and judgemental.

Procedures of direct influence include the various ways in which the caseworker tries to promote a specific kind of behaviour on the client's part such as consulting a doctor, or managing his money in a certain way. There are many situations in which techniques of influence are thought to be appropriate: often a client is not ready to think things through for himself or strong cultural influences upon his expectations of the worker may lead him to interpret refusal to give advice as indicating incompetence or lack of concern. The very anxious person also sometimes needs direction. When a strengthening of a client's control of his impulses is a casework aim direct influence often involves urging the client to control his behaviour better. Conversely, when a client demonstrates too much control or rigidity in his behaviour the social worker's influence may help him to relax the controls. It is often difficult to disentangle these procedures of influence but the following distinctions can be made.

(1) Advice can be given in the form of information, for example about services or resources available.
(2) Advice can be given about courses of action.
(3) It needs to be remembered that requests for advice can mask requests for other kinds of help, such as giving an opinion about someone's actual or proposed behaviour. Suggestions or orders can be made on the social worker's initiative.

When social workers or probation officers help clients to find jobs, apply for financial aid, control their impulses, or manage their use of alcohol or other drugs they are engaging in the process of social control. The aim of all these activities is to help clients to get along better in society, that is by conforming to social norms rather than by deviating from them.

Probation Officers' Views

It will be seen that altogether fifty-six probation officers were involved in the project described in Chapter Two. Twenty-six completed a postal questionnaire. Thirty were involved in the supervision of the probationers in the project and I refer to them as the project probation officers. Although the two groups are discussed separately this is to some extent an artificial division as some of the tabulated information indicates. The people who dealt with the postal questionnaire however were all asked to comment on a single case whereas the project probation officers, of course, were dealing with 100 cases between them. Another difference was, necessarily, in the content of the questionnaire. The postal respondents were asked specifically about the conflict experienced by probation officers in their responsibilities towards clients and to the community.

Table 3 (1) *Purpose of probation: probation officers' views*

	Project probation officers	Questionnaire probation officers		
	n = 30	n = 26	n = 56	%
To set limits for probationers and to provide treatment, i.e. to counsel and assist the client, help him to gain a better understanding of his situation, and to use this in changing his behaviour	27	24	51	90
Help with family relationships	2	1	3	6
Help with practical matters or material aid	1	–	1	2
To meet the individual needs of the client	–	1	1	2

The following statements about the purpose of probation were made by the project probation officers. All of them described one purpose of probation as offering psychological help. One reply of this kind was as follows: 'It is to help clients to function, give support where needed, and to be a friend and listen to their problems.' That reply was given by an officer in the 40-44 age group who had two years experience following professional social work training. 'Probation is a means by which an individual through a relationship with a significant other is helped to become able to manage all his affairs in such a way that he is able to live as an independent person who can deal with difficulties and problems in an appropriate manner; it means helping them to help themselves.' This probation officer had one year of experience following professional social work training. He was in the 24-29 age group. A direct entrant in the 45-49 age group with three years experience saw the purpose as 'support, encourage, and at times chastise (verbally), to listen to and share problems and to be a confidant'. He was more explicit than some officers in mentioning befriending the offender, adding, 'to be a friend when the rest of the world seems against them'. The next quotations show how the probation officers sometimes gave 'mixed' replies to the question: they illustrate those replies where behaviour control was stressed rather more. The purpose is 'to advise, assist, and befriend (still) and control at times in an effort to avoid further court appearances and to function in society as it is.' This was the view of a probation officer in the 35-39 age group who had one year of experience after completing professional social work training. Following direct-entrant training one probation officer had between eleven and fifteen years experience and was aged between 45 and 49. He saw probation as providing moral support, parental influence, and discouraging the 'tendency to take the easy way out: to instil respect for other people and their property'. Following professional training the next officer had between five and seven years experience. He was in the 35-39 age group. He also saw probation as providing support, 'stabilizing work habits, and home situation; relieving tension in the home'. One of the younger probation officers (24-29) age group) with two years experience was a sociology graduate and was also a direct entrant. He thought it was 'perhaps foolishly dangerous' to answer the question about the purpose of probation briefly but gave some ideas. It was: 'to give an opportunity for the client to discuss his experience and feelings in the interview and provide a safety valve for his feelings. It was to enable client and probation officer together to analyse client's situation and attempt to ease or solve problems; to interpret client's problems to his family and vice versa. It was to act as a bridge between the client and to various institutions he may have difficulty in dealing with and to provide advice on any problems with such institutions. To educate socially and sometimes morally and make client aware of possibilities open to him, and to provide selective material aid in times of financial stress. To help find work and accommodation where necessary. To provide a structured framework in which the above functions can be operationalized and in which the client can be reminded of his responsibilities as laid down in his Probation Order.' 'Probation is to enable the individual to live at a satisfactory level to himself within the law. The inadequate may need material and practical help. This has a double purpose in demonstrating that someone cares about their predicament, and also that there are other ways of improving your situation than shoplifting or doing a meter break. The undisciplined may need an element of discipline or the parents may need an authority figure for support. The aggressive can benefit purely from ventilation of aggression.' This latter probation officer had three years post-training experience, was in the 35-39 age group, and had taken professional social work training.

A probation officer with over fifteen years experience since professional training, aged between 55 and 59, saw the purpose of probation as helping 'the client to live a more socially acceptable life, to help remove obstacles to attaining that, and to help the client to greater insight into his weaknesses and strengths so that he may be able after probation has finished to maintain progress made. To provide in suitable cases training in the community as an alternative to institutional training. The establishment may see it as an inexpensive form of treatment and favour it because of that.' Some of the probation officers who were a further stage away from their basic training gave replies where the emphasis seemed different, in that it was more a standard or even stereotyped one.

The tendency here was to give the 'text book' response or the 'official version' with no further comment. Here are some examples. One of the older probation officers, in the 55-59 age bracket, professionally trained in social work with four years post-qualification experience, said that he thought probation was to advise, assist, and befriend and/or to save the expense of a prison sentence. One of the short answers to the question about the purpose of probation was 'to befriend, advise, and assist and build up the ego where weak', given by a probation officer with professional training, eight to ten years experience, and in the 40-44 age group. An officer in the same age group with five to seven years experience, trained as a direct entrant, said that probation is 'to assist those who are unable to decide for themselves, to reach a reasonable solution to their problems, by other means than committing offences against society.'

The small group of project officers might be thought of as being in the middle part of a continuum of all 'basic grade' probation officers. If probation officers are considered in categories according to age, training, and experience, these officers seemed to fall into a normal curve in relation to the categories. There were two probation officers in each of the lowest and highest age groups. Their experience since training was variable in length with most of them having had between two and five years experience since training. Twelve had non-graduate professional training and eight were direct entrants. There were no exceptionally highly academically qualified officers and the direct-entry probation officers were well distributed in terms of age. The probation officers' views below were given in replies to a number of questions or compiled from multi-faceted answers. This made it difficult but not impossible to interpret them: it involved reducing their answers sometimes to single categories; for example, it will be seen that what the probation officer saw as the main or primary purpose of probation or what seemed to be the more important feature of his replies were used. However, only thirty replies were involved and it will be seen that three-quarters of the officers had what may be described as a therapeutic orientation to their work. It seemed that their main concern was to provide help and psychological support for the individual probationers in one-to-one relationships usually in office interviews. The result can be related to a study of probation officers' ideologies in Britain, and to a study made in the USA.

The British study (Hardiker 1977) explored the extent to which probation officers subscribed to certain 'treatment model' assumptions about criminal behaviour. Some officers appeared to subscribe to treatment model ideals more than others but all probation officers were treatment orientated towards some of their cases and not to others. Their treatment preference seemed to relate to the seriousness of the offenders' criminal history and personal problems. The probation officers' treatment orientations appeared to correspond with the recommendations they made in their social enquiry reports. A treatment orientation and a recommendation for either probation or custody appeared to result from an assessment of problems. The probation officers' treatment preferences seemed to be related to the objective and subjective stresses in their cases. They seemed to use both notions of justice and of treatment in various combinations. It seems that control agents use a commonsense approach rather than a positivist model. In probation it seems to be both a combination of the 'responsibility' idea that offenders have free will and the treatment idea that offenders' behaviour is determined (Hardiker 1977).

Hardiker does not agree that 'responsibility' and 'treatment' models are systematically incompatible even though they might coexist in the probation service. She noted that the more serious an offender's criminal record and personal problems the more likely it would be that the probation officer would think his behaviour was somewhat determined. She went on to argue that a 'treatment model' of crime might suit social workers very well because it might provide a framework within which they could assess a case and relate their assessment to an intervention. It might be that a treatment orientation became a euphemism for social control and lead to an unfair presentation of a case. But there was also the possibility that a probation officer's vision of a case is liberating because he was able to provide a picture of the context which explained the degree of constraint an offender was under. In a study in the United States the purpose of probation was given as control by 26 per cent of probationers but the majority of officers considered their principal purpose was treatment (McEachern 1961:213-17).

Although it is an oversimplification to divide the probation officers into too sharply defined groups the evidence in my study suggests a tentative formulation about their attitudes in relation to their period of experience since training. The criteria which were used in tentatively classifying probation officers' attitudes were: (a) whether their replies referred only to the 'classical' function of probation officers, 'to advise, assist, and befriend' clients (with additional comments such as those quoted in this chapter, but which did not indicate any questioning of the basic function or qualification of it), or similar responses such as 'assisting the probationer and trying to help him avoid committing further offences'; or (b) whether their replies were more broadly based, suggesting for example, how assistance to individual probationers might be provided through interviews with the probation officer and ways in which the probation officer could work with members of probationers' families and people in other networks in the community in which the probationer was involved or could become involved. Two categories of probation officers' attitudes or perceptions were used therefore. The first category could be referred to briefly as having the 'stereotyped' view which implied a limited or narrow view of the functions of the probation department. The second category could be referred to as having the more 'flexible' view. In these cases probation officers saw the functions of the probation department as assisting their clients in a wider variety of ways and also as having a role in interpreting these functions to other groups in the community such as other social agencies, employers, educational institutions, members of the legal profession, and others involved with offenders. These categories are similar to those employed in an earlier study (Day 1970) of social work practice but by eliminating a 'middle-of-the-road' group of attitudes the present attempt is to achieve a clearer distinction, while recognizing the necessarily

Table 3 (2) *Probation officers' views of functions of probation*

Probation officers' views	Number of probation officers according to their years of experience since training			total	%
	1—2 years	3—4 years	5 years or more		
'Stereotyped'	1 (2%)	1 (2%)	16 (28%)	18	32
'Flexible'	14 (25%)	14 (25%)	10 (18%)	38	68

tentative nature of the classification.

Most of the probation officers trained between 1962 and 1975. It should be borne in mind that during that period there were developments in training leading to some emphasis on work with several family members and with groups. This emphasis was growing during that time but in practice one-to-one interviews were still the main method of work and of course this was reflected in training. Some of the probation officers who were 'young' in experience, that is closer to their training in time, seemed to have rather different attitudes to the work in contrast to some of the probation officers at the other end of the spectrum. It seemed that the closer they were to training the less set they were in their attitudes for example, in the sense that they were less steeped in the 'traditional' view of probation. I have to qualify this generalization because of certain notable exceptions at different stages in their careers. One probation officer of long experience for example was far more liberal and flexible than two of his far less experienced colleagues. He, and another probation officer of more than five years experience, was enthusiastic in helping in the project while some 'younger' probation officers were very hostile to it and did not see it as offering any stimulus to further learning. Of course there are many factors at work here, some of them more personal and therefore more private in nature. But the general view, outlined above, of the relationship between training and the effect of later experience in the field seems credible in the light of other research.

An example is a study which set out to explore the hypothesis that the direction of change in attitudes towards education occurring during time spent at college by student teachers will be reversed during time spent in schools (Edwards 1975). Examination of the period of initial training provided considerable support for the hypothesis. During academic work at college students' attitudes seemed more radical but when the students were on teaching practice they became oriented to the 'culture of the school' and less radical in their attitudes. When the period of time from entry to initial training to the second year of teaching was examined marked similarities were seen between the effect of teaching practice and the effect of the probationary year. The respondents tended to become less radical and more concerned with the instructional role of the teacher. The effect of the post-probationary year on teachers' attitudes was towards greater radicalism and less 'instructionalism'. The effect of initial training upon the educational attitudes of students was considerable. Finlayson and Cohen (1967) showed that there were considerable differences in the role conceptions of student teachers and head teachers. The latter group were more concerned about conformity, class discipline, and good order than the former. They were more inclined to reject activities in which children formulated their own rules of behaviour, opportunities for children to learn from their own experiences, and for them to discover their personal difficulties with teachers. The student teachers on the other hand were less in favour of interpreting right and wrong for children, less inclined to use punishment and to be strict on discipline, thus placing less emphasis on immediate conformity than the head teachers.

Of my initial sample of 100 probationers, fifty-one were supervised by probation officers under the age of 40 and forty-three by probation officers aged 40 or older. The probation officers over the age of 40 included one with one year of post-training experience, one with two years, two with three years, and one with four years. Six of them had five years or more experience since training. The probation officers over the age of 40, the group furthest away from their training, emphasized encouragement and psychological support in their plans for helping their probationers and seemed to place less emphasis on assertive or directive work. *Table 3 (3)* on the following page summarizes the numbers of probationers in different age groups supervised by probation officers in different age groups.

Table 3 (3) *Ages of probationers × ages of project probation officers*

Ages of probationers	Ages of probation officers	
	24–39	40+
Under 21	18	16
21–29	16	11
30+	17	22

The actual type of training a probation officer had received appeared to make little difference to his plans for helping; the direct entrants and the professionally trained groups seemed equally divided as far as their orientations were concerned and there was no difference between the groups in whether probationers felt probation officers understood their situations. The length of the probation officers' post-training experience seemed to make little difference to probationers' feelings about whether probation officers understood their situation and the same held for the probation officer/probationer relationship as it was seen by probationers.

The probation officers were asked for their views on what should be done about the probationers' situations. All of the probation officers said that probationers required a degree of supervision or direction. They did not mention support and encouragement in replying to the question about what should be done about probationers' situations and/or behaviour although later in their questionnaires they indicated that support and encouragement were appropriate. As far as this group was concerned, the training, experience, and age of probation officers made no difference in their replies to this question.

When they were asked about the probation officers' influence on their behaviour more probationers said that probation officers had influenced them when the probation officers had five years experience or more. It seemed that of the factors examined the age of the probation officer may be more important in affecting probationers' perceptions than other characteristics such as type of training. I have suggested that the closer a probation officer is to his training the less likely he is to be influenced by the traditional culture of probation. (Probation officers who have kept up-to-date by refresher courses might also be included.) This suggestion requires further investigation.

The case summary which follows gives a clearer picture of the complexities and uncertainties involved in the perceptions of probationer and probation officer. In this case the probationer's and probation officer's views seemed to correspond in that they agreed about a large number of subjects. It will be noted however (see the foregoing discussion) that the probation officer saw himself as easy going. The probationer described him as firm but kind.

CASE SUMMARY

A married man aged 39 was given a suspended sentence and placed on probation for one year after being charged with theft. He said that probation had helped him with his marriage and family problems. 'I talked to the probation officer. He talked to the wife. Things started to improve after that.' He thought that there were pressures on his wife who suffered from colitis and they had a daughter with spina bifida. 'We were just not talking to each other. We just had too much to do. We did not get a chance to be husband and wife. It helped us to have the help of the probation officer.' There was financial hardship for the family and the probationer had stolen previously. He said that he wished that he could have been offered help when he 'first started stealing: I wanted to be found out...did not know who could help me'. He was relieved about being placed on probation and had thought he would be sent to prison. The probation officer's views of his client's situation were similar. He thought the probationer appreciated that the judge recognized the existence of his difficulties which had been referred to in the Social Enquiry Report. The probation officer referred to 'the tense, unhappy marital situation and the problem in communication between the couple. The husband felt he got little credit for what he did do for the family — wife regularly pressed for more money. He tended to seek solace in drink. Also, wife ill with colitis, three children with congenital problems — one spina bifida. There has always been pressure on him ... He has consulted me when pressures were building up ... I feel that he regards the present situation as much improved. He would see probation as intended to help him and me as a "sounding board" for his ideas, feelings and problems.' Like the probationer the probation officer said that they had a good relationship. He said he had 'possibly' influenced the probationer's behaviour whereas the probationer said definitely that he had. The probation officer had discussed 'ways of easing the difficult situation as regards the handicapped child. He'd already thought of everything I suggested.' He saw himself as easy going in relation to the probationer and thought that this was how the probationer saw him. The probationer said that the probation officer 'calls a spade a spade. He gives sympathy but does not pull his punches. At the first interview he told me there was to be no messing about: he made it clear what the rules were. He talked things over with you rather than told you what to do'. This man said that his own relationship with the probation officer had been 'pretty easy going. But he can be strict as well. I'd say that really he is firm but kind although he listens. He is friendly too.' On the purpose of probation the probation officer said 'advise, assist, and befriend still reasonably appropriate. Help the probationer to help himself, understand why he has committed offences, try to develop certain aspects of personality mainly with the objective of preventing re-offending, helping him increase his ability to cope with difficult situations without responding in an inappropriate manner.' This probation officer was in the under 30 age group and had six months experience since training. In this case, of course, there were some obvious pressures and stresses. The probation officer seemed to be a reliable (strong) figure to whom the marriage partners could turn and he seemed both to have a clear perception of their situation and understanding of the part he could play.

The next section deals with the views of the probation officers who were contacted by questionnaire. The response rate was very good: twenty-six replies were received out of a possible total of thirty. A postal questionnaire was devised in order to increase the range of views of probation officers on the issues of 'care' and 'control', and on their approach to their work and general views on the purpose of probation. The circulation of the postal questionnaires was limited to three probation areas. Altogether thirty questionnaires were sent for distribution to three Probation and After Care services. Twenty-six replies were returned so that the overall response rate was regarded as good. The respondents almost without exception appeared to take a great deal of trouble in their replies. It is thus possible to give carefully thought out views of probation officers on the topics.

The tables which follow give some brief information about the

Table 3 (4) Breakdown of probation officers by age and training

Nature of training	Probation officers*	Age bracket						Total	%
		24–29	30–34	35–39	40–44	45–49	50–54		
Degree and applied social studies	P	2						2	4
	Q	4	6	1				11	19
Non graduate CQSW	P	3	3	5	4	3	2	20	36
	Q		5	2	2	2	1	12	21
Direct entry	P	1	1	1	1	2	2	8	14
	Q		1					1	2
Home Office entry	P								
	Q						2	2	4

*P = project group; Q = questionnaire group

Table 3 (5) Breakdown of probation officers by experience and training

Nature of training	Probation officers*	Years of experience since training										Total	%
		1	2	3	4	5	6	7	8	9	10+		
Degree and applied social studies	P	1										1	4
	Q	1	1	2	1							11	19
Non graduate CQSW	P	3	3	4	4	3	1		2			20	36
	Q		3	1	1	1	1	3		2		12	21
Direct entry	P	1	1	1	1	2	1	2				8	14
	Q			1								1	2
Home Office entry	P												
	Q										2	2	4

*P = project group; Q = questionnaire group

probation officers who replied to the postal questionnaire and the probation officers who took part in the other aspect of the work, that is those probation officers who were seeing the probationers interviewed for this research. One of the reasons for carrying out the postal survey initially was to increase the representation of probation officers' views. In view of the length and content of their replies the information obtained exceeded what had been expected. Being able to discuss an apparently fictitious case and to 'stand back' so to speak from their day-to-day involvements in their casework may well have encouraged these probation officers to write freely about a very difficult and important aspect of their work, the dilemmas of control and care, and to comment on the purpose of probation as they saw it. From the point of view of this project the contribution made by all the probation officers was valued and the response to the postal questionnaire was particularly good.

Probation officers were asked to study the brief case history given below and to give their replies to the following questions after reading it. 'Do you agree or disagree with the way the probation officer perceived his task? What factors or additional information about the probationer's circumstances might lead you to define the probation officer's task differently?'

The case history was as follows.

'A man aged twenty-five has a history of heavy drinking over a period of five years. He has appeared in court seven times during that time and found guilty of offences associated with his heavy drinking including assault and dangerous driving. He was placed on probation for two years. The probation officer saw it as his task partly to help the probationer to keep out of fights and away from care when he had been drinking, and partly to assist him with the problem of his intake of alcohol or giving up drinking alcohol altogether. He was also going to press the probationer to go to a psychiatric out-patient clinic and to meetings of Alcoholics Anonymous. He justified these ideas as being in the best interests of the community (by helping to avoid serious driving accidents and violence) and also as helping the probationer to deal with his emotional problems.'

It will be seen that a large number of respondents expressed some disagreement or were in some way dissatisfied with the way the case of the alcoholic and violent man was dealt with. Analysis of these replies is a little curtailed but I think the main areas of concern are

Table 3 (6) *Client with a drink problem*

Probation officers who agreed with the way the probation officer perceived his task	6*
Probation officers who disagreed	20

(*agreed in view of the serious nature of the problem)

Table 3 (7) *Probation officers' comments on actions relating to the tasks*

Probation officer needs to 'start where the client is'. He/she should make plans with the client rather than for him, build up a personal relationship and restore his self-respect, and in general help him to be more self responsible.	23
Probation officer does not possess magical powers, e.g., to help probationer keep out of fights and cannot act as escort twenty-four hours per day.	2
There is little help the probation officer can offer the persistent and heavy drinker, except to be available at times of crisis.	1

Table 3 (8) *Factors which should have been taken into account by the probation officer or additional information which would be helpful*

Probation officer should enquire into the client's motivation for drinking, his family, social, and cultural background and any stresses he experiences.	24
Probation officer should know more about client's emotional state.	2
Probation officer should know why client placed on probation.	1
Need to enquire about availability and adequacy of treatment facilities.	1

clearly shown in the summaries above. It is of particular importance to note the high valuation the respondents placed on the client's self-determination and self-respect. It will be noted that in addition to seeing this as an important moral principle respondents saw it as of 'technical' importance in trying to help him.

In looking at the factors which should be taken into account it will be seen that the social and cultural background was emphasized. (Note that some replies referred to several points here.)

Views on the Roles of Probation Officers

Fifteen probation officers saw conflict between their court duties and their professional ideology and thought that this conflict caused problems. The probation officers who were aware of conflict but said it did not cause problems seemed to identify more with the court and a 'letter of the law' approach than the other probation officers. The impression given was that they would apply the rules very strictly and thus avoid the necessity for weighing choices about interpreting the rules with social work aims in mind. It seems there-fore that the first group of respondents were more flexible in their approach although this did not imply unscrupulous disregard for the law nor any desire to undermine it — rather the contrary. Finally, and unexpectedly, members of the group who thought that the conflict did not cause problems said they were able to deal with potential conflict because of their professionalism and strong sense of identity in the Probation and After Care Service.

A number of officers were not too happy with the way diagnostic or descriptive categories were used in the postal questionnaire. This is reflected in the results; it can be seen (*Table 3 (11)*) that 'anyone if necessary' is used to deal with individual needs. That probation officers should both set limits and provide support is in a sense the

Table 3 (9) *Views on conflict between court duties and social work ideology*

Agree: there is a conflict	15
Disagree	11

Table 3 (10) *Ways in which probation officers dealt with conflict between court duty and social work ideology and response of probation officers who saw no conflict*

Probation officer aware of conflict but denies that it gives rise to problems and sees probation in limited terms.	3
Probation officer accepts that there is conflict and is open about this and may indicate it to his clients. He tries to encourage both the probationer and himself to view the relationship as one where power and authority conflicts are present. He interprets the probation rules carefully.	12
Probation officer feels there is no need for conflict to arise for a 'professional'. He is not coerced by anyone (e.g. court does not tell him how to do his job).	11

Probation and After Care officer's job and I quote one respondent's comment on this question. Most respondents were still against making probation a punitive measure (*Table 3 (13)*).

Table 3 (11) *Ways probation officers differentiated between probationers in their approach*

Probation officer set limits for:	
psychopathic person	2
markedly immature person	2
resentful person	5
acting out client	5
alcoholics	5
mentally retarded person	2
adolescents	1
anyone if necessary	3
Probation officers provided support for:	
neurotic/psychotic people	3
young mothers with financial problems	1
family problems	1
anyone if necessary	20
Probation officers set limits and provided support for:	
subnormal people	1
drink dependent people	2
recidivists	1
for most clients because these are the two basic ingredients in most probation relationships	2*
for all clients	11
number of probation officers who said you could not generalize in this way	7

*Several probation officers said that they would provide support and set limits for all groups of clients as necessary. 'There should be no reason why a probation officer cannot set limits and be supportive and this should be the indicator of a good probation officer' sums up their opinion. Two probation officers said 'I do not see why control and support should be incompatible'.

Under the general purpose of probation one respondent suggested that where there was a finding called 'non conviction' this could enable probation to be used, thus 'allowing a court to exercise caution in the absence of information on an offender — an avoidance of unnecessary expense without abdicating the right of oversight'. The respondent who added 'work with family' was among the twenty-two probation officers whose responses were in the first category.

The replies to the questions on care and control and the general

Table 3 (12) *Views on whether probation should be a substitute for another kind of sentence*

Yes: for isolated and inadequate people	1
Yes: for any clients with problems	2
Yes: for political offenders	1
Yes: for meter breakers and shop lifters	2
Yes: for drug and alcohol abuse	2
Yes: for more positive reasons	2
Probation always is a substitute	1
No:	15

Table 3 (13) *Probation officers' views on who probation should be a punishment for*

Some younger clients	1
Middle class swindlers	1
No one	22*

*But many respondents felt their clients themselves saw it as a punishment because of stigma being attached to probation.

Table 3 (14) *Probation officers' views on general purposes of probation (questionnaire respondents)*

To set limits for probationers and to provide treatment, i.e. to counsel and assist the client, help him to gain a better understanding of his problem(s)/situation and help him to use this understanding in changing his behaviour.	24
Help with family relationships	1
To meet individual needs of clients	1

purpose of probation may not be surprising to practising officers. They are interesting though in linking up with another part of this enquiry in which the views of probationers and probation officers were obtained in personal interviews. Their replies are given in *Table 3 (15)*.

To illustrate the replies of the probation officers who responded to the postal questionnaires I am paraphrasing what they said and using quotations from the questionnaires, in order to stress points which appeared important to the respondents or simply because they seem necessary to express the respondents' meaning. The views of two probation officers are given below. The use of clearly defined contracts with probationers is becoming much more widespread in

Table 3 (15) *Purpose of probation as seen by probationers and probation officers*

	Probationers replies	Probation officers' replies
To set limits for probationers and to provide 'treatment', i.e. to counsel and assist the client help him to gain a better understanding of his situation and to use this in changing his behaviour	90	18 (90%)
To provide supervision during a trial period when the probationer could re-adjust	none	none
Help with family relationships	3	1 (5%)
Help with practical matters or material aid	7	1 (5%)

the service and both of these officers found it desirable and apparently useful to their clients. Another general point which occurs in these summaries is the stress laid by probation officers on respect for the probationer and encouraging him to exercise choice in appropriate situations.

EXAMPLE

A probation officer (non-graduate CQSW and in the early thirties age bracket and with five years experience) made it very clear that he saw the help required by the probationer 'very much in terms of directive casework and contractual agreement. The client appears to be too "damaged" to accept any pussyfoot or arrogant approach' no matter how well intentioned this was. This officer would not recommend a probation order if the alcoholic and violent client would not agree to a strictly framed contract. He emphasized that some form of contract should be agreed before the probation order was made so that the client had formally agreed to the 'treatment' described. You could not *press* a person to recognize a problem such as alcoholism, which by its nature is not easily admitted to. Other factors which would lead him to define the probation officer's task differently were the client's wife and children and their attitudes and the attitudes of the client's and other close relatives. It would be helpful to know about the client's sociability and patterns of social behaviour, and also the extent to which alcohol was recognized as a problem to the probationer himself and to other people.

He saw the purpose of probation as to control or limit probationers' behaviour and to help the client in changing his behaviour. In addition it was 'to introduce the client to a better position of sociability by using other resources and members of the community, for example, volunteers and clubs'. He did not agree that there was a conflict between being a servant of the court and a professional social worker. He thought it necessary to define limits with very immature, and mentally retarded clients 'and others as and when it seems appropriate to do so'. A supportive relationship was appropriate for 'short-term clients who I am sure can consequently readjust, i.e., dependency can cause havoc at the end of an order'. Whether probation officers should be dealing with psychopathic, neurotic, and psychotic persons was questioned. 'I appreciate the grey areas between the extremes but the further one moves to the extreme the less likely it is that the probation officer will have anything to offer.' Probation should not be a substitute for another kind of sentence and it should be a punishment for no one.

EXAMPLE

A probation officer (with a law degree and applied social studies qualification (CQSW) in the age bracket 24—29 and two years experience) disagreed with the idea of referring the client to Alcoholics Anonymous or for psychiatric help if he was not interested. He saw the task as 'to encourage any attempt to control his drinking and to facilitate any contacts the client may wish to make... To try to find alternative interests and occupations to take him away from the pub and to point up the positive results of sobriety.' It would be helpful to have information relating to a root cause for the original heavy drinking of an emotional or personal nature. He saw probation as having three components: punishment, control of behaviour, and counselling. Necessary limits were agreed in the majority of cases and support should be given to: 'Any client whose level of coping in a situation necessitates it, because he will not be able to cope otherwise. The level of support given obviously varies.' Probation should be a sentence in its own right (not a substitute) and the need for it judged by the needs of the client even though a tariff system might demand another sentence. Probation is always a punishment since the sanctions of the court are made clear in every case. The probation officer's conflict between caring and controlling 'is inescapable since the officer's obligation to implement the order of the court and the fact that he is seen as associated with the court, rather than the client, will often negate trust, frankness, and acceptance in the social work relationship and cause treatment plans to be altered because of the client's return to court etc.' He dealt with conflict: '(a) by clearly stating my position as a probation officer with regard to the court and client; (b) by drawing up and keeping to a social work contract which defines how far the social work aims can be followed before the conflict becomes too great.'

This probation officer was particularly clear in expressing his views on dealing with probation officer's conflict. His reply covers points made by other questionnaire respondents.

Summary: The Results of the Postal Questionnaire

(1) Thirty questionnaires were sent to probation officers in three Probation and After Care Services and twenty-six were returned.

(2) The majority of respondents had some criticisms to make of treatment suggested in the case of a man with problems of alcohol and violent behaviour.

(3) A high proportion of these comments were related to the principles of respect for the person and self-determination.

(4) The importance of social and cultural background was emphasized in an equally high proportion of comments.

(5) Less than one third of the respondents did not agree that there is a conflict for probation officers between their obligations to the court and professional social work ideology.

(6) Of the probation officers who agreed that there is a conflict twelve dealt with it by being open about it if appropriate with their clients and by recognizing that the probation officer/probationer (parolee) relationship involves inequality of power and authority, although this does not mean that a partnership is not feasible.

(7) Most respondents disagreed with suggestions about the provision of psychological support in relation to specified 'diagnostic' categories. They felt there were some clearer indications for setting limits in terms of these categories but even then tended to qualify their remarks.

(8) Probation could be used instead of other kinds of sentences for isolated and inadequate people, and for meter breakers and shop lifters. (Most of these were by one person or two people and the answers were therefore varied.)

(9) The majority of respondents said probation should not be a punishment (i.e., all respondents except two).

(10) The general purpose of probation was seen as setting limits to behaviour and providing a supportive relationship in which the client could work on his difficulties.

Concluding Discussion

Thirty probation officers were involved in the supervision of probationers and twenty-seven of these officers saw probation as helping the individual through assisting him materially, and through counselling, helping him to gain a better understanding of his situation if possible, and helping him to modify his behaviour. This seems to be a large category but a dual concern is implied. It is to help not only the individual in his relation to society but also society in its relationships with the individual. This follows the notion that casework has a functional concern with the welfare of the individual and of society. Thus all of the officers said that one purpose of probation was to offer psychological help in some way when this was appropriate (that is in cases where not just material aid was required). Another function was a traditional one, that of befriending probationers although this was seldom expressed in this way except by longer serving officers. Like many of the probationers (90 out of 100) project probation officers saw regulations or control of probationers' behaviour as an important object of probation. Their role was an authoritative one in which they were expected to try to induce probationers to conform to socially (or legally) acceptable standards of behaviour. Some of the longer serving or older probation officers gave 'text book' replies with little further comment or quoted the Probation of Offenders Act.

The probation officers who were closer to their training in time expressed different attitudes to their work than probation officers at the other end of their careers. The closer they were to their training the less set the probation officers were in their attitudes; they were less steeped in the 'office culture'. There were exceptions. One probation officer of considerable experience since training was noticeably more liberal and flexible in his approach than two less experienced colleagues. But the general trend seems credible in the light of other research quoted. The evidence about teachers' attitudes is suggestive and lends support to an increasing body of opinion about the training of social workers. It may be that there is some truth in the charge that social work teachers may too easily lose touch with the realities of social work practice. This may well lead them to be unrealistic in their views about what social workers should be doing and to fail to prepare students properly for the difficulties of applying theory to practice. Such a situation is unlikely to be resolved until there is greater movement between social work teaching and social work practice and greater and clearer recognition of the importance of supervised field work. For many if not all 'professionals' there appears to be a need for periodic re-training or 'topping up' of training in order to keep up-to-date and to broaden horizons or develop fresh perspectives again.

If probation officers as a group are thought of as being placed along a continuum it would seem that in terms of training and experience most of the officers in this research spanned the middle of the range of basic grade officers. How does length of time since training, and the officer's experience during that time, affect his attitudes to his work and his role? We have no straightforward answer to this question but it is possible to put forward some suggestions. For example research on the attitudes of teachers is accumulating. One study contrasted the attitudes of student teachers and head teachers; the latter were more conservative and expected greater conformity from children than the first group (Finlayson and Cohen 1967). They found similar tendencies when student teachers were at college and when they were in teaching practice, and later in their careers. The tendency was for their attitudes towards education during time spent at college to change during time spent in schools, in the direction of becoming less radical and less liberal. It has been shown that distinct changes occur in teachers' conception of their roles, as they move from being students, to going to teaching practice, and then becoming fully fledged teachers. After one year in teaching the woman teacher sees herself in her role differently from the way she originally thought she would be. She sees herself as *less* happy, relaxed, perceptive, confident, and inspiring but as *more* blaming, demanding and impulsive than she had imagined at the beginning of training (Wright and Tuska 1968). Another study found that over a three-year period teachers became less concerned with pupil freedom, and more concerned with establishing a stable orderly classroom with the importance of academic standards being stressed. The change was accompanied by a decline in the tendency to attribute pupil misbehaviour or academic difficulty to the teacher or the school (Rabinowitz and Rosenbaum 1960). The peak of radical and liberal educational attitudes appeared to come in the second year in the college of education followed by a distinct decline in the third year (Edwards 1975). It seems that the teacher must in the first few years of his career come to terms with the realities of life in school. How much of the change in attitudes of a teacher after training is attributable to the influence of the attitudes of other teachers to which as a member of staff he is under pressure to conform, and how much they are to do with the practical problems of managing a class which damage the ideals of education acquired in training is not clear. It may be that similar attitude changes occur in the course of probation officers' careers and in the careers of other social workers.

A case illustration is given to provide examples of some of the results and shows a probation officer exercising a firm but kind influence on the probationers, who expressed a positive response, saying that the relationship was a friendly one, and that the probation officer listened and tried to understand.

The second part of the chapter dealt with the results of a postal questionnaire returned by twenty-six out of a total of thirty possible replies. The questionnaire which was different from that of the project probation officers' (who dealt with individual cases) included a short case history as a focus for some questions. A high proportion of the replies related to principles of respect for the person and self-determination. As well as being orientated to counselling the replies indicated concern with sociological factors. Where conflict between the interests of the community and the welfare of the client was involved it was suggested that the probation officer should be open about this with the probationer and recognize that the relationship involved inequality of power. This would not imply that a working relationship was not possible. The general purpose of probation was seen as the setting of limits to some aspects of behaviour and providing a supportive relationship in which the client could be helped to work on his difficulties. Like the highest proportion of probationers the highest proportion of all the probation officers, fifty-one out of fifty-six (90 per cent) perceived probation as combining personal counselling and helping in the control of behaviour.

An interesting commentary relevant to these observations is seen in the point of view of one radical writer and practising social worker (Simpkin 1979:155-57) who said that welfare need not necessarily be oppressive and it should be acknowledged that social workers play some part in maintaining social control. Some control, he argues, even if it does initially constrain the individual, can be necessary and beneficial. He counsels radicals not to repudiate control unless they follow through all the implications of this stance. The control aspect of social work stems both from their being state employees and from the nature of social work itself. He sees the social worker being expected and needed to act as mediator between individual and individual and between individuals or groups, and the state, as well as being an advocate of reform. He argued that it is difficult but not impossible to practise a social work which minimizes control and at least opens up some possibilities for development. Unlike teachers and policemen social workers are privileged in being licensed to criticize as the institutionalized conscience of society. The difficulties or strain involved for social workers, to which Simpkin refers, reflect ambiguities and difficulties facing them as they attempt to analyse, implement, or modify social policy. Conflicting ideologies may be found in legislation as well as agency rules and most social workers seem to subscribe to several ideologies which they see as applying to different aspects of their situation. Sometimes an ideology is not implemented because of conflicting ideas and/or interests. On the other hand an ideology may be adopted as a way of making sense of a situation so that it is a subjective mechanism for resolving strains (Smith 1977). Another way of dealing with conflicting expectations is referred to in discussing probation officers' roles above. This involves them in studying and closely adhering to the regulations governing their work and this contrasts with a more flexible approach and possibly a less strict implementation of rules in some cases.

4 Social Work Practice: Power and Influence in Welfare Agencies

In Chapter 2 I reviewed some work on consumers' views of social agencies which could influence the organization and practice of . social work. There are problems in using research on consumers' views but, in addition to these it is worth questioning how much power or potential power clients have. There seems to be some force in the argument that the power of the client, community, and the professional constituencies are far too weak compared with powerful legal, organizational, and governmental influences on social work (Payne 1979:234). Conflict between the various patterns of power and responsibility is inevitable in Social Service Departments and Payne argues that the policies of the organization, the political system, legal responsibilities, the needs of the community, and the standards of social workers in managing their work all have an important part to play as influences on Social Services Departments. Some notion of the position of social work in relation to these social pressures must be arrived at but it is hard to draw a general conclusion; the issue has to be worked out in individual situations as they arise. Payne's argument is persuasive although it should be possible to detect trends in social workers' views and responses to social pressures, and how these affect their relationships with their clients. Analysis of the roles of social workers in Probation and After Care and Social Services Departments, and in particular the ways in which they persuade, influence, or coerce clients is difficult and rather subtle. Not only is analysis of some slippery concepts required, so that part of the discussion has to be at an abstract level, but also the organization's influence on the social worker has to be considered. There are a number of perspectives on this question and, as with discussion of other topics in this book, the area is a controversial one: I propose to draw on some recent work on the identity crisis of social workers in local authority Social Services Departments which I

find convincing on the descriptive level and, with some qualifi-
cations, on the analytic level too. This work usefully looks at implications for practice and from this concrete starting point the discussion of questions of control in health and social services and related organizational issues can proceed.

The Identity Crisis of Social Workers in Local Authorities

A continuing preoccupation in public debate and in social work
literature is the identity of contemporary social work. This is reflected in discussions of social work's crisis of identity — in arguments about its value, its confused aims, and lack of coherent ideas
about methods. Satyamurti (Parry, Rustin, and Satyamurti 1979:89)
succinctly summarized a number of factors contributing to the sense
of crisis. She wrote:

> 'Part of the explanation for it lies in the the growth of radicalism
> in higher education since the late 1960's, which has affected
> many more people than would identify themselves as politically
> left wing, and has led to a scepticism towards individualistic
> explanations and solutions of social ills and to an 'end of ideo-
> logy' with respect to casework. Another factor has been generally
> increased reluctance to take social inequality for granted and
> consequently a greater awareness, not always formulated, of the
> shortage of available resources. But another factor, to which little
> attention has been given, relates particularly to local authority
> social workers' position as state employees and to what may be
> seen as a gradually crystallising contradiction between different
> elements of their occupational role. On the one hand social
> workers are supposed to provide a caring service, responsive to
> the needs of the client. This is what most people have in mind
> when they become social workers, and social work in this sense is
> part of a long philanthropic tradition. But local authority social
> work also had its roots in the poor law and is directly involved in
> control functions towards the deviant and dependent.'

This passage of Satyamurti is clearly relevant to a discussion of
social work and social control and she provides an historical perspective on the subject. While I agree with some of her major points I
differ from her in seeing a *necessary* contradiction between caring
and controlling. It seems that many social workers do find difficulty

in accepting unrealistic expectations of the controls they should exercise over clients and I would argue that some of these expectations
(such as some instanced by Satyamurti) are fatuous and impracticable
(even if their desirability was acceptable). I also argue that there is
a tension between caring and controlling which cannot be resolved in
an absolute sense. But in some situations there is agreement that
caring about a person can also involve exercising control over his behaviour, depriving him of choice, or limiting his freedom of action
because it would be harmful to other people and/or to himself.
Satyamurti's argument is that incorporating the caring and controlling aspects of welfare (analytically inseparable, but until recently institutionally distinct) into the role of local authority social worker,
confronts social workers with *irreconcilable* objectives and is a major
factor contributing to the sense of crisis. I hope to analyse this
suggestion further, referring to Satyamurti's work and to points of
agreement as well as difference. Satyamurti (Parry, Rustin, and
Satyamurti 1979:90-6) considered the care and control functions of
social work in the late nineteenth and twentieth centuries and proposed that 'it [social work] first has to be thought of as submerged
in the general development of intervention in the welfare field by
the state, and by large scale, organized private bodies.' The development was made up of complex factors, concern about the poor
physical condition of men available for military service, pressure for
reform from various directions, and fear of social unrest being some
of them. But the development of the welfare state should not be
seen in monolithic terms: different facets of welfare provision had
their origins in differing political, intellectual, and moral climates.

Satyamurti discussed changes in the poor law and the voluntary organizations and noted that the exercise of authority and control was
an important aspect of social work although redeemed and disguised
from the worker (if not the client) by a relationship in which concern
for the individual was central. After the Second World War came the
major reorganization of social services, the demise of the poor law,
and a rethinking of the distribution of care and control functions. For
the first time (except for the probation service) trained social workers
entered the statutory sphere bringing a further development in the
convergence of care and control functions by fusing them within a
single occupational role — that of child care officer. The functions of
care and control further merged from the 1940s onwards.

'During this period the range of powers and duties vested in local authority social workers has greatly increased. Many of these powers and duties involve the exercise of authority, within the framework of a relationship that is ostensibly focused on the good of the client but where there is room for substantial difference of interpretation as to what the good of the client is. The whole area of work with young people arising out of the 1969 Children and Young Persons Act is a case in point. The reorganization of the personal social services in the 1970's has meant that the control functions involved in work with old people, homeless families and the mentally ill have been added to those involved in child care work as part of the role of the generic social worker and this has made social workers more conscious of their role as rationing agents and authority figures.'

Social Distance and Social Work Relationships

Professional and occupational groups have their own specialized languages which are often unintelligible to outsiders and which have several functions. One of the most esoteric of these languages is that of medicine. The doctor's emotional situation is a difficult one and is reflected in the use of language to maintain social distance from patients and any involvement with their future: he must not allow himself to think and *feel* them as individuals. This is seen in the habit doctors have of calling patients by the names of their diseases. Doctors have learned to withdraw their emotions from the state of the patients and have replaced their own ability to imagine and empathize with them in order to retain their objective professional judgement. The plural pronoun 'we' is used to make sure that the doctor is not alone nor out on a limb. Saying 'we see a lot of that' is a way of identifying themselves as members of a knowledgeable elite. In medical training (though perhaps less frequently nowadays), doctors have been systematically taught scientific-sounding euphemisms and terms to be used when patients are present. Because of his emotional situation it is difficult for the doctor to use vernacular language although of course it is sometimes necessary to do so with the patient. He may have recourse to a kind of jocularity or drollery, seen for example in talking to a patient about her hysterectomy: 'We're taking out the cradle but we're leaving in the play-pen.' Some interesting parallels are seen in the study of social workers' attitudes by Satyamurti mentioned above.

Several social workers in her study said that although they disliked being professionally aloof, in practice they felt they had to maintain some social distance between themselves and their clients. Otherwise it would be more difficult to exercise authority if the need arose. Sometimes what they had in mind was an eventuality involving direct coercion—a compulsory reception of a child into care or admission to psychiatric hospital, for example. Perhaps more often, in the case of families, the authority situation they most readily envisaged was one in which the client asked for money and the social worker would have either to refuse or impose conditions on the client. Social workers seeking to maintain distance from their clients had an interest in sustaining client stereotypes. One such stereotype was to perceive clients as irresponsible, disorganized, and dependent. In some cases it seemed that clients learned to behave in a dependent manner, being encouraged to do so by their social workers—whether consciously or unconsciously. Stereotyping the client as child-like enables social workers to adopt the role of parent, but may make it necessary to deny or invalidate aspects of the client's behaviour which do not fit in with the stereotype. In addition to stereotyping social workers had other shared conceptualizations of clients' needs, of their roles in relation to these, and symbolic features of interaction. One interpretation of this was that the social worker diminished the client's status as an adult and citizen; this was reminiscent of, though more subtle than, the ways the person receiving poor relief in the nineteenth century was stigmatized and diminished (Satyamurti in Parry, Rustin, and Satyamurti 1979:98).

Satyamurti referred to a range of linguistic and classificatory devices by which social workers distanced themselves from their clients and instanced the word 'manipulative' as just one example. Sometimes these devices were used to avoid pain: a complex and stressful experience on the client's part would be described by the social worker in flat clinical terms for example. Words like 'manipulative' or 'difficult' were used to invalidate clients' claims which were seen as threatening to engulf the social worker with demands. Social workers had a kind of 'seige' perspective which led them to feel that people had to be deterred from approaching the department, the

area of financial aid being the statutory activity that occasioned
most worry. As far as management was concerned the solution was
that social workers were to exercise controls in giving money. Ideally
these would ensure that financial problems would not recur and
would also deter potential applicants so that the receipt of help
would seem less attractive. This was done by social workers visiting
and making thorough assessments, asking personal questions,
perhaps collecting the rent, possibly insisting on administering the
family allowance money. Thus the client would experience a number
of disagreeable consequences if help was given. There was a widespread view that a social worker should resist client pressure to give
financial help and should have some alternative to offer. At one level
social workers shared this view and often felt depressed and guilty
about giving money. On another level they were conscious that often
clients got into financial difficulties because their income was inadequate, and felt concern for peoples' needs. They were caught in a
dilemma between care and control, that is between a wish simply to
help and a wish to behave responsibly by the department's standards.

I think that problems arise in making these and similar interpretations and comparing them with alternative perspectives (like some
of those given here). One difficulty is that some people are able to
communicate their feelings of humiliation and both they and an outside observer who is aware of some social workers' and social security officials' attitudes can, to some extent at least, understand the
feeling. The observer's 'understanding' rests on seeing how the interaction between client and worker seems to elicit or heighten feelings
of humiliation or being treated as inferior. In many cases feelings of
resentment, humiliation, and fears of an impersonal welfare system
are experienced by people who are *not* treated disrespectfully by
social workers or officials, who may try to minimize or reduce feelings associated with dependency in the way they offer help. The
situation becomes more complicated when people seeking to provide
a service feel that they are being required to operate rules or procedures which may be demeaning to their clients. If clients perceive
this they may behave in ways which they think are expected of
them: the social workers' apprehensions are correctly read by the
client who then colludes with the worker. Disentangling complex reciprocal perceptions of this nature is hazardous. There is reason then
to look for interpretations in addition to, or as alternatives to, the

cribed here. The symbolic ways of maintaining social dis-
tween people are sometimes part of the accepted idea of
nal behaviour. They include, in the case of social workers,
not using Christian names or not permitting the client to use the
social worker's Christian name although the social worker calls the
client by his or her Christian name. They also include discouraging
clients from showing interest in the social worker's personal life and
not accepting hospitality or gifts from clients. Satyamurti found that
few of the social workers in her study valued these aspects of professional behaviour but they did not feel safe in changing such
practices (Parry, Rustin, and Satyamurti, 1979:98).

There are some difficulties in discussing symbolic aspects of behaviour at a general level. It needs to be recognized that a great deal
depends on how individual social workers perceive the psychological
state of individuals seeking help or even being sent for help. The
ways in which people address each other do appear to be of considerable significance in interaction and as Satyamurti implies they
involve value judgements. The reinforcing of feelings of subordination through the one-sided use of a first name (that is social
worker to client) is distasteful to many and also seems to carry the
risk of being counter-productive. It raises questions about what
training in social skills potential social workers are given and what
ethical assumptions may underlie them. It seems odd that a group of
social workers should find it necessary to continue with practices
they see as being forms of defence against their clients, rather than
working in a more positive way, for example through openly recognizing and helping to ease an unequal relationship. In itself this
discussion seems to illustrate lack of consensus or a degree of confusion about professional ideology and suggests a need for further
analysis in order to identify different, competing, or complementary
ideologies. This could be of positive help to clients who may find the
variety and vagaries of social workers' behaviour rather bewildering.
The question of maintenance of social distance and clients' feelings
about it is discussed in a stimulating book by Hugman (1977) who
argues that for many clients distancing by the social worker is hard
to accept and that they would prefer the social worker to 'act
natural'.

To Satyamurti the ways social workers distanced themselves from
their clients were strategies of survival both to enable them to handle
situations involving them in exercising control and to reduce the

pain inherent in their work. Being closely associated with clients' suffering, possibly contributing to it, and being able to do relatively little about it were seen as sources of social workers' pain, made more difficult to bear through lack of (or poor) supervision, so that social workers had to operate largely alone. Satyamurti pointed out that she did not want to suggest that the social workers in her study viewed their clients entirely as a threat or that they derived no satisfaction from their relationships with them. But the social workers seemed to be driven back on each other as the main source of satisfaction and support and this tendency was an important influence on the organization of the social work team. The support of colleagues was of very great importance to social workers' survival in the job and it was apparently more important than anything offered by senior social workers. Dependence on colleagues and commitment to them militated against the introduction of innovations and team meetings were almost invariably outpourings of dissatisfaction or grievance against others and were rarely occasions when problems were resolved or tackled.

Concepts of Social Influence

Persuasion refers to attempts to induce beliefs or actions through arguments, pleading, or urging. This implies that the persuader relies on moral or psychological pressure or the force of logical argument to attain his or her goal. It seems that persuasion may best be characterized as a gradual process, moving in stages such as gaining attention, comprehension, yielding, retention, and eventually, overt behaviour or attitude change. The persuader may be seeking behavioural conformity or attitude change, or both. Coercion refers to situations where the change agent is able, because of his or her power base, to exercise restraint, force, or physical control over the victim. This implies that the coercive agent is able to do more than manipulate information. He or she is in a position to control the environment and possibly corrupt and/or abuse power and authority. It is expected that the victim will give way or obey the change agent. A precise distinction between coercion and persuasion is difficult to make and the terms influence and control are often used interchangeably. The terms used to denote social influence processes carry implicit value judgements and elicit rather negative emotional responses (McGuire, in I. de Sola Pool 1973:225-26). In the social sciences language is

used not only descriptively but also promotively, that is to communicate not only how things are but also how they ought to be.

In analysing coercion and persuasion consideration of norms and
context affect the account in two ways. First, the vocabulary that is
used (which is everyday and non-technical language) is coloured by
moral judgements. Using such vocabulary means adopting a set of
views about right and wrong. Second, in applying this vocabulary a
set of rules is required and these are bound to reflect the social situation of the user. The meaning of the words has to take into account
the social context. It may be agreed that coercion is bad but people
may have different views about whether a particular event is or is
not coercive. Such problems of course are not peculiar to these
terms nor are they confined to the social sciences. An analogous
argument may be put forward about the vocabulary used to describe
responses to persuasion or coercion. The words used, compliance,
conformity, deviance, and obedience to authority, are all imbued
with value judgements.

Personal Relationships and Types of Power

It has been argued that control is a neutral concept. Everyone living
in some form of group is controlled in some way by that group. But
in social work the word takes on a more specific meaning since in
many instances the relationship between social worker and client is
not voluntary. The concept has no emotive value other than that we
give it but it is often linked with authoritarianism and rigidity. This
analysis is taken further by Tutt in his description of different kinds
of power (see Tutt (1979) who quotes from the original article by
French and Raven (1959)).

French and Raven's description of the power structure within
personal relationships can be applied to social work. Five types of
power are distinguished.

Reward Power. The social worker has this power over the client and
can use it to reward behaviour he or she wishes to encourage. The
use of certain allowances for clients, offers of holidays, and inter-
mediate treatment activities could all be construed as reward power.

Coercive Power. The client is punished if he or she does not behave
in the required way. This is the converse of reward power. It is
illustrated by allowing attendance centre orders to be issued for
breach of a supervision order (Criminal Law Act, 1977).

Legitimate Power. This exists when the controlled person has an internalized system of attitudes or beliefs which includes recognizing the right of the controller to control. A number of clients will accept that the social worker may legitimately order their lives. Other professionals apparently have far greater legitimate power, for example doctors in giving orders about diet.

Referent Power. Operates when the controlled person identifies closely with the controller, and this is seen as the basis of much of social work.

Expert Power. The controlled person accepts the greater knowledge of the controller and consequently accepts his or her control. Although closely connected with legitimate power it is different. For example a client may accept a social worker's advice on how to claim benefits because of the social worker's greater knowledge rather than because the client sees the social worker's power as legitimate.

Processes of Coercion and Persuasion

Where is the dividing line between the individual's self-control and external control drawn? The difference between self-control and control by others rests only in who is manipulating what stimuli. All behaviour control is stimulus control and awareness is the key to self-control because it enables the individual to manoeuvre his or her own sources of stimulation (London 1969:269-70). In studying individual responses to coercion and persuasion one is dealing with complex relationships, for example, between the sender (variables such as the structure of the communication, the kind of appeal, the sender's trustworthiness), and the receiver (variables such as primary or other group memberships, initial attitude, and psychological responses).

Jahoda (1959) wrote a comprehensive paper on the question: using a concrete example, the position of people on the issue of capital punishment, her analysis assumed that before external influence is brought to bear everyone accepts capital punishment as appropriate for certain crimes. After some influence has been brought to bear, some people hold to their position and some change. The analysis indicated eight processes contributing to the result. There is the person who though reached by the campaign does not change his mind and feels at ease about his position. (This is independent dissent.) A second type of person adheres to his previous position but feels uneasy. (Undermined independence.) The third category (independent consent) describes a person who has changed his mind, following disagreements with others but is now again at ease. The fourth process involves taking a stand against one's own conviction, private opinion remaining as before. This process presupposes very strong pressures on the person. (It is referred to as compliance.) Where a person regards the issue of capital punishment as peripheral and does not change his mind or feel any conflict about it this position is referred to as compulsive resistance. This type of behaviour appears unreasonable and would be expected in those who lack the essential ability to respond to external pressure.

In the next process a person has strong views on issues associated with capital punishment (e.g. an American liberal concerned about Russian spies). These factors touch on his feelings about the issue; his frame of reference has shifted. (Expedient resistance.) Where there is no involvement with the issue and the position is changed without creating conflict no strong influence is necessary. (This is conformity in the narrow sense.) Finally emotional and intellectual investment in the individual's system of beliefs makes it expedient to go along with social pressures. (His agreement is expedient conformity.) The scheme defining eight distinguishable acts has the property that one and the same person can perform any one of them, depending on the subject matter, the social influences which are exercised and the conditions under which this occurs. The scheme does not underrate personality factors and time span. When the individual's life space is dominated by the past there is inability to conform. When the present is dominant independent dissent will be unlikely and conformity will be the rule. Independent action is most likely when the time dimension is balanced between past, present, and future.

Social Work Practice, Theory, and Ideology

In a critical assessment of social work theory and practice it was argued that social work activity has been grossly oversimplified to fit theoretical assumptions about the nature of society and ideological positions. This falls hard on social workers who have to deal with some of the most difficult people in society (Fowler in Jones 1975:94-8).

Statements about objectives are often so sweeping in their claims as to be useless for the purpose of discussing methods of work. They often imply that social work is mainly concerned with individual care and totally ignore the issue of control. Thus you find uncritical acceptance of Rogers' client-centred approach which suggests that therapy and authority cannot coexist in the same relationship. Until only fairly recently the social work profession has given little attention to the idea of the social worker as a powerful figure. Social workers have tended to disclaim the role of authority and the idea that power is used in practice. Thibaut and Kelly (1959, in Goldstein 1973:280) refer to three kinds of control accruing to an individual whose power lies in his superior position.

Fate control exists where the rewards one desires depend on the choices or whims of another. This is not to say that the social worker controls the destiny of the members of the client system. But many existential issues are influenced by the practitioner, particularly by his choices for action based on how he evaluates the problem and what outcomes he anticipates. Whimsicality cannot be excluded; human choices can be made on the basis of momentary impressions, new ideas garnered from a recently read and appealing book, or how the practitioner feels at a given moment. In any event, the decisions and choices of the social worker do affect the subsequent sequence and direction of events. Decisions to accept or reject the presenting symptom in terms of importance, the involvement of another member of a family in the treatment of a marital problem, the inclusion or exclusion of a group member, or the selection of data for presentation to a policy-making body are obvious examples of how at least the immediate life experience of others can be influenced by the control of the social worker.

Behaviour control is the power one has to influence changes in the behaviour of another, usually through varying his own behaviour. In a sense, this control points to a major intent of the social worker — the deliberate development of the influence and leverage needed to bring about changes in the way clients behaviourally deal with problems. Examples are numerous, particularly in the imbalanced relationship in which the subordinate may seek cues and direction for the behaviour that he believes is expected. The social worker employs direct means of behaviour control in the form of guidance, direction, interpretation, and information giving: and indirect means by symbols that convey reward, approbation, or reinforcement.

Depending on the task or goal, the social worker approaches those persons related to the problem either as a power figure or as an authority figure. The social worker is a power figure when he is acting on behalf of the social welfare community and its statutory provisions for purposes of social control — for example, as a child protective services worker, as a probation or parole officer, or as a member of an institution. The social worker is an authority figure when he is acting on behalf of the social welfare community and its institutionalized systems of skill, resources, and knowledge designed to ameliorate pernicious social conditions — for example, with the intent to organize residents of decaying neighbourhoods; to work with youth groups; or to offer services to the poor, the ill, and the ageing. In the first case, the social worker carries delegated power — the right and the ability to bring about change through forms of direct control. In the second, the social worker carries delegated authority — the right and ability to bring about change by the employment of special skills, competences, and resources. This analysis of different kinds of control is helpful in making distinctions between power and authority which will be illustrated later. An important value in casework and counselling is individual dignity and emphasis on the client's right to select his or her own goals. However, it has been argued that the right is not absolute and the social worker cannot aspire to be totally non-directive (Davison 1965:21).

The probation and after care officer is clearly seen as an agent of social control because of his identification with court and penal settings. It will be helpful to place the control function in context by looking at other kinds of situations where social workers are involved and where their control functions are 'coercively' and 'persuasively' exercised. First we can examine work with or on behalf of children and their families, and the power social workers have in helping them. An illustration of a case of child abuse will be quoted, and this will be followed by a short case summary about a sixteen-year-old girl in foster care, and then a longer account of work with a family will be given. Work with a mentally handicapped person and his family has some parallels with some of the probation cases quoted. From being resented initially the social worker came to be seen as a helpful authority by family members. I then discuss situations in which clients are unable or unwilling to take decisions for themselves and where the social worker places limits on their freedom of choice.

A preliminary discussion of developments in social work with children may be of value in considering these cases. The Children Act of 1948 was the direct result of general concern about children deprived of normal home life. In the child care field social workers work to help children, foster parents, and natural parents. The social worker is responsible for pursuing the interests and welfare of the child and in carrying out the legal duties which are involved. A great deal of this responsibility is shared of course with a range of institutions, resources, and other people including parents and foster parents. The social worker's authority in relation to the welfare of children and families has points of similarity with the use of authority in other areas of social work. Thus under children's legislation a social worker may institute court proceedings to gain parental control. But if the parents or guardians fail to appear at court with the child it then becomes the responsibility of the police to execute the summons. But once a Fit Person Order is made the social worker may remove a child whatever the wishes of the parents or the child. (In a way this is similar to the social worker's action as mental welfare officer.) A social worker may also apply for a warrant empowering him (or her) to enter a home to search for a child said to be in need of care. In a similar way a mental welfare officer may gain access to a sick person who is said to be a danger to himself or others.

The supposed dangers of abuse of power have been discussed (Handler 1968) on the basis of a very limited study of the work of children's departments in England in the 1960s. Handler's main findings are presented here. He noted that Section 1 of the Children's and Young Persons Act, 1963, authorizes children's departments to try to prevent family breakdown and the reception of children into care by means of casework and, if necessary, assistance in kind, or, in exceptional circumstances cash. It was noted that the departments had connections with the administration of justice. Children may be brought before juvenile courts if they commit offences for which an adult would be sent to prison or if they refuse to attend school. Children's departments have authority to investigate and to bring children before the courts for care, protection or control. If a case is proved, the child may be committed to a local authority (in practice, the children's department) under a fit person order. The local authority (i.e. the children's department) is vested with the same rights and duties as a parent and can seek modification of the orders.

Children's departments have the authority to receive children into care. This is voluntary action on the part of the parent — although in poverty situations we must be sensitive to what 'voluntary' in fact means — but the departments also have authority to prevent the return of children, or to assume extensive control over children who return if the parents can be proved unfit. In other words, children's departments possess legally established punitive weapons and they can be one of the key factors in the forcible regulation of children, including removal from the home and institutionalization. Child care officers admitted that the departments are often known and feared as the agency that takes the children away and that they are trying to live down this reputation.

Children's department's clients came to them by various routes which included the police, for example when their help was sought for settling family disputes, helping with problems, or because of delinquency. Families were referred by education authorities and housing departments. Under the 1963 Act children's departments can pay off rent arrears or help prevent evictions by means of other arrangements. Health workers such as health visitors notified the departments of cases of child neglect. Families themselves sought help, for example, if they wanted children to be taken into care. Handler asked about the effects of referrals on the casework relationship. In the legal-punitive cases — delinquency, truancy, neglect, and cruelty — the caseworkers had to use threats. For example, if the child or the parents did not change, serious punitive sanctions might follow. The caseworkers were being honest with the clients; and the clients were entitled to know the consequences of alternatives.

Punitive legal sanctions constitute only one part of the reward and punishment system administered by the departments. The total system of rewards and punishments is developed out of the relationship between the agency and its clients — *why* the clients and the children's departments are dealing with each other and *how* they are dealing with each other. The reasons for the relationship affect significantly the character of the relationship.

It was on the benefit side that the more subtle authority implications came out. In many departments there was considerable reluctance to give financial assistance. It was departmental policy to avoid paying bills outright or immediately. When a family was faced with eviction because of rent arrears or debts to the Gas and Electricity Boards, the child care officers would negotiate with the authorities and during this period would attempt to work with the families. The 'plan' was to find out why the families did not pay the bills and to try to get them to rearrange their affairs so that family economics could be regularized. Punitive tactics were used. Child care officers let electricity remain off for considerable periods (but only in the summer) in order to induce more cooperative efforts. There were cases where departments have let families be evicted and rehoused in welfare accommodation to induce them to view their situations more 'realistically'. In one case, the children's department wanted to assume control over the children but the mother refused. The department lacked the statutory grounds for involuntary control. It deliberately withheld financial help until the home broke up and the mother had to ask the department to receive the children into care. According to Handler the operative social work principles in the children's departments were remarkably similar to those of the Charity Organization Society, founded about 100 years ago. The close supervision of the spending of money was little different from the old system of relief in kind: that is, poor people cannot be trusted to spend money that isn't 'theirs'. It was suggested that the image that most social workers had of their relationship with their clients (referring to child care officers in the 1960s) was patterned after the private psychiatrist/client relationship. In that relationship, the client voluntarily comes to the professional for help and the task of the professional is to examine the so-called 'presenting problem', establish a therapeutic relationship, and work out a 'constructive' plan of rehabilitation or at least devices for controlling the more destructive or obnoxious forms of behaviour. The client, in this private arrangement, is dependent in the sense that he or she feels the need for professional help, but the core of the relationship is voluntary. There are no legal, economic, or overt social compulsions. The professional, therefore, feels free to give his advice and the client, to a considerable extent, is free to take it or leave it. But it was argued the crucial difference between the psychiatric model and the child care officer relationship lies in the differences in the social characteristics. The children's department stands in a very powerful position *vis-à-vis* the client. The agency is a dispenser of rewards and benefits (which includes the staving off of more serious sanctions) that the families sorely need. These rewards and benefits are levers that the officers use in the casework plan. The casework plan means changing behaviour to conform to what the child care officer thinks is proper.

Handler found that child care officers had adopted the therapeutic rhetoric of the psychiatrist — their role was to get behind the presenting problem and restructure the family to abate major problems and to prevent them from recurring. (This, of course, is what preventive work means in the law and what the officers are charged with doing.) But people who came to children's departments had specific, tangible requests — a child to be received into care, a threatened eviction, an electricity cut-off, a truancy notice. Nevertheless, according to the social work rhetoric, disposing of the immediate problem is unprofessional, potentially destructive, and can create even further dependency. All casework services have to be in their terms 'constructive' parts of a 'plan'. From this viewpoint the coercive aspects of the casework relationship were not primarily due to lack of professional training or the personalities of the officers. The coercion stemmed from the structural position of the agencies which gave them enormous power over clients. Child care officers were authority figures. They were extensions of other authoritative agencies — the police, the schools, the health agencies — or the key to desperately needed benefits. Although these suggestions are serious and important the evidence assembled to support them was not impressive because it was derived from a brief visit to this country and visits to only a few children's departments (Handler 1968).

Cases of neglected or ill-treated children have aroused great public concern in recent years when several dramatic cases have received wide publicity. It is often very difficult indeed to decide about the welfare of children and elderly people and social workers have felt very vulnerable to criticisms of their work. There has been concern about failures to protect children through removing them from homes where they are thought to be at risk. Social workers have thus found the issue of social control a difficult one. They have been anxious about the implications of their role for the liberty of individuals. The first case summary from the field of child care is of a family where child abuse occurred.

THE WILLIAMS FAMILY

Mr and Mrs Williams had married when they were both aged eighteen. At the time with which we are concerned they had three children, boys aged five and three and a daughter aged one who had been born prematurely, had had to be placed in an incubator, and was frail and underweight. She was seen by a paediatrician who found nothing physically wrong. The health visitor continued to feel concern about her failure to thrive and her unresponsiveness. She noticed a bad bruise on the child's thigh and was not satisfied that this was caused accidentally as Mrs Williams said. She referred the family to the Social Services Department.

When the social worker saw Mrs Williams she at first denied any difficulties but then said she had been upset by the separation when Denise was born. She had not felt she was 'her' baby when she came home. Her experience with her own mother was of rejection: they had a bad relationship. She felt jealous when her husband paid attention to Denise. The social worker gave Mrs Williams phone numbers which she could ring at any time if she felt worried at all. Mrs Williams telephoned late one night. She felt an overwhelming urge to attack Denise. The social worker visited and arranged a medical examination. No serious physical injury had occurred but the social worker sought a place of safety order. Then a care order was made and Denise was placed in a temporary foster home. The social worker continued to visit Mr and Mrs Williams who felt very angry and resentful at the social worker's action at first.

Comment

The social worker exercised the control function in order to protect the child. Child abuse is often associated with separation at birth, early marriage, and poor relationships between parents and their parents. The situation appears to be clear cut from the summary although this is unusual. But the social worker interpreted Mrs Williams' phone call as a call for help and a danger signal and felt that it was necessary to act quickly.

In the next illustration as in the first one the social worker has to take account, not only of legal requirements and departmental policies but also the needs and motives of several people in relation to the interests of the child. The illustration shows the control function being exercised in relation to all these factors.

KAREN

Karen, a sixteen-year-old girl, was in a satisfactory foster home where she was being difficult in her behaviour. The foster parents were tolerant as far as they could be but the difficulties arose because Karen was determined to leave the home and live with another couple who appeared to be trying to seduce her into leaving. The social worker considered that this last home was not suitable. Karen was told by the social worker that the department had considered the proposed move very carefully and it had been decided that she must remain in her present foster home.

She burst into tears and abused the social worker and the difficult behaviour continued. The social worker visited one week later. Karen talked more than she had ever done before about her feelings for her natural mother. When her mother had told her to do anything (for example, to go to bed at a particular time), she had insisted that Karen obeyed 'because she does not really care what happens to me'. To the social worker the implication seemed to be obvious. The girl felt that the social worker did care for her. With her help she gradually settled in the foster home.

Comment
This summary provides an example of the social worker's role in controlling or allocating resources, in this case foster home care. It seems to be important to note the way in which the social worker exercised authority here. Karen's suggestion about a different foster home was listened to and investigated. The reasons for refusing the request were given: if they had not been this could well have been interpreted as a sign of not caring. Karen saw the social worker's use of her authority as indicating that she did care about her.

In the next case the social worker is carrying out the control function formally in respect of a nine-year-old boy but is also concerned with wider aspects of the family's welfare and influences the situation in a number of ways.

THE PATERSON FAMILY

Mrs Paterson was a widow aged thirty. She and her family lived in a council house in a district where there was a high incidence of delinquency, crime, and psychiatric problems. There was a serious housing problem and material conditions in the area were poor. The community was racially mixed but there was no evidence of serious tension. Mrs Paterson's home was of a slightly higher standard than average in the area.

Mr Paterson had died suddenly of heart failure in 1975. The six children were well nourished and clean. There were two girls and four boys whose ages ranged from twelve years to one year. The youngest child had been born eight months after Mr Paterson died. Mrs Paterson was having difficulties with Paul, aged nine, because of persistent truancy and problems of behaviour at school (when he attended) and at home, and in controlling her eight-year-old boy Brian. A social work assistant visited several times but more intensive visiting started six months later. A social worker visited once or twice a week and made good relationships with Paul and Brian. In the third week the social worker, Jean Smith, made a visit when she recorded a longer interview with Mrs Paterson.

'*18 November.* I visited to see how the boys were getting on. They have not been away from school so much recently and I hope they will continue to attend regularly. Now I am more worried about the eldest girl Jenny. She seems to be staying away from school and helping her mother with the younger children quite a lot and I have told Mrs Paterson of the dangers of letting her have time off school so regularly.

'As I was leaving Mrs Paterson told me she was having another baby in six months time. She seemed uneasy; apparently she was concerned that her mother was listening as she was there at the time of my visit. A neighbour appeared and I said I would go back the next day.

'The next day I asked her how things were. She said it was "all off with him and I'm having it adopted. I feel ashamed and can't believe I'm pregnant. What will people say about me? My mother told me not to tell you anything about it." I felt that Mrs Paterson had criticized herself and said this to prevent me from criticizing her. So I asked her what she meant in a surprised tone of voice. She said, "You must think I'm a tart as well as stupid." I said that while she might feel confused and ashamed there was no reason to feel I had condemned her for her behaviour. What good would it do if I did and how would it help her? She seemed to be surprised by this and eventually said that condemnation would not help. I hoped that she might at the same time see that condemnation of herself would not help either although I did not say that for fear that Mrs Paterson may have felt I was making little of her problems and did not understand her feelings.

'In order to make Mrs Paterson more comfortable by thinking that I knew more of the situation than I did I asked her if the man I met the other day was the father. She said, apparently relieved, that he was. "Mr Hirst is twenty-four and I'm twenty-nine." Again it seemed that she was expecting criticism of the age difference and she said it in such a way as to give the impression that the wicked old woman had seduced a young boy. I did not take her up on this but tried to indicate that their relationship was more natural by asking whether she loved him. Again she seemed surprised and replied that she did but that he had just treated her as a bed-partner. "Don't think I am being crude, but that was all I was to him," she said. "In any case it is all finished now. It wasn't him that finished it, it was me." She said this in a rather childish way. I risked making a mistake but felt that Mrs Paterson was tending to feel like a martyr, and that finishing with her boyfriend was her final stroke in directing everybody's condemnation onto her. I therefore said that I thought she had deliberately antagonized Mr Hirst by telling him she intended to have the child adopted. Mrs Paterson petulantly agreed with this. In order to increase her self-respect if only at a later date, and even if it were not true, I then added that Mr Hirst would not then have regarded her merely as a bed-partner. She seemed to see the apparent "logic" of this. She added however that she would not marry him as she had enough of marriage the last time. In order to get Mrs Paterson away from her "martyrdom" I encouraged her to tell me about her marriage.

'Mr Paterson had not been as good as all that. She had not told anyone about it as he was dead and it was therefore unfair but he had not treated her well. He made great demands on her, was at times cruel towards her, and did not maintain her properly. He gambled and that was all he thought about in addition to drinking. I turned the interview back to the present and said I was not suggesting that she should marry Mr Hirst, I wanted her to realize though that there could have been warmth and other positive aspects in her relationship with him. I asked her how she would cope with another child: it would be hard. I had presupposed that she would keep the baby for I feared that the talk of adoption, i.e. of getting rid of the baby in her eyes, may have been a euphemism for abortion. Mrs Paterson lives in a subculture where abortion is practised or at least attempted, and the earlier meeting I had broken up could well have been discussing this. At the same time I did not wish to influence Mrs Paterson in her decision, but felt that it would be better and more constructive for her to think in terms of keeping the baby for she could always change her mind later on.

'Mrs Paterson did not notice, or was not startled by the change I had imposed for the moment and went on to relate the various worries she had and the plans she had made. The two older boys would perhaps go into care; the two-year-old could go to sister-in-law's, and the rest of the children could live at home with grandmother coming to stay there. I think that Mrs Paterson's failure to realise the change of emphasis showed her true feelings, and that in her mind she had not been thinking in terms of keeping the baby.

'We then talked about general matters, mostly those concerning social service benefits during and after the pregnancy. Here again, however, Mrs Paterson had earlier felt that such benefits, in fact all benefits, were not paid in respect of illegitimate children. By this time I hoped that some of the woman's feelings of shame and despair had been removed or at least brought to the surface as I feel that she must see such feelings being unconstructive as far as the pregnancy is concerned. She had even twisted the story about the putative father to the extent that her self-respect was in question. I had thought we had made as much progress as was possible that day and so I ended the talk. I hoped that in doing so Mrs Paterson would feel relieved that she did not have to tell me everything that day or in the future.'

The social worker was authorized to supervise Paul Paterson, who was placed under the statutory supervision of the local authority Social Services Department.

Comment

In this case, the major step taken was concerned with Paul, but the single parent family also had a variety of other needs and difficulties and the social worker attempted to influence the members in different ways indicated in the summary. Whether or not the social work is regarded as of satisfactory standard here it will be seen that in addition to influencing Mrs Paterson the social worker took into account the family's material and financial needs and gave advice about obtaining resources. In these ways the social worker acts as a 'controller' as well as an enabler in trying to help Mrs Paterson think about the future and possibly come to terms with or to feel differently about her present position: 'I said ... there was no reason to feel I had condemned her for her behaviour.' The summary also illustrates another aspect of influence in the way the social worker structures the interview. She is very clear and open about her part in the interview and one has the impression that she and Mrs Paterson get on quite well together. This leads one to be at least sceptical of charges sometimes made about social workers (as here) abusing their position by 'being manipulative', but the evidence presented is not decisive.

The next example is drawn from work with a mentally handicapped person, and his family. From being resented the hospital social worker comes to be seen as a helpful authority who interprets the ideas and feelings of different family members to each other as they try to set limits to behaviour and to encourage self-reliance.

TOM RYAN

Tom Ryan, nineteen, who was mentally handicapped (subnormal) was admitted to hospital on a court order after stealing some tools. There were four other children in the family, two of whom had attended special schools. The parents were angry and refused to see the social worker who called to see them soon after their son's admission. They resented the fact that Tom had been admitted to hospital after his first offence and had been found to be subnormal. Tom had a stormy time in hospital for the first two months but gradually settled down to a responsible work routine which seemed to give him considerable satisfaction. One year after admission the parents asked for him to return to their care. A hospital social worker visited them. They were still very hostile but superficially cooperative and wanted to help Tom as much as possible. It was agreed that Tom could go home if employment could be arranged for him: the high level of unemployment meant that there was a delay of some weeks. The parents accused the hospital of making difficulties and making it an excuse for not letting Tom go home. A social worker found it impossible to make a working relationship with the parents. A minor crisis altered the situation. Following a quarrel Tom was now facing abuse and comment wherever he went in his home area. He got into a fight and the police intervened but took no action beyond informing the hospital. The social worker visited Tom and his parents. It was possible for her to show that she was aware that returning home presented difficulties and that she and the hospital wanted to help in overcoming them. Mr and Mrs Ryan seemed to accept this. They eventually became able to drop the pretence that all was going well and confide in the social worker. Tom had had a quarrel with his parents who had forbidden him to go to an away football match with his girl friend. They feared he would get into trouble with other fans. Mr and Mrs Ryan asked the social worker to reinforce their authority. Tom seemed to be indignant about the parents' veto: his reaction seemed to be out of proportion. The social worker discussed things separately with Tom and Mr and Mrs Ryan and found that Tom had told his girl friend that he had been to hospital and was still a patient there. The social worker said she appreciated that the parents did not want Tom to get into trouble when his discharge from the hospital was near. She was able to explain his difficulties to them and his need to stand on his own feet. Perhaps some compromise could be reached by letting him go to the match but insisting he came back on an early train or bus.

Comment

This case provides an illustration of a gradual change in attitudes (on the part of the parents) towards a social worker whose intervention was first resented and towards whom the family felt angry. The social worker is seen as an authority, being influential in 'taking Tom away'. Later, the social worker is also seen as a potential helper when the family experience difficulties. She is asked to act as a persuasive authority by supporting the parents' attempts to help their son avoid getting into trouble.

The two case summaries which follow describe action taken by social workers when clients are not able or not willing to decide for themselves. The effect is to deprive the persons involved of their liberty and to place limits on their freedom of choice. The examples are of social workers acting as mental welfare officers under the Mental Health Act of 1959. In these cases the social workers are part of a statutory procedure which involves a person who is thought to be ill in admission to hospital, and the individuals are deprived of choice of action in these circumstances.

MR AND MRS KYLE

Mrs Kyle was twenty-eight, married, and with a child of four. She was a fairly quiet, shy, and reserved person but was happy at home caring for her family and she seemed to have a good health record.

But between six months and a year previously she had started to withdraw more into herself and to spend more and more time away from her husband and child. Her husband had noticed that in conversation she gradually produced more and more odd ideas about many things. She believed that brown eggs were brown and not white because they were laid in the dark, and that potatoes could see because they had eyes. Her family regarded many of these odd thoughts just as eccentricities.

One day Mr Kyle went out to the pub and the shops, and on his return about two hours later, his wife was sitting rigidly in a chair and seemed unable to respond to his suggestion that he would help her (she was all right when he had gone out). Her eyes had a glazed look and when her husband lifted her arm it remained in a raised position even when he let it go. She did not speak. When her husband continued to try to force her to get out of the chair she became violent. Mr Kyle felt very alarmed and was not certain what to do. His wife seemed to have changed very suddenly and he felt unable to understand it. He fetched the doctor who examined Mrs Kyle although she did not answer his questions rationally. Mr Kyle said she did not seem to know the doctor, or know where she was, or what was happening. The doctor said that he could not treat her at home: she would have to go to hospital.

He discussed this with Mr Kyle and then telephoned the psychiatrist and the social worker. They arrived at the house together. The psychiatrist agreed with the family doctor that Mrs Kyle required treatment in a psychiatric hospital. He and the social worker discussed this with Mrs Kyle and she again responded by talking in an irrational way and then became very violent again, and said she 'would not go anywhere'. The husband seemed to be under consider-able strain as what was involved in compulsory admission to hospital was discussed with him. The doctors completed and signed their recommendations and the social worker dealt with the application. He suggested that Mr Kyle could accompany them in the ambulance if he wanted to but the husband said he would prefer to remain at home.

Comment

This case illustrates the way the medical and social work professions assess the needs and situation of the person and weigh social and psychiatric factors in deciding to use statutory powers to compel admission to hospital. In this way the person's psychological state and the social context (the family, neighbourhood, and community resources) are factors in the decision whether or not to exercise control.

MISS FORRESTER

Miss Forrester, aged seventy-four, was admitted to the local general hospital when the neighbours contacted the police. They had not seen her for several days: she lived alone in a flat and had few visitors. She tended to avoid her neighbours so no one saw much of her, but lately she had seemed forgetful, muddled, and aggressive. The policeman who broke into the flat thought she might be dead but she was found to be suffering from pneumonia. The GP thought her flat was in a terrible state. It was crowded with furniture and all sorts of oddments, books, papers, ornaments, and clothing, and the kitchen was full of unwashed dishes.

After being admitted to hospital her general health improved quickly although she was still rather frail, suffering from arthritis, mild diabetes, and was hypertensive. She was also very independent and liked doing things for herself. She was discharged from hospital to the care of her GP and visits were to be made regularly by a health visitor. The hospital social worker had arranged for a volunteer group to clear up her flat before she went home but Miss Forrester insisted that her chest of drawers and wardrobe should not be touched: the social worker agreed to make sure that this condition was observed. She also agreed to accept a home help although she was not happy with this. Things went well for several weeks but then Miss Forrester quarrelled with the home help because she felt she was not doing things 'her way'. Both the health visitor and the GP found that the neighbours complained about Miss Forrester's behaviour and said she was 'crazy', shouted at them, seemed very aggressive, and 'did not seem to know where she was: she seemed confused and dazed sometimes'. She did not eat proper meals and neglected herself. The neighbours were involved when she had an accidental fire in her flat, when some cinders fell from the fire and caused the carpet to burn. Miss Forrester seemed to be even more confused then and the doctor was asked to come. He telephoned the social services department and said that she should be admitted to a home for elderly people as a matter of urgency. The duty officer obtained the above information from the doctor and the health visitor and attempted to obtain some personal details from Miss Forrester. She seemed confused and her talk was rambling: she seemed to recall living with her mother and sister but did not seem to know where she was or what day it was. During this interview she grabbed at one of the drawer handles and spilled the contents. It seemed that the drawer was packed with various medicines some of which could be dangerous drugs. She became very angry and wept and shouted at the social worker. The social worker phoned the doctor and the area officer for assistance because it seemed unwise for Miss Forrester to be left alone. When the doctor and senior social worker arrived and discussed the situation, the senior social worker disagreed with the doctor's original recommendation. They eventually agreed that another course of emergency action would be necessary, and that Miss Forrester should be admitted to hospital for observation and possible psychiatric treatment. The doctor and the senior social worker tried to discuss this with her but Miss Forrester still seemed confused and wept as she talked about her mother. When the consultant psychiatrist saw her he agreed that it would be in the interests of both Miss Forrester's health and safety and that of her neighbours that she should go to hospital. She would not agree to this and became violent again: a compulsory order to admit her to hospital for observation was made.

Comment
There was considerable uncertainty, early in the story, about the help and treatment Miss Forrester needed. The general practitioner's

view that she could be cared for adequately in an old person's home was not shared by the social workers who assessed the social situation and observed Miss Forrester's disturbed behaviour. The decision to exercise compulsion supported by the consultant psychiatrist and the senior social worker was based on both areas of assessment (the social situation and the nature of the psychiatric disturbance). They shared responsibility for ensuring that statutory action was in the interests of the patient and the general practitioner also agreed with the decision as he took part in the later attempts to reach it, saw that an old people's home would not be a suitable environment, and that Miss Forrester required nursing care.

DISCUSSION

In the cases described here the social worker's intervention seems to be justified and it can also be supported by considering the possibility of harmful results if action had not been taken. The situations where the control function is exercised are often ones where the best interests of the people concerned are very difficult for anyone to decide. But when crises occur emergency action needs to be taken promptly if further harm is to be avoided. If social workers experience difficulty in their feelings about exercising authority this may lead to attempts to avoid taking this kind of direct action and in its turn this leads to clashes with society and other workers and can be detrimental to the client. At another extreme are those social workers, whose number is now dwindling, who appear to see themselves as simply another arm of the law. The problem, often reiterated, is that of balancing responsibility to society, the statutory requirements of the department, and the interests of the client. It is possible that some qualified workers attempt to avoid the dilemma by leaving this part of the work to unqualified (or less qualified) staff. (Some may move to other settings or agencies where statutory duties are not required.) Although compulsory action may be in the interests of all concerned workers may fear that by using authority in the emotionally charged crisis situation they may damage their future relationships with the client in some way. But there is evidence which indicates that at this moment of crisis, given skilful handling, the initial step can be made to build up a good relationship. Some workers find it difficult to recognize that when a client has ceased to be able to make decisions which are in his own interest and in accordance with the requirements of society, the client needs a controlled and effective caseworker. We already know that there are skills in statutory work which make it possible for people to be compelled to leave their usual environment without excessive discomfort. These are casework skills in which social workers use their powers of social diagnosis, apply their special knowledge of psychotic illness and attempt to assess the degree of anxiety and fear, so that hospital admission is carried out without unnecessary distress. The worker who sees his casework skill as a separate process will approach the prospect of doing an admission in a state of confusion, reluctance, and apprehension. The sick and distressed patient looking for an understanding worker who can use his authority to control and contain him will find his needs are not met.

Summary

One pressing problem which social workers face is vagueness about objectives and about methods of work. This carries the danger that the issues of power and influence of the social work profession are neglected. Social workers, it has been argued, have tended to disclaim the role of authority by maintaining the fiction of non-directiveness. This may be mainly because both social workers and their clients have mixed attitudes and feelings about authority, and this has affected their exercise of it and their response. Taking the social worker's attitudes first their feelings about the role may have been influenced by their psychological knowledge or democratic ideals. Also social workers have not been united in their views on professionalism and this may have been an important influence. Various forms of control accrue to a person whose power lies in his super-ordinate position. Contact control refers to the power of one person to keep another in relationship ('We will meet...'). It is the setting of certain conditions of the relationship. Where the rewards one person desires depend on the choices of another person this is referred to as fate control. The social workers' decisions and choices affect the sequence and direction of later events. (Examples are decisions to accept or reject the presenting symptom or including or excluding a group member.)

The third form of control is termed behaviour control or the power the social worker has to influence changes in the behaviour of another, usually through varying his own behaviour. This points to the social worker's influence which is needed to bring about changes in the ways clients deal with problems. For example the subordinate may seek cues and direction for the behaviour that he believes is expected. The social worker uses direction, interpretation, and information-giving as direct means of behaviour control.

Much of the discussion of 'problems of authority' or 'issues of social control' in relation to social work is carried on in rather an abstract way and there is sometimes an apparent failure to recognize the actual situations with which social workers have to deal. Social workers (and not only probation officers of course) act from time to time as agents of social control in giving or not giving material or professional resources, in removing people from their homes against their wishes, or the wishes of their relatives, and in attempting to influence their client's behaviour. The coercive and persuasive control functions of social workers have been examined by using disguised case histories or summaries from areas of work other than probation. This was preceded by an examination of the concept of authority.

The social worker may be thought of as using authority when the client sees that he or she is someone who has the right and the ability to pronounce on his actions. One kind of authority is that granted to an expert. All social workers have this kind of authority, for example, because of their knowledge of the social services and of the agency in which they work. Authority in an organization may be seen as a device which is used when human beings are engaged in a task. It is thus a special form of legitimized power which is created in order to get the task done properly. The social worker has authority as an agency representative: agencies control resources, services, or rights which people want. Making a money grant, or the granting of freedom to an offender can be made conditional on a client undertaking to act in some particular way. If the conditions under which resources are made available are accepted unwillingly the client may have stronger feelings of resentment to authority than he might have felt in different conditions. Social workers have authority deriving from powers that are enforceable through the courts, or that enable them in emergencies to take action against the wishes of the people concerned. Power affecting personal liberty can only be used in clearly defined circumstances and with proper safeguards. A probation officer can take a probationer back to court for punishment of his original offence only if precise conditions can be satisfied. The third source of authority in social work comes from the social worker's own knowledge and experience. The effectiveness of the authority of knowledge depends entirely on the client's recognition of it.

We can now discuss other perspectives, which are not necessarily incongruent with points made already. They have been recognized as problem areas for some time and readers may find the territory familiar. In this case familiarity will not lead, I hope, to contempt, since the issues are live ones and the debate will no doubt continue. The question of social work professionalism is discussed in relation to power in organizations and the potential tensions between bureaucratic and professional norms are analysed. I then discuss control, power, and authority in social services and this is followed by a summary of a radical critique of welfare professionalism. Finally the argument is put forward that social workers' behaviour and attitudes towards their employing organizations affect the service provided for their clients.

Social Work, Professionalism, and Power in Organizations

The term 'bureaucracy' is often misused; in the present context it will be taken to refer to a particular form of organizational structure. Its main characteristics are a form of hierarchical authority based on official positions and a system of rules governing the rights and duties of these positions. Labour in the organization is specialized and controlled by detailed rules and regulations for dealing with specific situations and individual cases. The aim of organizational control is to ensure that the rules are obeyed: workers have to be supervised and particular attention is given to recruiting the 'right people'. It has been argued that social workers are less than fully legitimated in their professional status within the bureaucratic organization. Compared with doctors and lawyers their training is short and relies heavily on other disciplines (sociology, psychology, and psychiatry) and in Britain a degree course in social work is a fairly recent innovation (Etzioni 1969). Social workers are thus less able to establish a right to professional autonomy in the eyes of other members of their employing organizations, and this underlines the tension between bureaucratization and professionalization. In their claims to professional status social workers have to face the fact that untrained people perform the same tasks as trained workers. But the more social work aspires to full professional status the more likely will potential conflict be within hierarchical organizations. However, as Lutz observed in 1964, the great effort social workers expend in trying to identify the characteristics that distinguish their profession contrasts with narrow provincialism in their practice and education. Fifteen years later some social workers still demonstrated sensitivity about their professional status and they appeared unnecessarily insecure. It was suggested that agencies were not responsible for the apparently delicate state of present-day social work. The failure to appreciate social processes and contemporary society in part accounted for its uncertain condition in Britain (Howe 1979).

Tensions between Bureaucratic and Professional Norms

There is not a high degree of consensus among social workers themselves as to the level of autonomy appropriate to their status; this serves to complicate the tensions between bureaucratic and professional norms. A number of writers (Leonard 1966; Smith 1970; Etzioni 1964 are examples) refer to conflict or potential areas of conflict between 'professionals' and 'bureaucrats' or 'managers' although for the social worker these roles may be blurred. Smith (1970) points out that the concern professional social workers have shown about the appointment of Directors of Social Work derives from concern about the relationship between professionals and bureaucratic structures, within the organization. There is a conflict between the principles of bureaucracy and the standards of professional practice, although bureaucratic and professional forms of organization are not opposed in all respects. In a professional practice the practitioner deals with each case according to his own professional judgement and refers to few regulations in doing this or in defining his own rights and duties. The bureaucratic hierarchy is markedly different because the bureaucrat's activities are clearly defined by rules and regulations and in all cases of doubt he must refer to a senior official.

Social Services Departments have attempted to introduce separate structures for administration and professional practice but have not been particularly successful although obviously there are marked differences between departments. But despite the attempt to separate the functions of social workers and administrators there is conflict and confusion when the two functions overlap. Discussing the emerging patterns of Social Service Departments from 1974 Younghusband (1978) said that many were still suffering instability and pressure from the 1970 reorganization and facing anxieties about 1974 local government changes. The increase of management levels, particularly of specialists, created confusing patterns of communication both at the centre and in the area teams, especially since clients needed more than one service. Frequently roles and responsibilities were not clearly defined throughout departments and there was a lack of close support for inexperienced workers. The role of senior social workers included both management and professional supervision responsibilities but many of them were newly appointed and urgently needed training for these different roles. For other staff such as qualified as well as unqualified social workers there was a lack of supervision and there were problems in keeping a balance between professional and departmental controls across a whole range of social work situations and in clarifying specialist functions (Rowbottom, Hey, and Billis 1974). In discussions with social workers about professional freedom it was found that they exercised delegated discretion rather than professional autonomy; choices had to be made within legal and managerial constraints. Varied administrative systems persisted sometimes with new and old ones running parallel because of resistance to change or a policy of achieving integration at a manageable pace. Many newly recruited social workers were inexperienced and ignorant of departments' administrative procedures. Formalized procedures were needed for the supply of resources to area offices but senior managers were often unaware of the pressures on area teams and there were anxieties about low professional standards on the parts of area teams (as well as managers). For various reasons, including the involvement of various divisions in a department being involved in one case, standardized procedures were needed for co-ordination (Younghusband 1978).

The social worker is more closely supervised by his seniors than the typical professional, and is not usually allowed the discretion of refusing his services to a client. Smith (1970) argued that the professional ideology of social work is not an accurate description of all aspects of the organizational hierarchy in practice. The role expectations of the social worker, as a professional, conflict with the hierarchical relations within the profession that at time closely resemble those of bureaucratic organizations.

Control, Power, and Authority in Organizations

Etzioni (1969) said that organizations could be analysed in terms of their control methods. Control and compliance with it may be based on coercion, or economic incentives or (in so called normative organizations) on the shared moral commitment of both supervisors and subordinates to the organization's purposes. He suggests that particular types of control are effective in particular types of organization. Etzioni's own view is that reliance on normative control, which acknowledges and respects the values held by individuals is the most desirable basis of behaviour in organizations. In addition to the norms or values of organizations themselves members of an organization have values which may or may not be congruent with those of particular organizations. An example is a situation where the norms and values which permeate the life of a community are brought by some of its members into the industrial organization in which they are employed with a subsequent influence upon the form of bureaucratic authority which the workers regard as legitimate (Gouldner 1954).

It is also commonly recognized that the possession of information may confer power on those possessing it. But clarifying responsibility for its use raises difficult problems, for example, if the information exposes mistakes or avoidable omissions of opportunities to help another person. When social workers feel that they should make representations to their employers or to government about underprivileged people or people who appear to have been unjustly treated they may find this very difficult. It illustrates the way in which social workers may be faced with difficult moral and/or political choices in deciding about the needs of individuals and the welfare of others (Day 1968).

In a study of the welfare profession, focused on occupations in institutional settings such as schools, psychiatric hospitals, or borstals, it was said that they seemed to be marked by forms of government and control quite unlike those of the virtuoso professions. (These are occupations that in certain crucial respects are subject to control by non-professionals even in setting professional objectives.) The welfare professions are rooted in the values of wider society which is vitally interested in them even though the practitioner's desire for autonomy is clear. Second, although there is a search for professional skills that will confer expert status 'there can be no complete withdrawal from the essentially social nature of welfare practice'. For many years teachers and prison officials have felt that there are simply too many people ready to tell them what to do and the people who train them are not immune from criticism. Another reason for the uneasy status of the welfare professions is that moving from practice to the training of practitioners is generally seen as promotion, while in the science-based professions it is not. The trouble then is political. Communication problems regularly conceal problems of power and in the welfare professions power and responsibility are seldom found together, and this is clearly the case with welfare planning which to be effective requires consultation with the practitioner. Poor quality in public debate and discussion lowers the morale of professionals or semi-professionals who are often not permitted to reply or comment (Nokes 1967).

Power and authority should be distinguished. Power is simply the ability to act in a particular way and to produce particular effects: the action taken is not necessarily legitimate. It cannot be delegated and individuals cannot be invested with it. On the other hand authority implies the existence of a right to be obeyed, which is acknowledged by those over whom the authority is intended to be exercised. Unlike power which is personal it incorporates the right to make decisions. When contrasted with power, and especially with power irresponsibly used, authority appears more positive. One type of authority may be delegated to positions rather than to individuals. This kind of authority, like that which derives from written rules, is essentially bureaucratic; it may be useful for some purposes but not for others. Official positions and regulations are not the only possible sources of authority in an organization. Authority may be accorded to individuals irrespective of their actual position in an organization, either because of their competence or expertise or because they are respected as persons. The idea that authority in organizations has various sources gives rise to questions about the basis on which individuals are prepared to invest others with it. However, Warham (1977) points out that no areas of authority can be so clearly defined as to encompass all the decisions work requires, and a corollary of the effective delegation of authority is a sensitivity on the part of those to whom it is given, to the situations in which it is important to refer upwards to a superior for advice, information, or instruction.

If one correlate of the authority of one person is the compliance of another, so authority in organizations must be perceived as embodying responsibility. Also, the person to whom authority is delegated assumes responsibility for the use of it. A superior cannot avoid this responsibility and this is perhaps one reason for the reluctance sometimes to delegate authority. Moreover responsibility is essentially personal: it cannot be defined in exclusively organizational terms. A further distinction has been made (Warham 1977) between responsibility, which is personal, and accountability, which is organizational, and it has to do with control. In a Social Service Department a social worker feels responsible for the welfare of a client. He is also administratively accountable to the Social Services Committee acting for the local authority. If members of an organization are to be held accountable the authority delegated to them should be reasonably clearly defined. They need to be helped to understand its limits. Also, they need to feel that the authority vested in them is real and that they are trusted to carry out the work. Third, the authority needs to be commensurate with the work that is to be done. A person needs to feel free to take the decisions which his work requires.

Control in Health and Social Services

Social work is carried out in organizations which are publicly sponsored, controlled, and financed (Brown 1975). The discretion which social workers exercise has been delegated to them and their positions are therefore exposed to public criticism. The social worker is in the position of being accountable and is in a structure of authority — a hierarchy, which may be felt to be simply a form of bureaucratic control. An alternative view is that the hierarchy may be seen as one through which authority and discretion are delegated and accountability is concentrated. In itself the existence of a hierarchy conveys little of the style of management of an agency. Unlike the probation officer the social worker in a Social Service Department is not individually and directly accountable to his employers for his work with particular clients. His immediate accountability is to his team leader. They are both part of a system which has the problem of maintaining appropriate balances between control as an instrument of accountability and the delegation of authority as an instrument of an individual social worker's autonomy in a professional capacity.

Among many factors affecting organizational control is the organizational environment itself. If an organization is to employ coercive measures it will need tangible support from other social groups. In framing legislation, for example, the state usually specifies the limits of coercive power it delegates to psychiatric hospitals or local authorities. The conditions for exercising coercive power are spelled out. The environmental conditions affecting an organization's normative power are not so clear, and little seems to be known about the effect of the organizational environment on control. First, it should be noted that there are marked differences between organizations in the pervasiveness of the norms which set standards of performance. For example hospitals are very pervasive in that they try to control most of the activities which go on in them. They make greater efforts to maintain control and highly pervasive organizations (some schools for example) may set norms for activities carried on outside the organization. A factor related to pervasiveness is an organization's scope, which is determined by the number of activities carried out jointly by its members. High scope enhances normative control because it separates participants from social groups other than the organization. In modern societies people tend to move constantly among different social groups. Relatively high separation and the low scope of many groups allows for the management of tension: for example, tension may be reduced by a separation of work and leisure groupings. Thus sometimes you hear social workers saying that they 'try not to (or do not) take people's problems home with them'.

The kinds of control used in organizations depend on the nature of each kind of organization and how leadership is distributed within it. It is then necessary to analyse the kind of power used and the degree of commitment of members of the organization (Etzioni 1964). In front line organizations the dilemma of those who occupy control positions is that they are responsible for making policy and maintaining standards of performance for the organization as a whole, while occupying positions from which this responsibility can least effectively be exercised (Smith 1965). The statistical returns and written records of organizations constitute a form of bureaucratic control. They are thought to increase speed of work and facilitate relations between supervisors and subordinates. But they may suffer from the disadvantage that they do not indicate changes in service to clients. The problem of demonstrating social work performance is not necessarily resolved by meeting bureaucratic norms. It is possible that the managerial and developmental aspects of supervision in social agencies can be confused or abused. Supervision is often seen as an educational process by which a social worker or trainee is helped to learn by reviewing his work with the supervisor. But this could be a subtle form of manipulation or control used by senior social workers who do not want to be seen as using authority directly. Thus Blau and Scott (1963) said that workers whose judgement frequently differed from their supervisors' might be regarded as being 'unable to accept supervision'.

Using this form of control a senior social worker (the supervisor) may assume that a junior social worker's non-conformity to agency procedures is due to unconscious motives. At first sight this seems to be a non-bureaucratic form of control but it can be used to enforce agency requirements. Conflict may be avoided by the professional's adaptation to tasks which originate in the bureaucracy. For example, such tasks may be redefined in terms of professional practice. Or organizational rules which appear harmful to clients may be placed in a theoretical context in which they are justified in terms of client welfare. The practice of questioning the worker's unconscious motives tends to elevate the superior into an omniscient power. Workers find that they cannot be right in any disagreement because their ideas are not accepted at their face value but dismissed as rationalizations to conceal unconscious resistance. However, typically in the bureaucratic setting, staff supervision has normally involved control and the direct use of authority. It has involved the checking of rules and laid down procedures. Strict authoritarian supervision has tended to decrease workers' job satisfaction and to foster a narrow concern with clients' eligibility for services and a reluctance to exercise initiative in interpreting needs. Such rigid authoritarianism tends to cause resentment among workers. The quality usually most appreciated in supervisors seems to be the ability to study a client and his situation in a calm way so as to encourage the worker to be constructive and able to learn from his experience.

Blau and Scott (1963) distinguished between social workers who were 'procedure orientated' and those who were concerned to provide a more widely conceived service for clients (whether casework or groupwork) who they called 'service orientated'. Procedure orientated social workers, as might be expected, were and are primarily concerned with checking client eligibility. They found that workers nearer in time to their training (i.e. with less than three years experience and who were popular and had group support) were 'service orientated'. Among those social workers with over three years experience the degree of group support did not seem to affect their orientation. This suggests that group support is important for newer workers in helping them with unfamiliar procedures and in not leading them to reject the service orientated approach derived from training. It was found that the prevalence of a service orientation in a group meant that individual social workers who were 'procedure orientated' experienced strong disapproval. Newly trained workers joining departments which are on the whole hostile to social work training and the professional behaviour and attitudes which it promotes confirm that they experience pressure to conform to the procedural attitude to the work. But as social workers become more professional, owing allegiance to standards external to their agencies, they become less amenable to organizational goals and procedures if these conflict with professional standards.

A Radical Critique of Welfare Professionalism

In a study of professionals in welfare bureaucracies Scott (in Etzioni 1969:117) wrote that 'disciplined conformity to authority was regarded as a sign of maturity'. As one supervisor explained to a recalcitrant worker, 'Maturity is involved in working with existing authority and in accepting it.' Another phrase often used to justify working within agency policy was that to do so was to 'accept the reality factors in the situation'. To resist agency policy was considered unrealistic and a waste of energies which could be devoted to constructive work.

It has been argued that aspects of professional culture can be deroutinized by 'radical' critics. It is important to recognize that this critique faces moral conflicts and uncertainties: it does not evade them. It is suggested that caseworkers have wished away moral and political dilemmas in the past. But the organization has not been seen as something entirely in accord with professional initiatives. On the contrary the latter are essentially liberal and employers may be ill informed and sometimes even not well intentioned. The organization is often regarded as hostile to proper professional practice. While it is acknowledged that clients and social workers may have different views of their objectives, differences in power are not admitted. They are 'on the same side' and this model of professionalism seems unable to see itself as other than benign. Within its boundaries the social worker is always an unambiguous helper (Pearson in Jones 1975:57-8).

A contrast is provided through a quotation from Pearson (1973) who suggests that it is false to say that would-be helpers can always help.

'It is comfortable to hold the simple view that physicians always try to help people, or at least never deliberately try to harm them. Unfortunately this is not so. It cannot be so. Modern society is a complex web of social relationships in which individuals and groups are in constant conflict. When physicians become entangled in such conflicts they are bound to help some and harm others. I do not deplore the existence of this fact but only its denial — especially when such denial serves strategic aims in an antagonistic relationship.'

It would be more proper for the psychiatrist to ground his actions in an open recognition of the possibility of conflict and Pearson argues that this adversary logic is not out of place in social work, referring to the client's perception of the probation officer as a 'copper's nark'. The dominant pattern of professional action and authority in social work generates the problem of clients perceiving social workers as inspectors or controllers — hostile figures. This pattern cannot incorporate the possibilities that organizational programmes might be inadequate or hostile to clients' needs, and the idea that they are adversaries. Pearson (in Jones 1975:57-8) argues that professionalism does not have to do with taking a wide view of the place of oneself and one's work in the world: it does not allow for a reflexive grasp. It means a narrow focus and this is not simply a problem for social work. It reflects how we conceive the organization of our whole social life. How many social workers ignore the illegal fiddling of their clients against the Department of Health and Social Security, an organization which social workers see as being unkind to themselves and their clients? How many probation officers turn a blind eye to their clients' breaches of probation orders?

Within the narrow view of professionalism the social worker is seen only as an unambiguous helper and various strategies are used to defend this view. Where he does not help, it is because he has insufficient skill or experience. In professional ideology the relationship of the organization to need is interpreted as the problem of 'authority', 'reality', and personal immaturity. In student training criticism of the organization is to be understood in terms of the student's personality and educational background. Organizational problems (the inability to meet client need) are related to an assumed personal failing on the part of students. If the social worker is not actually robbing the rich to feed the poor he is aiding and abetting the offence. Social work is in a position where it seems that many practitioners wish to do more than hold the hand of the distressed client and would galvanize that hand into a clenched fist. The social worker's identity is not only a managerial professionalism: what cannot be ignored is a view of the social worker 'as an enragee with more of an eye for the main moral chance' than is usually acknowledged. A sense of the need for professional consensus is false: 'social work is not and probably never could be a consensus profession, its very guts being in the operation of moral choice' (Pearson 1973).

The Client, the Social Worker, and the Organization

It has been argued that attempts to describe organizations may not necessarily correspond to reality (Warham 1977). Individual departments may fit typologies which have less to do with their nature as sub-systems of statutory social services than with their own characteristics as unique organizations. If a front-line organization is one in which the real power to influence policy lies with members at the periphery and at the bottom of a line structure departments will vary in their capacity to enable staff to influence service provision. A paper by Brenton (1978) took up the question of authority and control in agencies, her main argument being that the workplace is a political system and that worker participation is not so much a pragmatic but a political matter in that it concerns the wider distribution of power. She said that making the most of the integrative functions of participation is all the more appropriate for the agency that essentially functions through the caring activities of people. The highly bureaucratic structures of Social Services Departments makes the harnessing of staff goodwill and commitment through participation of some importance. The argument that service organizations should embody the values they seek to promote was advanced in relation to social work training some time ago (Day 1966). It was said that a social work school is providing a service for students. It might have imperfections or inadequacies but represents an attempt to express certain values and to use 'good' administrative practices. Its capacity to do this would depend on the larger organization to which it belonged. Brenton advances a similarly strong argument in relation to the exercise of power in social services organizations. They should embody the values they seek to promote.

The trend of Brenton's argument hinges on the degree of real control exercised by social workers as a valid counter weight to managerial authority. The constraints of statute and public accountability are recognized but the investment of time and energy in collective decision making may be compensated for by greater effectiveness in reaching agency goals. Further, the agency should be accountable to those whom it exists directly to serve. Agency professionals who are nearest to the client, in addition to having first-hand knowledge and understanding should be articulate and able to influence agency decisions in order to achieve effective realization of its goals. Thus the argument for wider power sharing and control involves a broader concept of accountability. What is sought is to redress the customary top-heavy administrative set-up in favour of the front-line workers and consumers of services. The first impressions of clients too are usually retained for longer rather than shorter spans of time. As far as the users of a service organization are concerned they seem to be of particular importance. This point will be taken up later but it is also important in the organizational context: it is to do with the reception arrangements in social work agencies.

Hall (1974) studied reception processes in different departments and found that receptionists without training and often without privacy for interviews could request information in public about people's personal problems and even decide whether a client should be seen, when and by whom. The advantages of hearing the clients' views are often referred to in the social work literature but there is an unfortunate tendency for the social workers' views to dominate. This situation is gradually changing but it must be acknowledged that it has problems, for example, in protecting people's privacy (Day and Eyden 1973). While Brenton's arguments in favour of greater participation and openness are appealing it remains doubtful how far they have or will be implemented. One hopeful sign is that some authorities have attempted to reduce the number of levels in their hierarchies. However the situation is changing in other ways too. Pressure groups have facilitated collective efforts on the part of clients to use or increase their power in relation to agencies. Public interest in prisoners for example, is strongly influenced by demonstrations by prisoners, and by reports of disruption or violence. The interest may be negative or punitive, but at least public debate is stimulated. This applies to other groups of disadvantaged people of course, including the mentally and physically handicapped. The extent to which they may achieve change could depend in great measure on the surrender of authority or power by professional groups.

The necessity for hierarchical structures is questioned on the grounds that for its effective operation the Social Services Department, as a front-line organization, needs a concentration of authority and resources at the point where the work is carried out. This is a pragmatic case for the recognition of professional autonomy in social work and it questions the utility of an administrative hierarchy (Glastonbury 1975). It has also been argued that as the Probation Service continues to develop as a professional social work discipline it is reasonable to assume that conflicts of interests will increase. It has the difficult task of balancing the concerns of several groups — courts, officers, and clients. In his study of the activities and interests of a group of probation officers Lynch (1976) found great concern for clients. Even with too high case loads when officers were asked to pass some cases to colleagues the officers did not do so even though this meant more work for themselves. The view that social workers will generally be content to operate within the framework of the organization's policy did not apply to this group. Three-quarters of the probation officers said that they were quite prepared to operate, and had occasionally operated, outside the framework of their department in order to provide what they saw as a professional service to their clients. The officers generally identified with the clients: this was where the bulk of the workers' interactions took place and where they derived much of the intrinsic satisfaction in the work. They rejected any suggestion that the senior probation officer should be given authority over how probation officers should spend their working day. The majority did not feel it necessary to keep their senior informed about all their professional problems but would discuss aspects of the work which appeared to interfere with the service given to the client. Thus they had a considerable degree of felt discretionary power.

Probation officers and social workers in area teams are front-line staff. The extent to which their organizations can build control mechanisms into the structure is influenced to a great extent by the nature of the work. Front-line workers have the power, because of their low profile and their specialist skills, to implement or not to implement the organization's directives as they affect their individual tasks. Thus the discussion so far has indicated that social workers' professionalism influences their responses to their employing organization and the power that they have to change its procedures. This is often overlooked although social workers take part in administration in a number of ways. Further, it seems that when they are able to study their activities (e.g. at a case conference or in a research project) social workers realize that in practice they have a greater degree of professional freedom than is often supposed, though they may not choose to exercise it. But 'social workers can influence and modify the organization they work in and contribute to policy making if they are not inhibited by fantasies about their own powerlessness and myths about the powers of others' (Day, Rhodes, and Truefitt 1978). If social workers in the front line do feel powerless, for example because of a large vertical hierarchy this bias towards vertical command and control may well make itself felt in the worker-client relationship, either to reinforce authority and directiveness or to produce a sense of frustration in the worker trying to be non-directive in an agency he experiences as directive. However ill-defined the social work task is, it is certainly not to induce passivity and dependence in clients but to help them attain the highest level of autonomy and self-reliance, which, in itself, is an exercise of power. The agency depends to a large extent on the internalization of this ideal by its staff who should be expected to mediate it to the client in a highly personal way.

I have referred in this chapter to professionalism and professional norms which are communicated to social workers in training and by their professional bodies, the Residential Care Association, National Association of Probation Officers, and the British Association of Social Workers. I will refer to the last-named body but first the potential support these organizations can offer to social workers should be recognized. When the history of professional social workers' organizations is written we will be in a position to assess the contribution they have made to helping clients and members as individuals and in the wider political arena as pressure groups. The historian will need to disentangle the growth of a larger professional body out of several smaller ones in the case of BASW, the reasons probation officers remained in a separate body, and the ways differences of views were or were not accommodated. An important example is the question of whether members of BASW should be qualified social workers or whether membership should be open to all people in social work posts. It is too soon to discover evidence about whether or not the decision to have a wider membership weakened the organization for example, as some have agreed, through reducing its credibility in negotiating with local and central government. One of BASW's serious problems has been linking its branches and maintaining adequate communication between its headquarters' secretariat and front-line workers and other members. To what extent did the circulation of its journal to all members facilitate this? When BASW's serious financial difficulties became apparent in 1980 some of its headquarters staff were made redundant very swiftly and the size of *Social Work Today* too was reduced so that its editorial content was diluted: this aspect of service to members obviously suffered.

I think it can be claimed that the Association has had a degree of success in influencing government thinking, for example in the help provided for vulnerable children and their families and in the mental health field. How far dialogue and reflection has been translated into action is open to question; social workers in inner city ghettos and those face-to-face with rural poverty would probably be very sceptical (to put it euphemistically) about this. It is, I repeat, too early to make a convincing assessment about whether and how the social work profession (to say that a united group exists is a large assumption) has been able to exert influence on behalf of clients and social workers. I suspect that more has been achieved within social work and in dialogue with other professions, medicine in particular. But BASW has found a voice in newspapers and journals and this should not be lightly dismissed. The question of involving clients in social services management poses some questions for social workers and these are similar to those which may arise in the course of helping. The British Association of Social Workers has considered that clients should be aware of the content of case records and how long they will be retained: local authorities have a variety of practices. The Association has also considered that clients should have the right to challenge professional decisions and to seek the opinion of another social worker. The client who disagrees with departmental policy and practice should be able to appeal to a special committee.

In his study of professions and power Johnson (1972:12-13) described how specialization in occupations created various degrees of social distance between clients and professionals. In his review of the literature he raised the question of the nature of the conditions or institutions in which professional people developed their characteristic sets of attitudes. He referred to different views of the place of the professions in society. They have been seen as inspiring a new moral order in society and as being distinguished from other occupations by their altruism. He discussed professionalism as a successful ideology which is espoused either wholly or piecemeal by groups who are unlikely to achieve control over their own occupational activities. 'This is not because, as frustrated social workers are sometimes convinced, the leadership pursues misguided tactics, but because there exist external conditions which are antithetical to the development of the form of institutionalized control under which the occupation is paramount and autonomous.' Johnson thus recognized the problematic position of social work in society also seen by other writers such as those I refer to above. Further, it is argued that focusing on the client-professional relationship places stress on variations in the social characteristics of consumers which give rise to variations in institutional forms of control. Different occupations are not uniform in character and development but are a product of different forms of occupational control (Johnson 1972:90; Younghusband 1978 Vol. 2:139-49).

The approach to social work employed here, based on the analysis of social interaction draws attention to the reciprocal influence of client and worker and their separate identities and aims. Simpkin (1979:39-40) observes that in this way the social work encounter has possibilities of conflict and change built into it. He describes a social work approach, the task-centred model, as typical of these developments since it is based on a commercial transaction — the contract. Although Simpkin refers to human rights in his later discussion he does not take account of the legal connotations of the idea of contract which to me are as repugnant as some ideas associated with commercial transactions which may involve dishonesty or trickery. He does show how a social worker may promise a certain kind of support to a client in exchange for the adoption or abandonment of certain behaviour. He suggests that social workers have welcomed the notion of contract because it enables them to suggest that they have something tangible to offer and because it suggests equality in the relationship, although this is spurious. The last suggestion carries conviction and this is reinforced by Simpkin's proposal that by focusing more on the initial negotiation than the outcome it would be possible to be both more realistic and open ended as well as fostering greater mutual understanding. He regards the purpose of the negotiation as not to arrive at an artificial bargain but to reach a degree of sharing so that by helping the client realize his potential he is also helped to exercise his power to stand up for his rights and to be a person. For this power sharing to happen acknowledgement and sharing of weaknesses as individuals has to happen. Social workers do not have to agree with clients any more than clients should agree with their social workers. To achieve a sense of each other in a real world recognition of difference and of conflict will be necessary and legitimate. For Simpkin the essence of working with 'difficult' clients is to convey the fact that the social worker too is a person who is ready to give but will not just permit the client to mess him about: this could require the use of statutory powers but the use of authority can be an occasion for personal growth. It will be seen from my discussion of the helpful use of boundaries with clients unable or perhaps unwilling to set them for themselves that I share this view of the helpful nature of setting limits for some people, and other work relevant to this topic will be discussed later in Chapter Five.

5 Social Work Practice: Authority and Control

A determinist approach to studying human behaviour involves working only within the framework of the natural sciences. How determinism and the value of self-determination are related raise difficult philosophical questions and it is necessary to ask how far social scientists do subscribe to all-embracing determinist theories. These topics and their implications for social work, taken for granted in earlier chapters, are explicitly discussed in the first part of this one, and the question of how far social workers are directive is then explored, and another topic dealt with earlier is discussed further, namely the way some people are helped constructively if social workers are directive. This is suggested by proponents of task-centred casework (Reid and Epstein 1972), by Goldstein (1973), and McBroom (in Roberts and Nee 1977). I will refer to the experience of changes in attitude during one year on probation as seen by probationers and probation officers and I will also refer to the views of other clients on the constructive aspects of the exercise of authority and the value placed on imitating the behaviour of people they respected.

Determinism and Self-Determination

What are the implications of deterministic theories of human behaviour for social work practice? Can they be reconciled with notions of personal responsibility and self-determination? The problem about the relationship between determinism and the principle of client self-determination arises in the following way. The principle appears to require that human actions are free: they are not determined by outside causes. There are various views on determinism, but the notion suggests that some human actions are predictable and that different stimuli will elicit various responses. How does this apply to the probationers or the clients of other social workers? Many social work problems are difficult to formulate only in behaviour-istic terms and have to take account of a variety of perspectives. A strictly deterministic approach might undermine human dignity and we have noted that social workers value client self-determination (as noted in the case of the probation officers discussed earlier).

The social worker's client is not viewed simply as a being respon-ding in a mechanical way within a triangle of forces. The two major forces are environmental pressure and internal drives (and Freud added the super-ego to these). This kind of determinism sees the person as a passive, coerced, reactive, and determined product. If the individual is ultimately the product of constraining forces and pressures in heredity and environment he is not responsible for what he does. If the delinquent is the product of his environment, of labelling processes, and of a particular and arbitrary set of social definitions of behaviour how can he be responsible for his actions? If general statistical truths like those about the failure of working-class children in the educational system are applied to individuals the result is self-fulfilling prophecy, and a dehumanizing of the individuals involved. Does the psychologist's view (or some psy-chologists' views) of people correspond to the image sketched so far? To a great extent it does. There are two contrasting positions which are relevant to discussions of values in psychology. The traditional, positivist position states that human behaviour and social institutions can be studied using the methods of the natural sciences. The other position asserts that political issues are inevitably involved: any study of social relations reflects the values of the student. It is argued that social science, by modelling itself on nineteenth century science has dehumanized people. Once people are treated as objects or things it is a short step to practising re-pressive social control. The extreme version of the positivist posi-tion suggests that the control of people is not controversial if it is regarded as 'scientific' while its opponents claim that this is just a benevolent mask used to disguise manipulative intentions, and it invites people to abdicate responsibility for their actions and encourages passive acceptance of the role of experts.

If the argument outlined so far is correct it seems to be im-possible to justify the notions of personal responsibility and self-determination. But these ideas seem to have validity in everyday life and it can be argued that actions can arise from the self and thus not be totally determined (Stalley in McDermott 1975:114). But is it correct to suggest that social scientists do subscribe to a universal determinism? In fact, traditional psychology does not assert that every act or thought is predictable in practice or in theory. What it does do is to emphasize many limitations on freedom which lead to the assumption that all conduct is determined and no act is free. Second, does the description above take into account the point of view of the acting person who is aware of having constantly to make choices and decisions? People are constantly deliberating and making up their minds how to act, how to decide, or to resolve a conflict. This process begins with the wish to achieve some objective. In everyday life a person wishes to achieve an objective, sees a way of achieving it, and then acts. The decisions which are most difficult arise when there is not one clear objective to wish for. When people experience conflicting desires it may be unpredictable which one they will choose to satisfy. So even if behaviour always arises out of desires and beliefs decisions about which of two conflicting desires to act upon are not necessarily predetermined. Two related points should be added.

Individuals are conscious chiefly when they feel in conflict, i.e. when there are problems to be resolved. If consciousness does not enter somewhere into the sequence of cause and effect it would seem to be a worthless aspect of the person. It seems that it is purposeful in that it can tip the scales at the moment of choice. But it seems to do more than that. It has the capacity for reflection on previous experience in dealing with current issues. The person with deeper knowledge and wider experience is freer than the person with more limited experience and skill, in selecting the most appropriate solution. It is important to note that all therapeutic approaches, including those based on positivism, assume that the aim is to lead the person to relatively greater freedom of decision. A person with a compulsion or a phobia seeks to be free from its domination and in addition free for a life that will be more closely related to his self ideal. The healthy, richly experienced, and mature person is able to modify and develop his own identity by looking at possibilities which are self-enhancing and excluding those that diminish him. There is a possible reconciliation in this line of thought between the freedom claimed by existentialism and the determinism claimed by positivism. Society has been likened to a theatrical performance in which people play a number of parts. If this analogy is pressed too far roles appear as external to the individual whereas the crucial ones are intrinsic parts of the self. This description of a social theatre makes it like a puppet show. But Berger (1966) argues that there is an essentially human quality of autonomy. People can look at the 'strings' which move them and they can reflect on their situations and deliberate about their future actions. It is possible to stand back, at least from some roles, to lack commitment to them and to the expectations of others (Berger 1966:198-99).

Further, as Berger argues, positivism treats all phenomena, including people, as simply a system of data or objects amenable to scientific study. People are regarded as a complicated aspect of the physical world and nothing more. It thus takes no account of the fact that a person is a subject and not only an object and that he is not only a part of the world but also an originator of meaning and value in the world. It fails then to recognize the way the world of objectivity can present itself as such only because man is not simply an object but also a subject. The idea of individual subjectivity challenges the presumption that 'true knowledge' is dependent on a transformation of consciousness from the standpoint of individual subjectivity to that of a detached impersonal spectator of objective reality. Analysis of a human relationship in scientific terms alone can only be partial and unsatisfactory as a guide to action. It has been argued that positivistic methods alone are insufficient to develop understanding of the nature of human beings. Allport (1969:570-71) pointed out that the methods of positivistic science seems to rule out the most appropriate tool, phenomenology. It is not sufficient to know how people react. One needs to know how they feel, how they see their circumstances, and what meanings they give to their lives. Thus what (or rather who) a person wants to become is important and from this position freedom lies in the person's general attitude towards life. In saying that a person is free to modify his identity or style of life one is not saying that he is liberated from all his drives or entirely free from his early learning, or that he does not feel constrained by cultural expectations. Accepting that all these pressures exist 'becoming' (to use Allport's word) is the process by which all these forces are employed by the creative urge to develop an individual style of life. The basic urge to grow, to seek unity and to pursue meaning is also a 'giving' and is more prominent than the propensity to give way to pressures.

One way in which a belief in determinism may be reconciled with ideas of individual moral responsibility is to insist that, for an action to be free, it does not have to be uncaused (non-determined) or unpredictable. When an action is said to be free it is usually supposed that a person was not acting under some kinds of constraints such as threats, physical coercion, or some kind of psychological compulsion. It is thus possible to show that there is a sense in which an action can be both free and determined. If a person chooses to drink tea rather than coffee, for example, this is a free choice but it may at the same time have been determined by personal or environmental factors. Arguments between determinists and the champions of free will are inconclusive since neither can establish the validity of their position. But being a person, being purposive, and being morally responsible seem to be related and such beliefs are of great importance for social work.

In everyday experience people make assumptions about the place of choice and free will in action. It is not unreasonable to suppose that actions have antecedent causes, that is to view behaviour deterministically. But it also seems sensible to pay attention to the choices people make about courses of action, and that involves examining their moral justification. It is important to distinguish between voluntary and involuntary actions in social work or other helping roles if confusion about 'caring' and 'controlling' is to be avoided. When an individual is constrained to make a choice his decision is still a real one. Choosing whether or not to be on probation is an illustration of this. The individual is acting under compulsion but his choice will have consequences: one course of action will have a different result from another. It is in sorting these consequences out that people may need help so that they understand what they are. When compulsion is exercised for the protection of other people it seems desirable that its purpose should be explicit. In this way choices are not obscured and the person making a choice has a sense of responsibility about it and does not feel undermined. The subject of influence may also be thought of in terms of making a choice. In helping people, whose self-esteem may have suffered, to do this social workers try to understand their clients as people, to increase their understanding of themselves and their situations and to exercise influence in ways which are seen to be helpful and careful. Thus for probationers in my study, for example, high value was placed on the helping relationship and through this they seemed able to avoid committing further offences. Such an approach emphasizes probationers' own perceptions of their situations and their own commitment to change.

The aims of 'care' and 'control' are the institutionalized expressions of love and concern, on the one hand, and of fear and distrust of nonconformity on the other. Their incorporation in social work practice ensures a permanent source of conflict for the social worker in his work with clients between the free choice of the individual and the demands of society. Social workers have acknowledged social work activity as the expression of care but have tended to neglect or ignore the expression of society's concern about nonconformity. This appears to be related to the maintenance of a fiction of non-directiveness which will be taken up next. Then the question of authority in social work generally, and its coercive and persuasive functions will be examined.

The Fiction of Non-Directiveness

Using the term counsellors widely, and including social workers, Halmos (1966) analysed the principle of non-directiveness and the ways in which this fiction was maintained. He pointed out that 'a perfect non-directiveness would be a negation' of the 'desire to be instrumental in bringing about a change by doing a service. The counsellor's desire to be "instrumental" in this way is an integral part of his professional motivation' (Halmos 1966:92). The counsellor's faith in non-directiveness is merged with a professional commitment to direct the patient to health, however indirectly this is done. But, Halmos argued, no matter how careful the counsellor, it is simply impossible to avoid arbitrary influence. In some cases this will exact from the client a measure of conformity or compromise imposed by the counsellor who 'not only takes his influential presence as a therapeutic tool for granted but...thinks it to be a most powerfully directive presence' (Halmos 1966:97). Where deliberate influencing is an explicit part of the therapeutic service a core of the fiction of non-directiveness is preserved but to focus attention on this is not to be reproachful about it. It just has to be recognized that non-directiveness is an element in the counsellor's faith. If the counsellor takes moral responsibility in the face of need for care then others should not complain. There is a paradox in it being desirable to cultivate the fiction of total non-intervention and in allowing the ideal of non-directiveness to perpetuate a fiction of its total possibility.

It seems that to restrain directiveness could be incompatible with giving help, because the empathy, sensitivity, support, and initiative required of the counsellor could make the aspiration to non-directiveness unrealistic and perhaps self-defeating. It is a necessary fiction in that it is an affirmation of faith in the integrity and uniqueness of the people the counsellor is committed to help. Social workers have tended to disclaim the role of authority or have tried to find ways of softening the concept of an authoritarian role, and this tendency has been attributed to psychoanalytic theory. Its basic ideas of neutrality and minimal intervention meant that an apparently forceful or assertive image was not acceptable. Social workers practising with groups or communities interpreted democratic principles and rights literally and they placed high value on the recognition of others' rights, equality, and cooperation. Thus, manifestations of power and control have been seen as the antithesis of these principles and an abuse of others' rights. But little reference was made to the fact that democratic participation is not spontaneous and that in the most democratic group, authority is a natural product of the participation and interaction that takes place within it (Goldstein 1973:93-8). These arguments have some force and are persuasive but I think the point needs to be made that psychoanalytic theory was sometimes misapplied or inappropriately applied.

Social Work and Authority

In general a person is in a position of authority when he is recognized as having the right either to enforce his decisions and issue orders or to make statements about subjects within his competence or jurisdiction which are generally accepted. Authority implies the right to be obeyed or believed. The subject of authority has been widely discussed and is often dealt with briefly in books about social work. It has been something of a 'dirty word' (Foren and Bailey 1968:xvii). The concept is not an easy one to analyse partly because of its emotive connotations and partly for other reasons. Different aspects of authority are present in many different kinds of relationships and situations.

One discussion (Timms 1964:11-12) refers to the social worker's agency or the setting in which social work is carried out. Social workers have authority partly depending on the setting in which they work. One kind of authority is based on knowledge, for example, specialized knowledge of the services of the social worker's agency, knowledge of the social services in general, and understanding of human behaviour. Thus the probation officer, for example, uses skills which he has in common with other social workers. What is special to the probation officer is the field in which he works, the probation, court, and prison structure, the rules and laws which govern his work, and the problems and needs of the offenders and other people with whom he works. Authority is the central characteristic of this field whether or not it is expressed in action. It is also an important aspect of the work of other social workers, for example, when they are authorized to exercise compulsion under the 1959 Mental Health Act or under children's legislation. It will be apparent that the term 'authority' will have different meanings in different contexts. It cannot be applied to a range of situations as if it had a single definition.

For example one way of defining authority is simply as legitimized power. Another way emphasizes the attitudes and feelings of those over whom authority is exercised. In this meaning of the concept authority is never given but is always contingent upon its exercise. Its exercise depends on the situation. It is possible to make generalizations about the exercise of authority by social workers but they need to be based on the realities and problems of practice. It was suggested above that all social workers may use authority and its use 'is not restricted to special fields such as probation. In assessing an application for material or financial aid a social security official or a social worker acts with authority when he determines eligibility. The youth leader uses authority in refusing to allow some kind of behaviour in the club room. The social worker selecting a foster home and the child guidance worker insisting that a child has to go to school are both acting with authority. In all three instances the social worker is primarily engaged in defining aspects of the client's role. Most actions involving authority are simply making explicit the role definitions governing the subordinate or dependent position. In the instances quoted the clients can question the authority figure in different ways.

The Use of Social Workers' Influence by Clients: Experience of One Year Probation

Earlier (pp. 28-9) I referred to the expectations male probationers had of probation, giving a brief summary and comment. This section is given over to probationers' views on their relationships with probation officers and how they developed. Probation officers's views will also be given. A distinction is made between the overt attitudes of probationers at the beginning, i.e. between those with negative and those with positive attitudes. Changes in probationers' attitudes are described and a case illustration will be given. Changes which occurred will be discussed together with factors which seemed to be associated with positive attitudes. Forty of the probationers had been on probation for one year or longer. Thirty-seven of them said that they were pleased they had been placed on probation and three of them felt indifferent or hostile to probation. The following account summarizes the views of ten of them. The probationers' own views are paraphrased or quoted verbatim while in some cases information from probation officers or their case records has been added. An analysis of the illustrations accompanies them.

Table 5 (1) *How probationers who had been on probation for one year (one-year probationers) felt about having been placed on probation*

Unhappy, resentful, a waste of time, indifferent	3
Relief, satisfied, grateful	37

Table 5 (2) *One-year probationers' view on whether they required help*

Probationer thought he required help from probation officer	14
Probationer thought he did not require help from probation officer	26

Table 5 (3) *Views on whether probation was intended to help: one-year probationers*

It was intended to help	39
It was not intended to help	1

Table 5 (4) *One-year probationers' relationships with probation officers*

| | As seen by | |
	one-year probationers	probation officers
Get on well together	35	32
Get on fairly well	5	8

Table 5 (5) *Views on whether probation officers had influenced one-year probationers*

| | Views of | |
	one-year probationers	probation officers
Probation officer had influenced thinking and behaviour	23	32
Probation officer had not influenced	16	8
Uncertain	1	0

Table 5 (6) *Views on kinds of control probation officers' tried to exercise*

| | Views of | | |
	one-year probationers	probation officers' ideas of probationers' views	probation officers
Strict	2	2	2
Easy going	15	4	8
Firm but kind	23	34	30

Table 5 (7) *One-year probationers' views of probation officers' friendliness*

Probationers saw probation officers as friendly	39
Probationer saw probation officer as unfriendly	1

Table 5 (8) *One-year probationers general view of probation officers' exercise of control*

Saw probation officer as directive	2
Saw probation officer as mainly permissive and less directive	38

It will be seen that all but one of the one-year probationers said that probation was intended to help them although twenty-six men said that they felt they required no further help themselves. Probationer–probation officer relationships were regarded as good by both parties in more than 75 per cent of cases. The probation officers seemed to think they had been influential in more cases than the probationers were able to allow. In sixteen cases the one-year probationers felt that the probation officers had not influenced their thinking and behaviour; their probation officers thought that they had not been influential only in eight cases. There were differences in the views of the kind of control the probation officers tried to exercise, more probationers seeing the officers as easy going but less probationers than probation officers seeing this as firm but kind.

Probationers with Negative Attitudes to Probation

EXAMPLE 1

One of the dissatisfied clients was interviewed on his last day on probation and this apparently had a striking effect in lifting inhibitions. He was the only probationer who said his relationship was poor. The probationer said that his probation officer was not friendly and he saw him as 'very strict ... so I don't take any notice of him'. The probation officer did not influence him. 'I don't like him much; he lectures; he's long winded and he goes on and on about little things. He's not much use. He won't listen to your side. He doesn't see things the way I do; he has to know it all so he blames anybody else. He's a big head. He talks over me. He does not help me at all; he just hinders me.'

This probationer had not appeared in court again since his first probation interview and he did not feel that he needed any help. He was still living in the same house, and still in the same job. He lived with his parents and had different girl friends from time to time. In addition to there not having been any marked changes in his circumstances there were no perceptible changes in his attitudes to his family (warm and friendly) or his bosses ('don't think highly of them') and while he liked company very much his mates did not influence his behaviour. He was in the lowest age group (i.e. under twenty-one). His probation officer had initially seen the probationer as an immature personality living in a delinquent neighbourhood. He rated the stress on the probationer as severe and said the probationer's capacity to plan ahead was poor. In contrast to the probationer's account, the probation officer saw family ties as weak and the probationer as being indifferent to his family. Father was seen as 'ineffectual and has little contact' and mother as being overburdened by the care of a large family. The probationer had previously appeared before a juvenile court for theft and trespassing and had been placed on probation. The probation officer's assessment was that the man had lacked firm supervision, his father working unsocial hours, and he seemed to be headstrong and unable to accept authority and advice. He first thought of probation as a 'let off' and was indignant that it made demands of him. The probation officer thought that a change in the probationer's attitude was necessary. The probationer seemed to come to see that supervision could be reasonable and that his feelings and difficulties could be understood. The probation officer regarded his exercise of authority as strict; the probationer saw him as easy going. This case probably provides an illustration of extreme differences in the perceptions of probation officer and probationer. At the research interview the probationer's very hostile attitude to and dislike of the probation officer was very evident.

One of the interesting and suggestive features of this probationer's situation was the lack of family and neighbourhood support and another is the view of the father as ineffectual and having little contact. It is possible to suggest that the negative feelings for the father were transferred to the probation officer as representing paternal authority, but the evidence also suggests a realistic base for the deep feelings he described.

The next example is of a hostile client, whose hostility seemed politically motivated. He developed a positive attitude to probation and to his probation officer.

EXAMPLE 2

A probationer aged nineteen was on probation for one year following a charge of theft. He had been on probation before following a similar offence. While he said he felt 'probation is a cover up for the capitalist system; it is a con trick' he said that 'probation could possibly be helpful'. He himself 'did not need help: I can accept responsibility' but 'the magistrates thought I needed help regarding money and getting a job'. As an International Socialist he mainly blamed the capitalist system for his difficulties. Asked what could be done about his situation he said that the 'bosses cause unemployment; it could be solved' (and this applied to his own situation). 'Taxes were spent on the royal family and on arms and yet expenditure on hospitals was cut. The government misuses money.' He thought he was placed on probation because 'they could fine me. I accepted probation as an alternative punishment but I have changed my views. The probation officer is a reasonable guy with a nice personality. He gets too personally involved and is too strict with his clients but he's become a good friend of mine. He talks things over with me although I tend to be independent and make up my own mind. But he's reasonable. He's prepared to listen even when we differ. He is firm but he's friendly too.' This probationer said he did 'not trust social workers generally because they do not keep to what they say' and he repeated his comments about dissatisfaction with the system when asked about the purpose of probation. His probation officer agreed that the probationer saw being placed on probation as a move of the Establishment against the working classes so as to keep them subjugated. The probationer seemed to expect the probation officer to be negative and authoritarian. 'At first the probationer was negative and hostile but later found it to be a useful "area" for exploring his own attitudes.' The probation officer thought that he had influenced the probationer 'by helping him to understand his own feelings and attitudes more clearly.'

In this example the client's ambivalent feelings are evident but he seemed, after a year, to be more positive about probation and towards his probation officer. He seemed to distinguish between the two in that he held to his views about the political aspect of social work as an institution supporting the status quo and as an agency of social control, while coming to see the probation officer not solely as part of 'the system' of control but as a human being who at least showed interest in his views even if he did not agree with him. This probationer certainly distrusted social workers and probation officers and saw them as negative and punitive. His general attitude was one of suspicion and hostility to a world which seemed to him to be hostile towards him. He appeared to use this belief as a way of justifying his views and his defence of himself in relation to the Establishment, and possibly as a way of avoiding personal responsibility for his actions. But as time went on he discovered that the probation officer was not just negative and authoritarian but was willing to listen to his ideas and discuss them with him. In the course of expressing his feelings of anger he seemed to develop friendlier feelings towards the probation officer and to respond to his interest and concern. Many variables are no doubt operative in probationers' perceptions of probation officers' exercise of authority. There is the possibility that the probationers' wishes or needs affect their replies, especially in the case of the more dependent probationers. Another important factor may be time and the effect this has on the probation relationship. The changes are subtle and not very easy to evaluate. It may be that as the relationship develops and as the two people come to know each other the relationship changes so that firmness, for example, seems to become less appropriate or necessary as time goes on. There seemed to be a definite trend in the probationers' views of the probation officers as easy going. Twice as many probationers assessed exercise of control in this way after one year on probation as at the beginning.

The following case illustrates a probation relationship which remained poor during one year of probation.

EXAMPLE 3

A single man under twenty-one, having no previous history of court appearances was charged with theft which he committed with a friend and he was placed on probation for three years. He appeared to accept the charges but was resentful about being placed on probation feeling that it was a waste of time having to report each week. He did not think he required help, feeling that he could manage without outside supervision; he had merely allowed himself to be influenced by friends and saw this as the cause of his offence. The probation officer regarded the probation relationship as 'poor'. The probation officer said that the man allowed himself to be drawn into the offences and did not really understand how this happened. The probationer may have been unwilling to reveal too much about himself; he may have been suspicious of authority. He did not talk about himself or his family easily and thus appeared to have difficulty in communicating. The probation officer thought that the probationer should be encouraged to be tolerant of other people and to make new friends, but did not think he had influenced the probationer's behaviour in the early stages. The probation officer found it difficult to say what he thought the probationer's expectations of probation would be. There was no social enquiry report and this made it difficult. The probationer said that the probation officer had 'a friendly face and talks about how I am getting on'. Probation officer and probationer appeared to agree that the probation officer had not influenced probationer's behaviour to any marked extent in the early stages. The probationer said that other people did not help him to make up his mind very much. 'I like to think things out for myself.' The probationer did find it difficult to say what his expectations of probation were. He was vague about this at the beginning. He thought probation was to stop people getting into trouble but 'I don't know whether it works or not'. At his research interview, the probationer said that he had not appeared in court again and there was nothing now with which he felt he needed help. He thought that probation was not intended to help him; it was a punishment as far as he was concerned. It was a waste of time; although the probation officer was friendly he thought that nothing need be done about the probationer's situation or behaviour because things were satisfactory. The probation officer did understand how the probationer felt; he realized that he was bored with his job and was trying to change it. He thought that the probation officer was easy going and did not influence his behaviour. The probationer regarded his relationship with the probation officer as only moderate; they got on quite well together. It was no better than this because the probationer regarded probation as a waste of time. He could not see that probation had been of any value to him. He had not committed any more offences because he did not want to 'get put away—I wouldn't have done anything even if I hadn't been put on probation.' He did not care what the probation officer thought of him 'unless it it would mean a discharge from probation'. There were no changes in his social life and attitudes to other people since he was put on probation and he said that his remained a united family. As far as dealing with problems was concerned he tried to forget them.

This probationer maintained a consistently negative attitude from the beginning of his period of probation to the end of his first year. To him it was a waste of time and a punitive measure. He regarded his situation as satisfactory and said that he did not require help. From his point of view his relationship with the probation officer was not very satisfactory because of his resentment about being placed on probation and because it had been of no value to him. He recognized that the probation officer understood what his attitudes were and shared the probationer's view of their relationship.

Probationers with Positive Attitudes to Probation

The next example is of a probation relationship which was seen to be good by both probationer and probation officer by the end of the year. At the beginning of the time on probation the probation officer saw the probationer as resigned and apathetic. But the relationship became a good one. Just as the order was about to be terminated the probationer offended again.

EXAMPLE 4

The probationer and probation officer agreed about the charges and that the probationer was resigned about being placed on probation. There were no things that the probationer required help with. Probation was to keep him out of trouble. 'The probation officer can help me keep out of trouble. I thought I'd be fined. I'd prefer probation. I would prefer to stay a probationer than to have to pay money. The probation officer puts me in mind of the foreman at work. He is quite nice, but not all the time.' Referring to whether he thought the probation officer understood his situation the probationer said 'Yes I think so. He saw my family and that helped'. He did not mind talking to the probation officer; he was easy to talk to. The probation officer listened to him but 'he puts you in your place really but it suits me'. 'He sort of helps you ... says, why don't you put some money in the bank?' Although he had preferred his junior school the probationer said he had liked his class teacher at the secondary school. (His attendance there was irregular.) 'This teacher joked with you but also kept you in order.' He disliked another teacher 'who was always shouting at you and did not give you a chance'. Probationer's best subject at school was art. He did not want to proceed to further education. The probationer said that his friends had a great deal of influence on him; really he preferred his own company. Mother too had a great deal of influence on him but she worried about him too much; she was the boss.

This man welcomed the framework of control that probation provided and aligned the probation officer with other figures of authority. He referred to the way the probation officer set limits but said that he needed this. At the same time he found it easy to talk to the probation officer and felt reassured by offers of advice. From statements the probationer made about his relationship with parents and teachers the probation relationship appeared to follow a similar pattern in which 'care' and 'control' were compatible. This case provides a clear illustration of a positive transference and the probationer seemed to be dependent on the probation officer.

EXAMPLE 5

A single man in the under-twenty-one age group was on probation following an offence of theft which he committed with other people by whom it was thought he was easily influenced. He had committed similar offences in the past for which he had been fined and placed on probation. His probation officer described his attitude to the charges as one of being resigned and thought he saw probation as a punishment; at first he did not think he needed help but the probation relationship became a 'good' one. His educational attainment was very low and he sought the probation officer's help in coping with filling in forms: 'I think he finds me useful over things he does not understand.' The probation officer noticed that the probationer tried to conceal his inadequacy and denied that he had any serious difficulties, although later he attributed his earlier offences to the influence of his delinquent friends and having nothing constructive to do. The probation officer agreed with this and saw his aim as helping to build up the probationer's self-respect and confidence. He had felt worried about being placed on probation but seemed to feel that the probation officer was understanding. The probation officer thought that the probationer trusted him and enjoyed talking to him. He thought that he influenced the probationer's behaviour by making him realize that he was the one to suffer by his delinquency. The probation officer described his exercise of authority as easy going. The probationer said he was firm but kind. The probation officer saw the probationer as an inadequate personality, very immature, and moderately mentally retarded. He thought that the gang had a strong influence on the client. The man's mother tended to exaggerate financial problems which the probation officer said were non-existent. The probation order was about to terminate when the probationer reappeared in court charged with theft. He was caught by a policeman in the act of stealing petrol from a car and was placed on probation again for three years. He thought that the reason for this decision was that he 'had not been in trouble while he had been on probation' but there was nothing that he now required any help with. Probation was to keep him out of trouble by reminding him of the consequences of offending. He did not mind being place on probation again, having become accustomed to fortnightly visits to the probation officer. Faced with difficulties, he tended to sit and dream and hope they would go away. Asked about the probation officer's view of his behaviour and situation and what should be done about them the probationer said 'he just asks about how things are and tells me to behave myself'. He thought that the probation officer understood him; he showed interest in him and they had a good relationship. The probation officer was 'easy going — he does not nag or tell me off about things'. The probationer was 'not really bothered' about what the probation officer thought of him. The probationer saw the purpose of probation generally as ensuring that a person did not get into any further trouble and as helping resolve practical and emotional problems.

This example could also be interpreted in terms of positive transference rather as the preceding one. But the probation officer here was not seen only as an external authority by the probationer. The officer also provided practical help in the form of direct teaching, for example, in giving explanations of forms and form filling. Goldstein discusses the social worker's teaching role and distinguishes between the educator, in the strictest sense, as someone who manages a learning process that has as its goal the acquisition of knowledge for growth and maturation or the development of special skills, and the social worker. The social worker manages a learning process that is primarily directed towards the acquisition of knowledge that will aid in the completion of certain tasks or in the resolution of problems related to social living. The more directive interventions of the social worker include the provision of instruction and guidance.

This probationer was defensive about his inadequacy, which he tried to conceal, and in this he was like many of the men in the population studied, at first either denying that they had any difficulties, or being unable to express what they were in words. Later with the development of trust in their probation officers and, in this case at least, with increased self-respect and confidence, they felt more able to discuss problems or deficits. Learning involves change in values and in this example the probation officer thought he had influenced the probationer through discussion of the consequences of his delinquent acts; he caused suffering for himself. He was thus helped to consider how he wanted to act in the future.

EXAMPLE 6

A probationer aged over twenty-one was employed as an agricultural labourer when he was placed on probation. He was unsettled in his job and said he 'saw no future in it' and he did not like the older men who disagreed with him ('people over forty – they don't agree with what you say'). He had disliked all his schools and all his teachers; they too had 'not been with it' and did not understand him. He would have liked to have gone on to Further Education to improve his employment prospects but said he married at the age of eighteen. He separated from his wife seven months before the research interview and since then had had casual relations with girls. He had no close friends and preferred his own company. His son was with his wife and the probationer was staying with his mother. She was separated from his father; this had occurred before he married. He recalled frequent disagreements between his parents but he had positive relationships with his two sisters and three brothers who he still saw frequently. He regarded his mother's attitude towards him as not friendly although he said he was attached to her 'even though she's done unkind things'. He felt that he got on best with his sisters; they 'all helped each other out'. They did not shun him because of his hair style and the way he dressed; his mother moaned at him about these things. He had been charged with offences in the past including theft, being drunk and disorderly, and committing a breach of the peace. He was fined for all of these but said the charges were not fair; the police picked on him. For the present he said the charge of breaking into a house was not fair and he was placed on probation for two years. He said that although he had not committed many offences if he appeared in court again he would 'get sent away'. He did not really need any help except in finding somewhere to live; he did not feel happy about staying with his mother. Really he could help himself or he could get help from his sisters; he had lived with them in the past and they had loaned him money when he needed it. He had also been helped by the Samaritans when he had been depressed. Again he could not recall the date ('I find it difficult to talk to you') but he had attempted to commit suicide. The Samaritans, 'a man and a woman, came and I went to a mental hospital for a month. I got depressed again when I came out but I haven't tried it (suicide) again. I still get depressed. The wife would not let me see the baby.' He felt satisfied about the help he had received from the Samaritans and from the psychiatric hospital. He had needed hospital treatment. He saw probation more as a warning than as being intended to help him. He would only have sought help from relatives if he had not been placed on probation. Generally he tended to blame himself for problems, to be apathetic, to sit and dream and hope that problems would go away. He was pleased that he had been placed on probation; it was better than being sent away. A man who had been in Borstal had told him about probation: 'They make sure you keep out of trouble and that you work.' He had expected himself that the probation officer 'would have been on to me more ... would be moaning' but this had not happened and he saw the probation officer as friendly and as trying to help him. The probation officer was not the kind of person he had expected at all. He had suggested: (a) that the probationer should get a job; (b) find somewhere else to live; and (c) try to be reconciled with his wife. The probationer agreed with and achieved the first aim but was more doubtful about the others. He felt the probation officer understood his situation; he himself felt able to tell him how he felt. He regarded the probation relationship as good and added that he was not a good talker: 'I can't talk a lot unless they ask questions.' He thought the probation officer was firm but kind and he pointed out consequences clearly (e.g. if the man did not pay maintenance to his wife). In general he saw the purpose of probation 'for them to keep an eye on you for the time they give you. To keep you out of trouble — that sort of thing'.

The probation officer thought that the probationer accepted the court findings: after the hearing he had told the probation officer that he had been depressed about the breakdown of his marriage. (He seemed to have accepted charges made in the past.) The court told him that he needed help and he appeared to accept this too. He thought that probation could be of help in reconciling him with his wife; his expectation was that the probation officer would tell his wife to return to him. The probationer was seen as being rather dull. He saw being out of work as a main cause of his difficulties but failed to see that this was by his own choice and to accept that the 'work habit' could have helped the marriage. The probationer's parents had separated eight years previously according to the probation officer. His father used violence to his mother, and towards the probationer. The probationer's own marriage was of short duration; he was physically violent towards his wife and she divorced him. He seemed unable to make a lasting relationship with a member of the opposite sex. He tended to be resigned in the face of difficulties and to blame other people. He was 'rather apathetic' about being placed on probation. His expectations of the probation officer were confirmed at first because the probation officer wrote to his wife immediately. The probation officer hoped for a marriage reconciliation and an awakening of the will to work. The probation officer thought that the probationer felt he understood his situation, thanking him profusely for writing to his wife. The probation relationship was regarded as good; the probation officer thought he was being firm but kind. When there was no response to his letter the probation officer hoped to encourage the probationer to accept the marriage breakdown and to adjust to it. He assessed the probationer as having a moderate character defect and as subject to severe situational stress (because of his domestic situation). His self-control, ability to plan ahead, ability to use ideas and to analyse relationships were all regarded as poor. The probation officer said that his thinking was concrete rather than subtle. He had truanted quite often from school and found learning difficult. There were no teachers he particularly liked. His educational level was thought to be low-stream secondary modern. The probation officer said that the probationer could not hold down a regular job; at his last job he had disliked his supervisors; he resented authority and when he did work was only interested in the money. The probation officer doubted very much if anyone at work took any interest in him. He had an irregular record of casual work on the land interspersed with periods of unemployment. He had 'never acquired the work habit'. The probationer was happy in his home district; he had lived there all his life. He lived with his mother; she appeared to accept him but the probation officer thought her attitude towards her son was ambivalent. (The probationer was subsequently admitted to hospital suffering from depression.)

Asked at the research interview how he felt about being placed on probation the probationer said he felt resentful. He was 'badly done by' and he did not consider himself guilty of the offence. He said the probation officer was 'a bit of a moaner at first but improved as time went on'. He was now applying to have the probation order discharged. The probation officer 'did not really understand the probationer's feelings and situation, and did not believe that he really was not guilty'. He had found it easier to talk to the probation officer as he came to know him better. He said the probation officer was easy going and he did not have any influence on decisions the probationer made. The probationer described the probation relationship as only moderate; they 'got on well on some things but not with others'. The probation officer had given his advice about maintenance payments but the probationer did not think he was willing to give any other kind of help. The general purpose of probation was 'to give you a chance before they send you away'. This probationer said he did not care what the probation officer thought of him, but had come to see him more regularly because the probation officer had threatened him; this was during the previous four months.

In this example the client's initial expectations of the probation officer were not fulfilled. Instead of a harsh or authoritarian person he found that the probation officer was someone to whom he could talk, who understood his situation, and how he felt about it. The client presented a range of very difficult problems ranging from unemployment, to problems of relationships in his marriage and with his mother. His attitudes to the probation officer seemed to be mixed and variable and the probation officer had to be directive at times; the probationer responded to this in a positive way although clearly he felt very resentful about being on probation.

EXAMPLE 7

A probationer in the under-twenty-one group was charged with theft and placed on probation. The charge was regarded as fair. Charges had been made against him before; when sixteen he had been fined for breaking into a club and stealing, and for using his cycle without lights and when it was in a dangerous condition. He said these charges were fair. He thought that being placed on probation meant that he would receive no more warnings; if he offended again he 'would be sent away'. It was to keep him out of trouble and to help him. The probationer saw a need for help in keeping out of trouble; he thought he had needed help since the age of fifteen and he had felt seriously concerned about his situation since his original court appearances. He had not experienced other difficulties earlier in his life and he did not understand why he had committed the offences. 'I did it without thinking.' Asked what could be done about his present situation he answered simply 'probation, nothing else'. He was happy about his home district and his accommodation and was employed as a labourer in a wood yard. He was happy in his job which he found easier than his previous one on a fishing vessel. He had also worked on the land. He liked the people he worked with and said his boss respected him and enquired how he was getting on, although he only came to the yard twice a week. He felt concerned about his mother who suffered from stomach pains: 'She's had it for some time and something might happen when I'm out and it worries me.' His father had left his mother 'when I was little — when I was a baby'. His mother was now thinking of remarrying. He had one younger sister and two younger brothers; they were not on 'very good terms' but he was on 'good terms' with his mother; she tended to worry about him too much. He said they were a united family despite the tensions with his siblings. He had one steady girl friend who influenced him a great deal for the better: 'She stops me from getting into a lot of trouble.' He was extroverted and liked other people's company very much. He went to a club with friends about twice a week. His 'main mate' influenced the probationer very much, for the better, and the probationer also influenced him. He had liked his schools mainly because he had 'good mates' there: he was not sure if there were any teachers he had liked. He disliked the mathematics teacher at the secondary school: 'He was bad tempered and strict and did not help you to understand; he smacked you on the back of the head if you got it wrong.' He 'had not bothered' to do any further education. He tended to respond to difficulties by blaming himself rather than other people and to shrug his shoulders, feeling there would be little that he could do. He was pleased he had been put on probation. 'My mates had told me about it and told me about reporting regularly. They said they got on with the probation officer all right.' He had feared 'it was two years away' (i.e. a custodial sentence). When he met the probation officer he said he saw him differently from other people he knew: 'He talked to you civilly and nicely.' The probation officer suggested that he 'should steer clear of people who got into trouble'. He seemed to understand the probationer's situation. 'I was late the first time but he was all right about it.'

The probationer described the probation relationship as good and thought that the probation officer told him what to do and influenced him by this means. 'He tells me to keep out of trouble.' He saw the probation officer as easy going and friendly, and the general purpose of probation as 'checking up on people; he helps them out and if they get into more trouble he'll speak up for them. He tells "them" (i.e. the court) that you are attending regularly and that might help you'. The probation officer said that the probationer's capacities were poor in many areas. His self-control, ability to plan ahead, to use abstract ideas (and analyse and generalize), and to perceive the possibility or impossibility of influencing events and to see relationships, were all regarded as poor. He was thought to be under situational stress, mild as far as employment was concerned, and moderate in relation to the family situation. The probation officer also said that the probationer was inadequate. The probation officer saw the causes of the probationer's difficulties as being that he was a 'product of a broken home. Parents divorced after having lived apart for some thirteen years. Has lived with mother since father left home.' The probationer associated with delinquents and appeared to blame his mother for the break-up of the marriage. His criminal acts appeared to be his way of 'getting back' at mother. He refused to listen to older people, had strong anti-authority feelings, and refused to work unless he was 'in the mood'. The probationer was told about probation by friends who themselves had been on probation. He was resentful, thinking that probation was a waste of time and that the probation officer was 'out to make life difficult for him'. Much work would be needed in 'firstly trying to form a relationship with him and then trying to get him to see his difficulties'. The probationer did not appear to feel that the probation officer understood how he saw things. He was 'very resentful'. He would 'answer questions but will not volunteer any information'. Because of his resentment and suspicion of authority the probation officer said that the probation relationship was poor at first. He had not influenced the client's behaviour although he was strict with him. The probationer would 'require firm kind handling, perhaps more firm than kind. He needs to see that he has offended against society and to accept the fact that his probation officer is trying to help him'. The probation officer felt that this would be an uphill struggle because of his client's resentment. Without a father he needed to be helped through the adolescent stage and to 'realize that authority figures are there to help as well as punish'. The client did not see any difficulties or realize that he had any. He did not think he required help; it was 'a bind having to report'. About family relationships the probationer was said to be hostile to his mother. He and his father were thought to be friendly.

Relationships with girls were very casual and the probation officer did not know whether his girl friends influenced him at all. He was easily led by friends and they had influenced him for the worse. He mixed mainly with delinquents and had been led into delinquency by them. The probation officer did not know whether probationer had any influence on other people. He truanted from school, especially during his last year. He did not like any school and had no particular liking for any teacher. He was 'slow to learn and very dull'. The probation officer assessed his educational level as low-stream secondary modern. He confirmed that mother suffered from ill health: a duodenal ulcer and high blood pressure. This affected the probationer's life but the probation officer did not say in what ways. The probationer was happy in his home district. 'All his friends are in the area.' This man appeared in court again and was sent to a detention centre for three months and then resumed his probation interviews. He was charged with causing damage and a breach of the peace and thought he was sent to a detention centre 'because the court knew my record'. He thought the charges were justified; his local football team had lost their match and he had become involved with a group of disappointed supporters. He thought that probation was intended to help by providing advice but he had already learned his lesson; he did not require any help now. He dealt with difficulties by talking to someone about them. He did not mind having been placed on probation because he blamed himself for his difficulties and found it was helpful to talk to the probation officer who he regarded as strict at times. But he thought the probation officer understood his point of view and he offered the probationer advice, although he denied that the probation officer had any influence on his behaviour. He said that the probation relationship was moderate; the probation officer soon told him off if it seemed necessary.

He cared about what the probation officer thought about him and had shown this by bringing his fine money to the probation officer who paid it in to the court for him each week. He had asked the probation officer for help in deciding what to do and the probation officer had helped by getting him a job as a seaman. He had felt more able to relax with the probation officer since his discharge from the detention centre three months previously. He had not kept his appointments regularly at first but he had come more regularly following discharge from the centre because 'I realized I'd be in trouble if I didn't'. He did not think his attitude to people at work had changed but with his friends outside work he said that he helped other people to make decisions to a greater extent than he had at the start of probation. 'I give them advice to prevent them getting into trouble.' The probation officer referred to the probationer being in the new job as a trainee seaman and said he had helped him in this. He said the probationer's attitude to work had changed. Now he appeared to want to work as opposed to feeling he had to work. As far as social contacts were concerned the probationer mixed mainly with delinquents and his friends influenced his behaviour a great deal. He was in frequent contact with his married sister and had a steady girl friend who had a slight influence on his behaviour; she tried to help him to keep away from his delinquent friends. On changes in the family the probation officer said that mother was more accepting of the probationer and seemed to nag him rather less. The probationer now believed that his mother tried to help him even though she nagged at him. The probation officer thought that he had influenced the probationer and helped in this modification of his attitude towards his mother. The probationer now accepted that the nagging was an expression of concern about him. The probationer's attitude towards detention centre training 'wholly accepting'. He now saw probation as possibly helpful. He still tended to blame himself for difficulties and reacted apathetically. The probation officer thought that at least until recently the probationer had seen probation as mostly a waste of time. The probationer felt that he did not need the probation officer to 'nag' at him. The probation officer thought that he (the probation officer) should wait to see how the probationer coped with his new situation and that was what was required at this stage. He did not know whether or not the probationer felt that he understood his situation, but the probationer now found it easier to talk to him than at the first stage. This happened when the probation officer told the probationer flatly that he did not talk to other people, and himself in particular, and told him not to sulk and act like a child. He thought that since then the relationship had been moderate and he thought that he had influenced the probationer in helping him to talk more freely. He thought that the probationer saw him as strict.

The probation officer's aim in this example seems clearly to involve measures aimed at facilitating the client's socialization and re-socialization. To a greater or lesser extent this comment applies to all of the examples given in the present chapter. In this case the probation officer seemed to try to enhance the client's competence to function more adequately in family and community groups. The probation officer tried gradually to help the client to acquire behaviour adequate to the demands of the roles he is called on to play. This man was regarded as being poorly equipped for performing an adequate repertoire of adult roles. The probation officer noted the probationer's early experience was emotionally insecure. This seemed to lead him to be dependent on his wife, who responded by being over-protective. In his turn the probationer reacted to this by periodically 'losing' various jobs. This client was typical of a number of 'inadequate' men in the population. He had had very limited opportunities indeed for learning important adult roles, having been brought up in children's homes and having been protected to a considerable extent by his wife. His social functioning had become so seriously impaired as to produce problems for himself and his family. However significant changes occurred as the record shows. The probationer himself said that he thought probation had helped him. The probation officer had obtained a money loan for him and had also attempted to help with problems of inter-personal relationships. The probation officer seemed to understand the processes of adult adaptation and the client was encouraged to be realistic about his financial and employment problems. The changes described occurred within a positive and warm relationship. The probationer saw his officer as understanding and showing concern and said he was like a good father.

The next case illustrates a probationer's dependence on his probation officer as someone with whom he could talk over his problems. The probation officer appreciated the client's need for counselling; at the same time he recognized that he 'needed' to be treated, as far as possible, as an 'equal'. At the beginning, however, the probationer saw probation as the 'lesser of two evils' in that he was likely to have received a sentence of borstal training.

EXAMPLE 8

The probationer who had been on probation for one year had a record of offences of theft and he had been on probation before. He was twenty-three. He 'accepted probation with relief as an alternative to prison'. He did not require material help now and preferred 'to be self sufficient'. He was separated from his wife and had found the probation officer helpful in relation to this. Now he continued to find it helpful to talk over problems. 'Yes probation was intended to help but whether it does depends on how you are matched to the probation officer. I definitely appreciate it now because it has been helpful discussing problems.' The probation officer was seen as being fair and relating to people well. 'I couldn't do that job.' The probation officer helped him to make up his mind about things, 'whether to split with the lass for good or to stay together'. On the purpose of probation he said that youngsters did not appreciate it but his short term at an approved school had helped him to do so. It was helpful for young adults: 'but you've got to appreciate it and want to be helped. Otherwise you are wasting your time.' His probation officer commented that if he had not been placed on probation he would have discussed his problems with friends but 'he thinks probation can help him as it is an opportunity for him to discuss things with an impartial adviser'. 'He did not respond to a direct authoritarian approach, prefers to think that we work together.'

The next case is of a younger probationer who emphasized his view on probation as helping him with difficulties; and not just as an attempt to avoid or prevent the commission of further offences.

EXAMPLE 9

Another probationer aged nineteen who had been on probation for one year welcomed probation rather than being sent to borstal. 'It might work out better. They took the line "Give him a chance and see what he makes of it".' Asked about things he needed help with he said: 'I can't define it but I suppose everyone needs help. You may have faults which the probation officer might see and he can tell you of anything really serious. You look back at your offences and they seem stupid; you've learned from making the mistakes. Probation means being helped with your behaviour, and having a talk with them. It's not just keeping you out of trouble.' Probation was intended to help him with his behaviour. 'You can voice your opinions ... I'd tell him if I liked community service if that was offered.' How did he feel about being placed on probation? 'Over the moon. On Cloud Nine. I dislike the idea of custody. On probation you're your own boss still; it's not such a big restriction as prison or borstal.' The probation officer was 'down to earth and frank. He's broad minded and likes a joke. It's like talking to your Dad about something but you don't have to be as wary as you do with your father. He's not really a friend, more like a guardian.' On whether the probation officer helped him to make up his own mind about things: 'I'd weigh up his advice but make up my own mind because he would not hold it against you unless you committed a crime. He would warn me and I would listen to his warnings.' The purpose of probation was 'guidance. It puts you on the straight and narrow. It's to make sure you get on OK and make a go of your life.' The probation officer said that the probationer was aware of his need for help with the question of accommodation and with emotional problems when he was placed on probation. 'He knew he was unsettled. He had been for several years following the break-up of his family. He thinks probation has helped him to stabilize his life.' At the beginning of the period of probation he was 'unconcerned and uncooperative'. Now, the probation officer thought they got on well together and he thought he had influenced the client's behaviour by being non-directive and providing the opportunities to think over problems and plan for the future. The purpose of probation in this case was to 'help resolve emotional problems'.

Changes in Attitudes to Probation

The next case is of a man who at first saw probation in very narrow terms. The relationship with the probation officer was poor at first but later was described by both people as good.

EXAMPLE 10

A married man in the age group over thirty with three children under the age of five was charged with theft of electricity (he reconnected his supply after it was cut off). He was placed on probation for two years. His only court appearances before this were for motoring offences. He accepted the charge and first saw probation as being of help in resolving his financial problems. He 'saw probation only in these terms and became resentful' when his probation officer 'disabused him of this idea'. According to the probation officer the probationer realized that his chronic failure to go to work and earn money was the reason for his difficulties. He obtained work within four months of starting probation with the active help of the probation officer, and his wife's strong encouragement. In this case, the probationer's expectations of probation were not met. But the probation officer said that the probation relationship became a 'good' one, probably because the probationer appreciated being made to pay his own way and was able to regain some of his self-respect. The probation officer's exercise of control, and the probationer agreed about this, was firm but kind. 'I am firm when he appears to be slipping.' The probation officer saw his principal aim in helping as encouraging 'a continuation of a regular work pattern leading to fuller restoration of self esteem'. The probationer came to feel that the probation officer understood his situation. The probation officer also worked with his wife who was very strict with the probationer and could not tolerate his shyness of work. With the probationer's encouragement she became a stronger support to the probationer who was very attached to her and their children. The probation officer saw his client as inadequate. He regarded him as a very immature man, being to some extent neurotic. He had difficulties in inter-personal relationships and tended to act out his problems. He periodically rebelled against his wife's over-protection or dominance by losing his job. His early life experience was apparently one of emotional instability and insecurity. His parents separated and he was brought up in children's homes from the age of three. The probation officer thought that his difficulties in relationships stemmed from his early experience and contributed to stress in his family or marriage. But his children were very affectionate to him and his wife had insight into his vulnerability and protected and guided him. He saw his mother occasionally but the relationship appeared to be superficial. When he had been on probation and employed for four months the probation officer found that the family tension had largely eased. Everyone in the family seemed more contented. The client tended to believe that helpers (the way he saw the probation officer in the beginning) might have magical powers. These attitudes, briefly recorded by the probation officer, were indicative of the probationer's behaviour in difficult situations. The probationer's account of the charge and his reaction to it correspond to the probation officer's. He said that he thought they (the court) should have given him a chance. 'But I was out of work and the probation officer thought it would help me get back on my feet.' Probation had helped him to obtain, and 'be more stabilized' in a job. The probation officer had helped him to obtain a loan of money from the Social Services Department. The probation officer had also helped him in his relationship with his wife. His unemployment had worried them both a great deal. What appears to be of special interest is the probationer's very positive reaction to recognition of his needs (seen by the probation officer in his terms) and the probation officer's help in dealing promptly with the immediate difficulties. The probation officer went beyond the presenting problem and in doing this he encouraged the probationer to be realistic about the situation (for example his money and work problems and his attitudes to them). The house was now rented in his wife's name because of his arrears in rent. He mentioned having seen another probation officer early in the proceedings who he thought did not understand his situation and was 'bullying'. Of his present probation officer he said that he did seem to understand and seemed concerned about him: 'he is like a good father.' 'He shows me the right direction; because of his job he has got to be firm but he is very kind with it. He talks things over with you; I do not feel nervous talking to him.' The probationer said that he sat and thought about problems, and he tended to blame himself for things rather than other people. He thought probation was intended to be helpful. 'It kept me out of prison and it has made me realise a lot of things.' This man did not appear in court again. At the end of one year he said he did not require any further help; he was in regular employment and felt that his financial situation was now under control. He was gradually repaying a loan made to him by the Social Services Department. He thought that probation had helped him to understand and to deal with personal problems. He now dealt with difficulties by talking to someone about them. The probation officer was prepared to listen to him carefully and discuss ways of dealing with problems and he found it easier to talk to him now than he did at the beginning of probation. He felt comfortable in interviews and was more relaxed now; the probation officer made him feel welcome and showed interest in him. He had helped the probationer to make decisions, for example about employment and finance, by talking things over and he was firm but kind. Probation had enabled the client to 'come to terms with problems and think more carefully about my actions and the possible consequences'. This probationer cared about what his probation officer thought about him and he had tried to demonstrate this by reporting regularly, and by listening and doing his best to cope with his situation. After six months he had felt more able to discuss private matters with the probation officer. Although his foreman and workmates had changed since he was placed on probation, he thought his attitudes at work had not changed. They were friendly and the foreman had given him more responsibility. He thought the foreman would help him if necessary because he was easy to talk to and seemed to take an interest in his work. His social life and relationships with people outside work had not changed. Relationships in the family had not changed since the first interview; he still had a good relationship with his wife and although he was living away from his brother and three sisters, family ties were strong. The probation officer said that the probationer still liked the people with whom he worked. He mixed mainly with non-delinquents; his friends influenced him only slightly and this applied to his influence on them. His wife told him what to do; she was firm but kind with him. He was happy to have a dominant partner; they were genuinely affectionate towards each other, and the children. The only source of tension in the family was when the probationer failed to get up for work; this did not happen often now. The probationer had not appeared in court again. He saw probation as helpful: 'He recognizes that it kept the family together.' The probation officer said that the probationer had no particular difficulties now, but if he had he tended to talk to someone (e.g. his wife) about them. He was pleased he had been placed on probation and he now kept in touch with the probation officer voluntarily; his wife also contacted the probation officer from time to time. The probationer had told the probation officer that he thought that he (the probation officer) understood his situation. The probation officer thought the probation relationship was a good one and that he had influenced the client's behaviour. He had gained in self-confidence and in a sense of his own worth and he now worked regularly. The way the probation officer exercised control varied. He had at times been very strict and at others more easy going, supportive, and encouraging. He regarded the client as inadequate and as a very immature personality. His abilities were regarded as generally poor but his self-control was fair. He tended to describe experiences in a concrete way.

Discussion

Some changes were perceived by these men and by their probation officers during their year on probation. Generally there were improvements either in their actual physical environments or in their feelings about their physical and human environments during the year. The three men who said they were dissatisfied with probation also said they were dissatisfied with their home circumstances. One of these men had been unable to obtain a job during the year on probation. He was of subnormal intelligence and had problems in social adjustment. His problems made him virtually unemployable. Seven men had become unemployed during the year, one having reached retirement. Seventeen men who would not have done this before said that they would deal with difficulties now by talking to someone else about them. They illustrated this by saying how they discussed things with their probation officers. It seemed that in the probation relationship the probation officer provided a model of behaviour which they could imitate and try to use in other situations. Thirty-seven probationers said that probation had been a good thing for them. It is probably important that these men's attitudes initially had been positive. Twenty-four of them had found that they were more relaxed with their probation officer; thirteen said this had not changed; they could still feel at ease in their interviews. There were also changes in probationer's perceptions of authority figures, a higher proportion of men seeing their probation officers as easy going than at the start of probation. When probationers felt positively about being on probation or thought that it had been of use to them and had not been a waste of time some features in their backgrounds or attitudes stood out. By this is meant that among the forty men certain attributes were found which occurred frequently. In half of the cases, for example, the probationers had received urgent help promptly with problems early on in probation. This giving of prompt attention in times of stress, whether it is associated with material or psychological problems or both, can be a form of realistic first aid. It is helpful in so far as it enables the person to cope better with his situation both currently and perhaps in the longer term. This aspect of helping is discussed in Parad and Miller (1963:150-52). A discussion of the comments of some satisfied clients who wanted material help referred to this form of aid as a main indication to the clients that social workers were concerned about them: this also applied to satisfied clients who were seeking help with inter-personal problems. Clients were often aware that efforts were being made on their behalf — for example that workers were contacting a variety of people (landlords, merchants, gas and electrical employees, local authority officials) in an effort to relieve their financial distress. This is aptly illustrated by one client who exclaimed 'they do things, they don't just talk'. 'They go out and do something for you. You feel as though they're worrying about you' (Mayer and Timms 1970:108-09). The act of providing material assistance, or taking some action on the client's behalf (if he is unable to do it himself at the time) can give the client a strong indication that the social worker really cares and is trying to understand and to help. For some probationers in the study they also seemed to be able to feel a lessened degree of shame about being in difficulties; this seems to be related to their feelings of worth and self-esteem.

In less than half of the cases a good relationship with the probationers' fathers was noted. A stable and compatible relationship with a girl friend or partner was noted in the same number of cases. The remaining factors which were noted were said to occur with much greater frequency. The development of self-confidence and improved self-esteem is noted in most of the cases for example. All of the probationers except two said that they were able to meet people socially on equal terms; they did not feel dominated by others. The probationer's perception of his probation officer as understanding or trying to understand his situation and attitudes occurred frequently. The variables which were found in the attitudes and backgrounds of men who had a positive perception of probation are summarized in *Table 5 (9)*.

Table 5 (9) *Variables in probationers' attitudes and backgrounds which seemed to be associated with positive attitudes to probation*

Positive attitudes to probation at the outset	32
Positive experiences (e.g. receiving help requested early in probation)	24
Probationer saw probation officer as being interested in him	36
Probationer saw probation officer as encouraging and supportive	36
Probation officer appearing to understand or trying to understand probationers' situation	35
Probationer 'close to' one or more of his relatives	32
Probationer having compatible and stable relationships with girl friend or partner	18
Probationer having 'good' relationships with father	19
Probationer being able to engage in social activities without being unduly 'dominated'	35
Development of self-confidence or self-esteem by probationer	35
Probationer accepted charge and findings	37
Probationer had not appeared in court before	33

(Note: more than one variable often occurs in any particular case; these figures refer to the group of forty cases.)

It is perhaps not surprising that probationers' and probation officer's perceptions are congruent in a number of areas since they had known each other for a year. The probation officers agreed with probationers about their understanding of probationers' situations. Their ideas about how probationers saw the probation relationship correspond with the probationers' attitudes in a higher proportion of cases than they did at the beginning of probation. At this stage no probationers were said to have problems or neurotic or psychotic illness, nor of character defect. No probationers were seen by probation officers as being affected by delinquent subcultural influences. On the other hand, some probationers were still thought to be under severe stress because of family problems and problems of unemployment, and twelve men were still regarded as being inadequate because of immaturity. The probation officers said that they had good relationships with thirty-seven men, and poor relationships with three. The probationers agreed with their assessments. Perhaps the main impression to be formed from this group of forty probationers is that more men in the group were seen by their probation officers as being capable of thinking about situations and planning ahead than were thought of as having poor abilities in these areas. The probation officers' perceptions seemed to confirm the general trends shown in the probationers' views. The probationers' group seemed to have more people who were quite capable of thinking about relationships and who seemed to be able to take a detached view of their own behaviour and its probable consequences.

Thirty of the probationers who had been on probation for a year said that their probation officers had influenced their behaviour for the better. It appeared that these probationers may have generalized from learning in the probation office situation to other aspects of their lives. As their perceptions of 'Authority' changed in their relationship to the probation officer it may also have changed in other relationships.

Helping Relationships and the Use of Boundaries

Irvine (1956) wrote that in working with certain 'immature' clients the social worker needed to use authority, give advice, and set limits. Essentially this involved an acting out of a parent-child relationship between client and social worker. A social worker was mentioned who set limits to the frequency and length of interviews and dealt with 'the greedy dependent demands of the clients for extra interviews like a firm and patient parent, showing sympathetic understanding of the wish for more attention while holding to the limits she had set'. Reviewing studies of class difference in parental roles Leonard (1966:71-6) said that one difficulty in Irvine's approach was that the client's expectations of behaviour appropriate to a parent would depend in part on his social class. In middle-class families relationships tend to be more egalitarian; parental roles are less differentiated and rigidly defined. In middle-class families the father is seen as a support to the mother and as a companion to the children as well as an authority figure. In the working-class family the father often remains a rather punitive figure. The lower the social class the more rigid and punitive is the father. It would be surprising if these culturally determined expectations were not reflected in the attitude of the client to the social worker as a parental figure. Differences in the exercising of authority in the family reflect different patterns of expectations and values (Leonard 1965). It is necessary therefore for social workers to be aware of the different expectations they may have from their clients as to what is appropriate parental behaviour. The social worker has to take account of the extent: (a) to which the client's problems are the result of a personality structure which has evolved from unique responses to personal life history; (b) to which they reflect cultural conditioning. If what social workers see as 'problems' are in fact culturally determined and supported by group norms, then there is less likelihood that those 'problems' will produce internal conflict in the client. The client of lower working-class status is likely to view the social worker as an authority figure. In some cases it may be appropriate for the social worker to use this authority directly. In other cases the social worker may need to recognize how the client regards his status although the responses may not involve direction or advice. To sum up, the social worker's and the client's expectations of the parental relationship may thus diverge not simply because of the client's psychopathology but because of conflict between their cultural definitions of the parent-child relationship.

Casement (Butler 1970:49-57) discusses the experience of emotional deprivation in childhood with particular reference to parental indulgence as a denial of rejection. He argues that the manoeuvres used by children to avoid the impact of that deprivation later become techniques for evading responsibility. In the relationship established between client and social worker people can make use of differing degrees of new experience as a corrective and as offering the possibility of personal growth.

Some clients cling to their conviction that skills of persuasion can again find a 'parent' who will give in to pressure as did their original parents. In some this is regression while in others it appears to be a demonstration of a point of childish dependence beyond which they have not grown (fixation). In either case the resultant collusion needs to be recognized and dealt with.

In working with a manipulative client it becomes clear that what is being enacted with the social worker is a repetition of childhood experience with the original parent(s). The manipulative techniques were learned as a child and found to be successful with parents.

A crucial factor in the child's basic insecurity is the parents' ambivalence; to the child it feels as if the parent does not love him. The parents and the child come to share a need to deny the rejection or try to. For some it is not possible — rejection becomes overt. For others, giving to the child or giving in feels more like losing than setting limits. Such a child however is deprived of many aspects of security. The demonstrations of loving are not convincing — hunger for love is not satisfied and the child craves for more. Anger is feared as destructive because parents are experienced as fearing it. Frustration is felt to be intolerable. With age this has a cumulative effect; a conviction grows that these emotions can only be dealt with by avoidance or removal; the child has to persuade a parent to do for him what he cannot conceive of doing for himself. When a person's tolerance of frustration is new and he has not learned to live within constructive limits and he later becomes a parent he finds it difficult to deal with his children's demands; someone else must be found to act as parent perhaps.

The social worker becomes a ready target especially when there is an economic premium set on 'keeping the family together' and the children out of care. The assumption is that the consequences of a life lived without limits (as in a child's dream world) can be shifted on to 'them' who are then expected to remove the problems. Often it is not easy to set limits and statutory responsibilities can compel a social worker to collude with the manipulative client.

One factor to be alert to is the seductiveness of the social worker's own wish 'to be good through giving'. This offers convincing evidence both to the social worker and the client that they care. Clients are not slow to sense vulnerability and to play upon this as with the original parent. It is not easy for the social worker to learn how to help clients to find ways of dealing with their own difficulties and to become less dependent. It is not easy to resist the manipulative client in agencies with statutory responsibilities where, for example, the safety of children might be bartered for payment of rent arrears or further delinquency for the price of a room. The setting of limits in practice involves social workers in self-questioning, leading to awareness of the significance of their actions and their effect on the relationship. Are they caught up in the easily established collusion with the client who prefers to be child rather than parent? Are they prepared to deal with this or do they prefer to avoid looking at its implications? For some clients it may be that they can attempt to resolve the problem once their responsibility is clarified. In some cases initial dependence on the social worker may need to continue. The usefulness of practical help should be continually reviewed and its positive or negative contribution should be assessed. When a social worker refrains from giving practical aid or is simply not able to, this could provide someone with an experience of coping with both the anxiety and anger engendered by frustration.

It can be found that these strong emotions need not be destructive or even paralysing, but can be released towards constructive ends. Interpretation can then clarify the experience both in terms of the original relationship to the parent where the skills of persuasion became established and in terms of the relationship with the social worker. Personality growth can thus develop from this, as the client is freed from the sterile reputation of his or her own bad experiences with parents. A new 'internal parent' can then become established. In this way the client's children can perhaps be offered a more hopeful childhood experience than had been the lot of their parents.

Casement suggested that not infrequently a client can be presented with a 'first time experience' of self-directed action. Subsequent capacity for putting their own anxiety to constructive ends can help people to see hidden strengths within themselves. Having once survived anxiety or frustration constructively a client is less able to maintain the belief that certain anxieties cannot at any price be survived alone.

It is always useful to ask 'why do I do this, for this client, now?' It may be filling in a form, dealing with rent arrears or other financial difficulties or speaking to a marriage partner. There are occasions when it is appropriate to use active help as an expression of concern. There are also occasions when the client may be able to do something for himself which from habit he has been accustomed to leave to somebody else.

Defensive Manoeuvres and Collusion

The psychodynamic approach in setting limits described above bears comparison with Jordan's (1970) work. He argues that social work theory does not see the transference as an expression of what is to be 'treated' because the function of a social worker is to 'treat' social problems. In the past social work, by trying to assimilate itself too closely with some aspects of psychoanalytic theory, had misunderstood what was happening in the client-social worker relationship. Jordan develops this by referring to defensive manoeuvres by which the client protects himself against unwanted feelings. Transference and counter transference reactions are spontaneous and inevitable and are not confined to therapeutic encounters. They are forms of projection; the figures projected are chiefly parental but the image of anyone who has been emotionally important to the client may appear. In psychotherapy the patient may identify with these early figures or with the therapist and these feelings and ideas need to be disentangled. The patient in analysis has to free himself from inappropriate or unrealistic projections and identifications. Jordan points out that a social agency does not overtly invite people to express their problems in the way the psychotherapist does. People with social problems are more likely to be prone to behaviour which could be described as impulsive, immature, or 'acting out'. Social work agencies, Jordan argues, invite the defensive manoeuvres from clients described above by offering help with social problems. The social worker is a sort of recipient of those parts of people's personalities from which they feel most in need of escape at times of social crisis.

People described as impulsive, anxious, and under social pressure provide many clues about the deficiencies of the traditional casework model. They refuse to play the game according to the rules of casework theory. By doing this they indicate the weaknesses of these rules. The biggest weakness is that the game is formulated in such a way that it often seems as if only the social worker has aims and plans and things he is trying to do to the client. It fails to take account of the things that the client is trying to do to him, and it may be that the worker's ego rather than the client's is under threat. What is the social worker to do about the problem of challenging the client while helping him face something he wants to avoid? Using case histories Jordan suggests that finding a way to do this is not best thought of in terms of matching a set of 'treatment techniques' to a set of 'psycho-social symptoms'. It is more a question of understanding how the role the client is trying to get the worker to play reflects a defensive or distorted way of relating to people. It involves finding a way of relating to the client that helps him discover that this way of relating is not as necessary for his self-preservation as he feels it to be. As Jordan demonstrates, this is very difficult but it can be done.

Probationers' and Probation Officers' Views after One Year's Experience of Probation

Both Hunt (1964) and Goldstein (1973) referred to positive aspects of the role of authority and their comments seem credible in the light of forty probationers' views after one year on probation. Hunt said that some external control of the individual can assist in the maturation process because it provides real and promised stability and can contain anxieties about aggressive and destructive impulses. Goldstein commented on the provision of order, focus, and direction and sources of control contained within the authority, influence, and importance ascribed to the social worker. With regard to the group of probationers who had been on probation for a year it is not surprising perhaps that their probation officers' and their own perceptions of their situations were congruent in a number of areas. The probation officers' ideas about the probationers' views on the relationship showed greater correspondence than earlier in the period of probation. One particular impression which emerged was that more men in this group were seen by their probation officers as being able to plan ahead and to think about relationships. Probationers and probation officers agreed that the probationers were able to take a detached view of their behaviour and its possible consequences. Another important point noted was that thirty of the men said that they thought that their probation officers had influenced their behaviour for the better. They seemed to have generalized from learning in the probation officer situation to other aspects of their lives. Their views of 'authority' seemed to change in their relationships with their probation officers and also changed in other relationships. These suggestions, as was said earlier, are tentative but I propose to pursue them further.

An Influence Paradigm and Social Work: Some Suggestions

Bandura and Walters (Jehu 1967:102-04) define imitative learning as the tendency to reproduce the behaviour of living or symbolic models. The use of models is very ubiquitous and in many countries the word for teach is that same as the word for show. Problem solving in monkeys and men is often observational learning. The subject looks at a situation, perhaps makes implicit trial and error attempts to deal with it, and then achieves a solution. Through the ability to to learn by observing instead of only through action, such animals may be helped by observing the performances of others. Monkeys have solved problems, without overt trial and error, by watching others solve them. Imitation may be described in terms of secondary reinforcement. The sounds made by a parrot's owner become secondarily reinforcing for the parrot by virtue of their association with the owner who provides direct reinforcement such as food. If later the parrot makes a similar sound by accident this will have reinforcing properties and will tend to be repeated. A baby learns to imitate its own sounds and then sounds made by others. But imitation by children, and imitation of parents in particular, may be reinforcing for children regardless of the act being imitated. Perhaps no single psychological theory will explain all examples of imitation. Since it can be expected that imitative responses will persist imitation is important not only for learning in childhood. There is a considerable degree of uniformity in behaviour: if people imitate or copy the actions, thoughts, and feelings of others they will 'keep in step' with one another. This facilitates cooperation in groups. Deliberate requests for information are basic in learning; also ideas or suggestions are picked up from other people without the subject being aware of this. As far as communication in general is concerned, experience and practice are necessary for increasing efficiency. This comes from observing and copying people such as parents and other family members. Later, school teachers and friends play more important parts. Attitudes, prejudices, values and interests are communicated by them and provide standards for judgements of self and others. To state this briefly not all communication is in the form of language. People are influenced by others when they copy their actions (imitation), their thoughts (suggestion), or their feelings (sympathy). New responses can be learned by reproducing a model's behaviour. In addition to transmitting new responses imitation can inhibit or disinhibit responses which the learner already possesses. Jehu (1967:107-11) cites experimental evidence supporting these points and a third effect of imitative learning which is to elicit existing responses of a kind which do not involve inhibition. A native returning to a district after prolonged absence recovers the local dialect more quickly than a stranger could acquire it. The model's behaviour serves to release similar behaviour in the observer. It is helpful to distinguish personal and positional models. A personal model is followed for the sake of his or her personal attributes. A positional model is imitated for the sake of the attributes pertaining to his or her social position. In imitating a positional model a person enacts a social role and not a personal style. It is also helpful to think of children in connection with imitation and the conditions governing the two kinds of modelling. Familiarity based on previous experience of interaction with the model, may well be crucial for personal models but not for positional models. A person's capacity for threatening a child, by punishment may help to establish him as a personal rather than a positional model. However it is difficult to produce experimental evidence for the occurence of imitation as a defensive reaction, although the claim that modelling may fulfil defensive functions is very plausible (Rycroft 1972:67). The process of socialization is based on the need for approval by other people and the emotional satisfaction of having the respect of one's reference group. These external influences on a person's actions change as development proceeds and the emotional investment becomes greater. Pleasure comes from the feelings of success in being like the model; it is painful to feel that one has let him down. The model is a certain kind of person, belonging to a particular group, and loyalty is extended to include this group. Identification appears to be a self-sustaining process because it passes to the learner the control of punishment and reward. This is similar to the child achieving some independence of external rewards and punishments when he internalizes his own standards (Erikson 1965:243).

In the process of teaching a skill a parent or teacher serves as a competence model. In learning language from the parent the trial and error, correction and revision process continues until the child learns the rules for generating and transforming sentences. A set of productive habits enable him to be his own sentence maker and his own controller. He learns the rules of the language skills, by interaction with his teacher-parent. The teacher or parent also teaches more than this. He passes on attributes toward a subject and toward learning itself. The teacher is more than someone to imitate. Potentially he is a competence model, or a working model, with whom to interact. As he becomes a language speaker the language of interaction with the model becomes part of the learner. He wants the model's respect and to share the model's values. The teacher becomes part of the student's inner dialogue. This seems to mean that the teacher is now not *just* a model to imitate: he is someone with whom to interact. There seems to be a human need to respond to others and to work jointly with them towards objectives. This reciprocity seems to be important for survival. It should not be confused with a motive to conform. Barker (1963) said that the best way he found to predict children's behaviour was to know their situations. Situations have a demand value that seems to have little to do with motives like conformity. Where reciprocity or joint action is needed for a group to reach an objective it seems that there are processes which carry an individual along into learning or acquiring a competence required by the situation. Although little seems to be known about the motive to reciprocate it seems to be a motive to learn as well. Children learn their roles in families and schools through reciprocal learning. This reciprocal learning may be seen in complicated games. A more specific example is the way a young child learns to use the pronouns 'I' and 'you' correctly. The mother says to the child, 'You go to bed now.' The child says, 'No, you go to bed.' The mother is amused: 'Not me but you.' At first the child feels confused but then learns that 'you' refers to himself when another uses it and to another person when he uses it, and the other way round with 'I'. Reciprocity occurs in the give and take of discussion. But if reciprocally working groups are to give support to learning by stimulating each member to take an active part there will be a need for tolerance for the specialized roles that develop, such as the experimenter and the critic. From the cultivation of these interlocking roles members get the sense of operating reciprocally in a group. The emergence of the role of auxiliary teacher can be encouraged, thus getting away from the oversimplified view of 'teachers and experts' higher in the hierarchy than 'students and laymen'.

The part played by the teacher or parent in the socialization of the younger person may be assumed to some extent or in an analogous way by the probation officer with his probationers. There may be differences in the intensity of the feelings involved and the attitudes of the people involved in this group of two, who may not know each other for a period any longer than one year. The purpose of extending the discussion is not to try to press the analogy too far but to take note of the importance attached to reciprocal influence. We need to learn more about this complex process: the study of perception indicates that the probationer's influence on the probation officer has to be studied as well.

To put this in another way and to develop it theoretically, the behaviour of both the probationer and probation officer is influenced by each other's behaviour. A number of variables are operative. In some cases the two people have no control over them. For example they cannot control their genetic constitutions, basic attitudes, and personality traits. The accompanying diagram (*Figure 5(1)*) may be used to illustrate a paradigm of reciprocal influence. The extent of their influence on each other may remain unknown to both people.

Figure 5 (1) *The perceiving-acting loop*

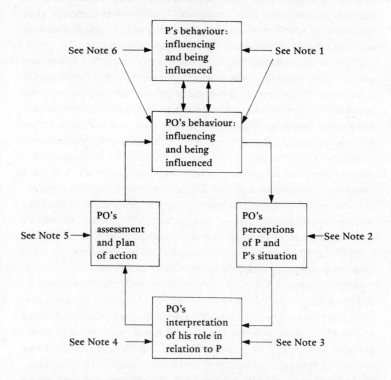

Note 1: The probation officer (or social worker) perceives his influence on the probationer's (or client's) behaviour and his own response.
Note 2: The previous experience of the two people affect their perceptions and future actions.
Note 3: The probation officer's perceptions of the probationer's attitudes towards probation and to the officer also affect the officer's interpretation.
Note 4: These perceptions also affect his interpretation of his role as probation officer.
Note 5: The probation officer's assessment of the situation helps to shape the probation officer's aims and his selection of social skills.
Note 6: The probationer perceives the probation officer's goals and his social techniques and the probation officer's response to his situation and actions.

Other factors in the diagram affect the processes of perception and interaction, for example, the aims of probationer and probation officer and how joint aims are perceived. The diagram indicates the 'experimental' nature of the probation relationship.

It will be seen that similar notes could be written from the probationer's point of view in his attempts to influence the probation officer: correspondingly, another dimension could be shown in the diagram by another loop in which P and PO interchange their positions so that reciprocal relationships would be represented. It will also be apparent that this is not a closed system.

Two kinds of factors might affect the situation. One group may contain environmental factors which may or may not be within the control of the people in the situation. (This also applies to some personal characteristics.) A second category are things of which the people are aware, such as some experiences which may affect their perceptions and actions. The process described is not a 'straight line' sequence, as if first there is a probation officer's behaviour, then probationer's behaviour and so on. Feed forward and feed back affect it; previous behaviour affects current behaviour. Present perceptions of probationers may be better understood in the light of earlier perceptions (if these can be 'known'). Changes occur over time. For example, among the study probationers some became more discriminating in their assessment of relationships: in other cases perceptions of authority seemed to be more rigid.

Simultaneously the probation officer: (a) may structure an interview and make the probationer aware of some of the goals that will direct their behaviour as well as defining their responsibilities as the relationship develops; and also (b) may perceive the consequences of the way he exerts influences on the probationer. Some of his perceptions may lead immediately to changes in his behaviour while others may take place over a longer time span, for example, in receiving information to act on in the future. It may be that the probation officer finds that he is not achieving his purpose in his interview (e.g. engaging the probationer's interest or encouraging his willing participation). He may then modify his behaviour deliberately: he could terminate the interview or adopt other tactics. The probation officer thus behaves according to his earlier perceptions of the probationer's behaviour. His behaviour may be intended to feed forward to new behaviour on the part of the probationer. Part of the probation officer's behaviour in trying to influence the probationer may include trying to enhance the probationer's self-esteem. The first part of the process is related to the expectations the probation officer has. These will be related to his existing information about the probationer and his attitudes towards this information. They will also be related to his thinking about the purpose of the interview and consequent plans for it. The second stage is when the probation officer tries to implement these plans: his actions in the interview. Third he perceives what happens in relation to his initial aims. The fourth stage is when he proceeds with the interview (or series of interviews) as planned or modifies his behaviour as a result of his previous interpretations. It is as if a perceiving-behaving loop develops for both the probation officer and probationer which involves perceiving, interpreting, and acting. The probation officer sets up an hypothesis about a possible relationship between his potential behaviour and its effect on the probationer. (The probationer also does this.) In effect he says (usually to himself), 'If I ... then the probationer will...' (do action (a), or (b), or (c)). After this hypothesis is devised the probation officer experiments and if a piece of behaviour appears not to be successful in helping the probationer move in the direction for which it was hypothetically designed the probation officer may alter his behaviour sequence, or draw on another part of his repertoire of social skills. An appraisal of social science theories which may be useful to helping professionals, based on the plans of intervention, refers to the monitoring of the process aimed at enabling the practitioner to closely observe the continuing impact of attempts to help (Bloom 1975:74). I would add that the client too could be involved in and helped by such monitoring. Verification of specific actions by the helper involves assembling evidence supporting or not supporting his hypotheses about likely effects: does the client respond to the helper's communications as predicted? How is feedback from the client used to modify plans so that goals may be attained? (Bloom 1975:108, 162) In this sense social work intervention can be regarded as a self-correcting process.

6 Social Interaction, Social Order, and Social Work

This chapter takes up topics mentioned earlier and develops them theoretically. In the introduction I underlined the importance of interpreting signals and symbols, and subsequent chapters attempted to explore the understanding of social work intervention by clients and social workers. The problems of the nature of social work and political activities were reviewed as a background to later chapters also in the introduction. Social work, I have said, is a political activity and one of its functions is social control. In social work with individuals and small groups social control is mediated in face-to-face interactions. The processes of socialization or re-socialization are ways of linking small groups with the wider society and from various approaches to the study of socialization I selected social learning in interpreting attitude changes in Chapter Five. What is central in social work and in politics is the process of communication and we can explore this further now.

Communication involves influencing people and the attempt to influence could be described as the basis for social interaction. If it were not the case there would be no point in meeting others. Social life, in other words, involves influence; it is impossible to avoid and it would also be undesirable since many social values are involved. Our capabilities depend ultimately on the adequacy of others' communications to us and the adequacy with which we can communicate with others. An understanding of society depends on study of the messages and communication facilities which belong to it. Communication can only be maintained when there is feed back from the receiver to the sender. If a system is closed, that is if it has no interaction with its environment, it will eventually cease to function. The system which survives has to interact with its environment. Such an interactive system is referred to as open and its most important feature is its ability to construct and use a feed back

mechanism. If a sender does not evaluate what happ
message and the receiver's reaction, and if the receiver
the sender's response or how he is affected by the mes
likelihood of communication breakdown is great. The same
may have different meanings for different people. To deal w.
gap in understanding both sender and receiver have to attach
symbols and meanings to the information they transmit. Adaptation
and control of human communication also serve to detect the effect
of the communication and to adjust it to what both sender and
receiver expect.

Being human means living in a world, that is to live in a reality
that makes sense of living. The life world is social in origin and in its
continuing existence. It provides meaningful order for people's lives
and this has been established and is kept going by collective consent.
To understand the life worlds of human beings it is not sufficient to
understand the particular symbols of interaction patterns. It is also
necessary to acquire an understanding of the overall structure of
meaning in which these symbols and interaction patterns are significant. Control and communication systems are always attempting to
counteract one tendency of messages which is the distortion and disorganization of meaning. Communication and control are thus essential to the person's inner life as well as his social life. Language has a
powerful effect on the kinds of order which can be distinguished and
conceived. It helps the individual to order his experience in his own
way. But cultural change is threatening and the rate of change may
disrupt the lives of people, individually and collectively, and this
leads to defensiveness. The problem is to achieve control in a multiplicity of conflicting value systems. Social institutions and relationships are best understood as constantly changing. Paradigms are a
means of ordering ideas and explaining how ideas seem to organize
themselves. Many of the most significant aspects of language and
social reality lead to reconsideration of aspects of social life that
are taken for granted. Language imposes differentiation and structure on the continuing flux of experience; the use of language
involves participation in its order. Further, it is not possible to
discuss human relationships without reference to meaning which
is usually studied through the interpretation of symbols.

Personal development may be regarded as a struggle between
the individual and society. It is a struggle for self-expression and
influence on the part of the individual and for his subjection on the

part of society. It is therefore inappropriate to conceive of man and society in one-sided terms. Social reality does not make the individual nor does the individual construct social reality but both statements are true simultaneously. The individual can only develop under the influence of his cultural and social environment but during his development this environment is changed. Absolute consensus is rare but smooth social interaction depends on some agreement between the parties about the definition of the situation and mutual recognition of each other's roles and aims, and agreement about the rules that will regulate their activities. Some ideas for a typology of social interaction have been proposed, one criterion being the extent to which social encounters are rule-governed.

Before I take up the question of the regulation of social encounters, using the interview as an example, I want to refer to the way communication makes it possible to reflect on communication itself (as well as social life in general). Such reflection may lead to disagreement with other people and might then be analysed in political terms. Social life, and particularly its political aspect, depends on reflective activity because collectivities frequently feel that they have to search for agreement about desirable or undesirable courses of action. Totalitarian states do not permit freedom of expression and societies which claim to place a high value on relatively open communication have subtle methods of censorship and control of views hostile to the establishment. Limits are also explicitly embodied in laws and regulations which most social workers may approve, for example, those about sexual or racial discrimination. Laws of this nature however raise controversial problems about how limits are defined.

The Interview and Social Interacting

Kuhn (Rose 1962:193-206) discussed the social work interview as a social act analysed by social psychologists according to symbolic interaction theory. The act was analysed in terms of its beginning, middle, and end. He argued that the goal definitions of the client and the social worker and their definitions of each other's roles were important aspects of the initial part of the act. In the middle part of the act the effects of differences in class, culture, personality, and temperament had not been studied to any great extent and this also applied to the end of the interview process. Kuhn argued that the interview was a special case of the act in which the individual reviews his past and present situations and actions with the aims of self-assessment and self-definition. The professional relationship was one which maximally assisted these processes of rehearsal and self-definition. Interviews, as social acts, are studied in three time phases. At the beginning the participants have the problem of defining the act, the social worker possibly perceiving it as one part of a series while the client may see it as a single incident. Before asking what is going to happen the participants try to define themselves and each other, although relatively little is known about this.

The end of the interview or the interview process has perhaps been the least studied empirically. Possibly there are important differences between the effects of the termination of a series of social work interviews and of the termination of psychiatric psycho-therapeutic sessions. This view is based on the respects in which the ends anticipated differ. In both cases an individual in trouble welcomes a supportive relationship which each is supposed to provide. But there is a demand for anonymity by the troubled person that is less well met in the social work situation than in the psychiatric situation. The social worker has no legal immunity from the obligation to give evidence in court. The client may therefore view the end of the relationship with mixed feelings aroused by the possibility that his confidence may be violated or at least that he would fail to achieve anonymity in some important respect.

Characterizing the interview relationship as one in which each person puts on a 'performance' for the benefit of the other seems appropriate. Each puts on his best 'front', that is the one most calculated to impress the other, but neither will be 'taken in by his own routine'. The social worker will endeavour to maintain the professional prescription of self-constraint and will be expected to probe the client about his situation and reactions. The sophisticated client may conceal his ideas or views or use them as a way of negotiating whatever it is that he thinks he can get to his advantage out of the relationship. (An example will be given later of this approach.) Each in his own way will engage in certain acts of mystif-ication. This could involve the social worker in using certain esoteric words in 'managing the scene', and referring to powers outside the interview situation. According to this view of the interview as a 'performance' the social worker justifies the use of mystification to himself in terms of the 'professional role' but its real use is to create or maintain the authority to probe for the client's dark secrets. This tends to diminish rapport. But control and rapport are both necessary, though paradoxical, requisites if the social act is to go as the social worker defines it.

According to the dramaturgical model of social interaction then interviews are regarded as encounters in which actors carry out performances. They have an openness to verbal communication, each participant performing a particular social repertoire depending on each actor's view of the situation. For example each actor may feel that he or she must put on his 'best front' because of the wish to impress each other. They may not be 'taken in' by the other's performance but may be motivated by a wish to cooperate with each other — to reach a working agreement. According to this interpretation the social worker may make use of his professional role in order to exert authority and power in the interview. The client may balance this by withholding information and try to negotiate the situation to his advantage (Goffman 1969:8-9).

Another approach is the role identity model of interaction where the two people come to agree or compromise on a definition of the situation. Once agreement on the problem and task is reached they can continue their interaction. Each individual thus supports the other's role identity (McCall and Simmons 1966:6-7). Thus this positive approach to the interview regards it as the context in which an individual discovers himself and establishes his own identity. The interview is seen ideally as a constructed situation in which an individual can express, at least in conversation, essential features of his past, present, and future. In this process the client is encouraged to rehearse his past actions, and assess evaluations which others who matter to him put upon them, to consider alternatives, and to imagine the responses of significant others to these. He can rehearse future acts and re-assess himself in the light of his performance. The prime requisite for the social worker would seem to be that he presents himself in this dialogue in such a way that will facilitate this rehearsal and self-definition. To do this it is necessary for the social worker to have achieved a degree of clarity about his own self-definition and a reasonable congruence between role ideal and role actuality. Further, it involves understanding the paradox of control and rapport and aspects of the interview for which each is distinctively requisite.

The ethnomethodological approach to social interaction emphasizes the ways people seek meaning in their experience. This
approach involves questioning how participants know what to do in
an interview. It suggests that as a result of social experience they
have certain role expectations and have learned various techniques
from everyday life. In the social work interview for example, the
client often expects that the social worker will seek certain kinds of
information. It is likely that the client will want to make a good
impression by giving information and by acting in a subordinate
way (Cicourel 1964:204-05). Social exchange involves the voluntary
actions of individuals being motivated by the returns they are
expected to bring. If A supplies a rewarding service to B then B is
obligated and must in his turn reward A. During the interaction
norms regulating the exchange are established, the most fundamental being reciprocity, but it may be that the individuals' interests
will clash. They may both then feel that the cost of offering further
rewards is not worth the benefits received. But if they are to profit
at all they must have a working agreement which will require
continued re-negotiation.

Berne (1968:36-9) provides analyses of the varied forms which
interaction may take and suggests that the underlying processes may
be more complex than they seem. Thus he distinguishes a 'procedure' as a series of simple complementary transactions while a
'ritual' is a stereotyped series of simple complementary transactions
programmed by external forces. An 'operation' is a transaction or
set of transactions undertaken for a specific stated purpose. Berne's
primary focus is on 'games'. A game is an ongoing series of complementary ulterior transactions progressing to a well defined predictable outcome. A game has a 'pay off' for the person initiating it and
his (or her) real motives are not immediately apparent to the other
person. The important point about Berne's contribution is the way
he illustrates the subtle and complex facets of interaction. According
to game theory man is conceived as a goal-making and purposeful
actor. In an interview each actor must be aware that the other has
goals and there is commonly an understanding by both parties of
the rules of the game. These may be subverted for example if one
participant diverts the attention of the other by changing the
subject.

Conflict arises if cues and messages are not perceived accurately,
for example, if each actor is using a different language or a different

set of interactional rules. The attempt to arrive at a definition of the situation is also a potential source of conflict. The powerful actor here has a better chance of imposing his definition of the situation. The social worker generally controls what is discussed and tends to take the part of leading actor (Lyman and Scott 1970:1). The initial meeting between client and social worker may be regarded as inherently a bargaining situation (Scheff 1969). This is because the social worker, like other professionals in similar contexts, can control the agenda by giving or withholding information and by deciding which resources can be made available. Where clients have a submissive attitude to authority figures or are referred because they are in conflict with authority in other agencies the social worker's influence may be increased. Where clients have had conflicts with authority in other agencies this may significantly affect social workers' interpretation of their problems. In interviews people seldom have equal roles in shaping interaction. Power arises from imbalance of exchange resources. Prolonged use of the resulting power by one party (the social worker) leads to resentment by the other (the client). The wielder of power claims authority and status but if there is shared awareness in an interview the client has more control over the definition of the situation. The client may not understand the way in which the social worker controls the interview. This uncertainty may reinforce the social worker's categorization of the client in terms of 'symptoms' for example. If there are communication problems the client may see the kind of help offered as inappropriate to his needs and terminate the association. The client's awareness of the social workers' powerful position may lead to feelings of inadequacy (again reinforcing the social worker's categorization of the client). The client may adopt defensive measures once he is aware of the unequal balance of power. He may avoid discussion of some topics and thus retreat or he could assert himself by taking special care of his appearance. Or, of course, he might defer to the social worker and do what he is told. The social worker could adopt some ways to reduce conflict resulting from awareness of the power inequality. The social worker could consider why the client's expectations differ and avoid premature placing of the client arbitrarily in a category (Fitzjohn 1974).

Multiple Perspectives

These different models of interviews show how the study of human behaviour and experience is in general beset by the problem of the multiplicity of approaches and theories related to it, and the different methods they use. This is due in large part to the complexity of the subject matter and of people, and the lack of control the observer has over his subjects (of whom, of course, he is one). The subjects are observers too, of course, and are likely to know they are being observed and may well adjust their behaviour to this (intentionally or not). (Such problems are found in other fields of study, physics and biology for example, but they are not so pervasive and theory is more coherent.) The most significant determinants of individual behaviour are ideas, feelings, beliefs, perceptions, attitudes, and values. These aspects of personal experience are not open to direct observation but can only be inferred from the behaviour and statements of a subject. This makes it very difficult to entirely avoid interpretation and the possibility of variability of observations. Precise description of a quantifiable nature is often impossible (Barker 1975). Knowledge is essentially a 'construction', a conceptualization depending as much on the characteristics of the conceptualizer as it does on the phenomena studied. Theories are not reflections of an 'outside' world but themselves confer meaning and organize information. Understanding may be said to consist of description and explanation although the two are often intermingled (Schultz 1971).

Theories differ in the *kinds* of explanations they propose but all assume that there will be antecedents of related events without which the behaviour in question would not have occurred, i.e. they are deterministic. But the kinds of causal analyses are very varied. For example in seeking to 'explain' the misbehaviour of a child the learning theorist would look for factors such as whether good behaviour has been sufficiently rewarded. The psychoanalyst might search for the meaning that the behaviour has for the child, for example, is it a sign that he is seeking attention? A biological theorist might look for an inherited need for a high level of stimulation. The phenomenologist would seek reasons in the experience of the child. How does he perceive the situation at home or in school? Is he bored? Is what he is offered irrelevant to his needs? (See Israel 1972) A phenomenological perspective is appropriate to gaining insights about the way a person experiences his world, and with the way a person's subjective constructions of the world are influenced by historical, cultural, and other environmental factors. Luckmann (1970) contrasts traditional and contemporary views of the 'life world', considering the changes that have occurred over time in people's subjective maps of 'reality'. Although it has been argued that experimentation in psychology may produce self-fulfilling prophecies the phenomenological approach is not a criticism of experimental method but it calls into question what it is considered appropriate to study quantitatively or precisely, for example from the point of view of behaviourism. The phenomenological approach, like any others, has disadvantages. It can be claimed that it has a degree of self-consciousness about the relationship between theory and method which is advantageous, but it should be emphasized that account needs to be taken of multiple perspectives.

The Regulation of Social Interaction

Interviews as one form of interaction can be regulated in a number of ways. Earlier in this book we saw that some social workers felt it necessary to maintain social distance from clients (Chapter Four). In those situations they were structuring the interview and we will now look at the role of verbal communication in this process. I referred earlier too to the ways in which social workers may collude with clients and this perspective provides a contrast in that the client is seen as manipulating the situation to rid himself of unwanted feelings (Chapter Five). In studying these questions further I begin by considering the notion of role taking as a fruitful one because it suggests a process whereby actors try to organize their interaction so that the behaviour of each takes its meaning from their ways of adapting to others. To conform to the perceived expectations of other people is only one way in which an individual's role playing is related to the role playing of others. The idea of social role as it has been traditionally used has been ambiguous and the theory of roles appears to have been a weak one. It has been suggested that role theory should be repudiated as a system of rigid cultural and mechanical determinism. This version of the theory suggests that roles are superficial and are adopted and abandoned: implications for the actor's personality are not recognized (Kluckhohn and Murray 1953: 53-67). In focusing on role conflict and role strain it has thus seemed to be a negative theory. There has been a lack of ideas about how roles function normally. More sophisticated conceptions of normal role playing and role taking (found in the work of Mead (1935)) contribute new and helpful ideas to the study of social interaction. On this basis the principle of role reciprocity reflects a changed perception of the role of relevant others. Interaction is a tentative process involving continuous testing of the conception one has of the role of others. The other person's response reinforces or challenges this conception (Turner in Rose 1971:20-40).

Discussing the roles that are undertaken and valued in human life (adult life in particular) Perlman (1968:4) wrote: 'what's in a role, in a vital role, is a *person* with his mind, body, feelings ... the word "person" emerged to express the idea of a human being who *meant* something, who represented something, and who seemed to have some defined connectedness with others by action or affects.' Perlman and Turner underline the notion of the actor as not only the occupant of a position for which there is a neat set of rules (a culture or a set of norms) but a *person* who behaves (and must act) in the perspective supplied in part by his relationship to others whose actions reflect roles that he must understand. Turner (Rose 1971:20-40) wrote that the role of alter can only be inferred rather than directly known by ego; testing inferences about the role of alter is a continuing element in interaction. Hence the tentative character of the individual's own role definition and performance is never wholly suspended. Social acts can be thought of as varying along a continuum, depending on the degree of structure inherent in the interaction. This structure concerns the orientation of the participants and their awareness of how they should behave in the situation. When the structure is high there is no doubt about the roles and how the actors will perform them. Each actor's goals are understood — for example when a bus driver or conductor collects fares from passengers.

In low structure interactions there are awkward silences or both parties try to speak at the same time. Each of them will then try to clarify the situation. If they make negligible progress or if their discoveries are distasteful to either of them they may withdraw and terminate the interaction. The impact of definitions and meanings on interactional structure has aptly been referred to as the definition of the situation: interactions can proceed only when to a large degree the participants have a common definition of the situation. In other words if an interaction is to proceed smoothly there must be some agreement between the parties and such consensus about the definition of the situation involves a recognition and acceptance by each of the roles and goals of the other, and agreement about the rules that will regulate their conduct. But in Goffman's (1969: 15-66) view absolute consensus is rare. It is not so much a real agreement about the overall definition of the situation as recognition of whose claims concerning what issues will be temporarily honoured, and agreement too that open conflict about definitions of the situation will be avoided. When the structure of an interaction is low (because it is not explicit) each actor will experience some psychological distress. There is considerable uncertainty and confusion. When strangers meet few clues are available to help either of them. When one actor is aware of the structure, but the other is not aware, clues are available to one actor as in the situation where a person becomes a patient of a psychiatrist.

Earlier I referred to the variety of types of social interaction. One criterion for differentiation would be the numbers of people involved but a system of classification has not been devised. Another criterion could be the extent to which action in social encounters is governed explicitly by rules varying from courts' procedures at the more formal end of the continuum to an informal social gathering, a party, where 'rules' governing behaviour are not written into a contract, but where people do have certain expectations about their roles. In two-person encounters the participants may play the roles of speaker and listener and in any dialogue these will alternate, both roles and their switching depending on their social skills. One function of language is to facilitate the definition of role relationships, and an aspect which has been studied in particular is that of forms of address — what one person calls another and what this signifies. Are there 'rules' which govern the selection of different forms of address? Brown and Gilman (in Giglioli 1972) show how a speaker can signal his perception of his social and psychological relationship with a listener by his choice of words of address. They discuss the use of pronouns of direct address in Indo-European languages which have two forms of 'you', and trace historically developments in using them. They designated these pronouns T and V, derived from the two Latin singular pronouns *tu* and *vos*, standing for familiar and polite pronouns (you) in any language, these pronouns thus marking something other than the simple distinction between singular and plural number. They argued that such pronouns are closely associated with two fundamental dimensions in the analysis of social relationships, power and solidarity.

Plurality is a very old metaphor for power. In Latin the plural *vos* was used to address the emperor and eventually this was extended to other power figures. Power, of course, is a relationship between two (or more) people and both cannot have power in the same area of behaviour. It is a non-reciprocal phenomenon: the superior says T and receives V. Freud spoke of kings, employers, and priests as father figures and reversed the terminology and this derives from the fact that an individual learning a European language reverses the historical order of semantic generalization. The individual's first experience of subordination to power and of the reverential V comes in his relationship to his parents. Later in his life similar asymmetrical power relations and similar norms of address develop between employer and employee, and soldier and officer. Freud believed that later social relationships would remind the individual of the family prototype and revive responses and feelings from childhood. In the person's history recipients of the non-reciprocal V are parent figures. The non-reciprocal power semantic only prescribes usage between superior and inferior and it calls for a social structure in which there are unique positions in the power structure for every individual. There was never only a single rule for the use of T and V in medieval Europe because society was not so finely structured. For members of a common class (people of roughly equivalent power) there were norms of address which were reciprocal. In the medieval period and later equals of the upper classes exchanged the mutual V and equals of the lower classes exchanged T. For many centuries in Europe usage followed the rule of non-reciprocal T and V between people of unequal power and the rule of mutual V or T between persons of roughly equivalent power. Very gradually a distinction developed in address between equals, sometimes called the T of intimacy and the V of formality.

It is possible that a single relationship will involve a conflict between the two dimensions of power and familiarity. Factors relevant to the choice to emphasize one aspect of the relationship rather than one another can be examined. In a West European family, for example, considerations of solidarity and familiarity would argue for mutual T among all members, but power differences between parents and children would suggest the use of T down and V up in the generations. Brown and Ford (1961) worked out semantic rules governing address in American English. They found that the most common address forms are the first name (FN) and the title plus last name (TLN). These function in three sorts of patterns in dyadic interaction: the mutual TLN; the mutual FN; and the non-reciprocal use of TLN and FN. The semantic distinction between the two mutual patterns is on the intimacy dimension with mutual FN being the more intimate of the two patterns. In changing from mutual TLN to FN it is the person of higher status who generally takes the initiative. The superior does this because the willingness of the person of lower status to enter into association can be taken for granted and there is little risk that a superior will be rebuffed. Thus each new step towards friendship is initiated by the person of higher status. To find a framework for describing of one person can act as an independent variable affecting the structure of an encounter. But changing settings, participants, message forms, and topics can all modify verbal behaviour. Work on restricted channels of communication in small problem-solving groups shows their interdependence. If communication channels change, other things being equal, patterns of interaction and role relationships change. If role relationships change then patterns of interaction change (Leavitt 1951).

Social Order, Meaning and Language

Developing the discussion of the use of language I want to review work on its relationships with meaning and social order, and to refer again to socialization. The so-called 'problem' of social order is often regarded as the central problem of sociology. One approach to the analysis of social control emphasizes the way in which society has a body of rules or norms of behaviour which have moral significance. This tradition emphasizes the consensual nature of much social behaviour. Social control is seen as a result of inter-related social institutions and ideas like socialization, social system, and authority. It refers to the fact that each person generally takes into account the expectations of others and not so much deliberate influence or coercion. These ideas of social control are challenged on the grounds that they are too simple and the idea of socialization requires investigation. This leads into the second tradition which emphasizes the disruption and lack of harmony in capitalist societies. It owes a great deal to Marx. Conflict and competition continuously make for instability and change. Social control is achieved by coercion and the exercise of power. The notion of socialization is often regarded as almost the only key to the understanding of social order (less attention is then given to social control). Socialization may be thought of as the complex processes through which individuals become social beings. It is important to note that emotional involvement plays an important part in socialization and that it is related to identity and the self-image. Man thus seems to construct his own social situations through social interaction and uses these created situations as standards for future action and, in turn, to train others to observe them. Where there are rules and norms there is deviance. In order to explain why men conform it is necessary to know those circumstances that make the difference between complying with rules and not complying, and this also applies to explaining why men do not conform. If not contained deviance is a threat to orderliness and to organization. But deviance should not be identified with social disorganization: in some circumstances it may aid efficiency. Deviant behaviour is behaviour that violates rules but like most definitions this one conceals some ambiguities. Social control refers to anything people do that is socially defined as 'doing something about deviance'.

Deviance may be conceived of as being created by society as we have seen earlier. In America and Britain emphasis is placed on social status and financial success. However opportunities to achieve these goals are not available to all people equally. The legitimate means to 'success' not being available people have to choose what to do. Most people will conform, trying to pursue success by legitimate means. But some members of society may resort to illicit methods while other people may 'opt out' and retreat from society; they have been unable or unwilling to succeed either by legitimate or illegitimate means. Deviation may take many forms. Some people become inflexible bureaucrats (ritualists or people who abandon the pursuit of success but insist on 'going through the motions' and regard the rules as sacred). Such people may not be regarded as deviant by others. People who become drug addicts on the other hand (retreatists) may be so identified and become subjects for treatment. Other rebels may attract very severe sanctions: the political dissident puts his life at risk.

Another view focuses on the reaction of society towards certain activities which are regarded as deviant. Societies create deviance by making those rules the infraction of which constitutes deviance. The question remains of why people who have been socialized deviate. And, again, there is considerable disagreement among members of society about who shall be considered a deviant. It brings us to the question of power. In a pluralist society it is found that certain groups have more power than others and will be able to impose their definitions of what is deviant upon other groups. In modern societies the task of rule enforcement is given to certain agencies, for example judges and policemen.

Not all the knowledge in society has the same status or equal validity. There are often firm controls over who gains access to different types of knowledge. Members of a community have to pass through certain rites of passage if they aspire to enter certain occupations, for example, passing examinations to obtain licences to practise a profession. Various kinds of objective knowledge become appropriate as thought and are expressed in language. Various professional groups in society and agencies of law enforcement are relevant to the control and distribution of knowledge, as are various government departments, commercial organizations, and welfare agencies. The members of these organizations have particular cultures which are more or less legitimized in society. Ideology is another very general term and is concerned with the influence that ideas have on social organization. It refers to a pattern of ideas which are said to explain and legitimate the social structure and culture of a particular group or society and which serves to justify social actions. An ideology often helps to integrate an individual's perception of social experience and his conception of his social world.

This processing and control of knowledge by particular groups and the development of ways of dealing with laymen and the power to manage the realities of others are all questions to do with the use of language. Language maintains control in social relationships. For example Laing (1971:43-6) discusses the psychiatric label 'schizophrenia' and suggests that the control established by doctors using it may be so total as to remove all power from the patient to see his own reality as valid. The approach to understanding social life described above sees reality not in a reified sense but as being produced by psychological and social processes. A central idea is that 'everyday consciousness' is reified: in using language people take for granted the reality which language structures and preserves. Many of the most significant aspects of language and social reality lead one to reconsider many ideas about social life which are taken for granted

(Hayakawa 1968:107-10). It is not novel to suggest that the cal continuity of society and social order rest largely on the vation of knowledge through language. Social order is defined all embracing frame of reference in a society that its members as social reality. Through social order objects, persons, and events are identified, arranged, and interpreted so as to give them meaning and thereby convey to people a firm sense of the way things are.

The term meaning has a central place in interactionist sociology. The notion implies significance, an interpretation of a situation, act, or idea and how to respond to it. Meaning is established only when the response elicited by some symbol is the same for the one who produces the symbol as for the one who receives it. Meanings are socially structured and socially transmitted. They derive from society, its institutions and language. They change through the process of social interaction by which men modify, change and transform social meanings. Words have meanings because of interpretations placed on them by social behaviour. Language is socially built and maintained and in acquiring it the structured ways of a group are acquired. Behaviour and perception, logic and thought come within the control of a system of language. Along with language people acquire a set of social norms and values. By using language we experience the world in a particularly ordered way. Language can be seen as the imposition of order upon experience. It imposes differentiation and structure on the continuing flux of experience. Further, language provides a fundamental order of relationships by the addition of syntax and grammar to vocabulary. It is not possible to use language without participating in its order (Berger 1967:20-1).

At this point it is relevant to discuss some aspects of symbolic interaction theory, with particular reference to social order. Duncan (1968:70-1) has pointed to the symbolic environment and how people can be stimulated to action by it as well as by stimuli from the physical environment. A symbol is a stimulus that has a learned meaning so that, for example, a chair means an object to sit on. A symbol also has value which is the learned attraction or repulsion people feel towards the meaning. Practically all symbols are learned through communication with other people and by this means it is possible to learn meanings and values from other people. Duncan discusses sociological 'explanations' of social order and says that if they are in purely environmental terms ('conditions', 'forces', or 'equilibrium') they are like explanations of the action of a play by its stage setting or of the playing of a game by the shape of the playing field. Nature may be outside human perception, or subject to immutable laws which we can know yet cannot change, but in so far as we communicate about nature we do so through symbols which we do create and do change. This does not make nature and symbols the same: having a baby is not at all like writing a book about the experience. But as we symbolize nature we make it a scene or stage on which we enact the drama of social order. The environment is symbolic and we act in and through symbolization of the environment and the laws which are symbolic as well as physical and biological. A symbol is something that refers to or represents something else. A sign, by contrast, indicates the presence of something. Language is full of symbols but signs are also often used that are not strictly descriptive. They include abbreviations, trade marks, or badges for example. Meaningless in themselves they acquire recognizable meaning through common usage. Briefly a sign is a construct by which one organism affects the behaviour or state of another through communication. A symbol is regarded by general consent as typifying or representing or recalling something by possession of analogous qualities or by association in fact or thought. What is called a symbol is a term or name or a picture that may be familiar but possesses specific connotations in addition to its conventional and obvious meaning. Thus a word or image is symbolic when it implies something more than its obvious and immediate meaning.

When we communicate about our environment we are acting in the realm of symbols and it is necessary to understand the laws of symbols as well as the laws of nature. We select stimuli which will provide the response needed (or felt to be needed) to provide order in our relationships. We see our environment in certain ways because we want to do certain things in it: it is an object of perception organized through symbolic forms. We are stimulated by hunger or aggression and also by our attitudes towards these stimuli. In so far as perception arises in communication it occurs within an act which contains a stimulus and an attitude towards this stimulus. Attitudes arise in imagining the result of responses. This imagery may be drawn either from the past or the future. Social relations are analysed on the basis of various theories of knowledge about society. Thus, for example, it is said that a social system depends on the extent to which it can keep the equilibrium of the personality systems from varying beyond certain limits so that the causes of social relations are seen in forms of association or the class struggle. Or it is said that social relations depend on 'good' or 'effective' communication and language comes to be seen as the final 'cause' of social integration. Belief in any kind of social legitimation leads easily to an elevated, ideal view of those ends for example 'social systems maintain themselves'. When we appeal to reason as a way to social order we assume that people are capable of reason and will follow it if and when they 'understand' it. Grounds for such a faith are no more demonstrable than any other supernatural beliefs. Health practitioners of all kinds link themselves with symbols of authority such as white coats for doctors and uniforms for different ranks of nurses. Different social groups have different kinds of illnesses, for example malnutrition means hunger in one society or relative poverty in another. Different occupations have different health hazards. As the efficiency of industrial production increases boredom sets in and monotony has a deleterious effect: the thinking of an individual is impaired, his emotional responses become childish, and his visual perception may be disturbed. Neuroses and some psychoses may be the result of malfunctioning in a group rather than a characteristic of pathologically isolated patients.

Social meanings arise in moments in which a symbol means what it does to the self because of what it means to the other. The self and the other are bound by a third element, the symbol, whose meaning in turn depends on the possibility of reciprocal responses of actor and audience. Rules cannot be secret: they have to be shared and it is their clarity which characterizes their use in social relations. The learning of rules is obviously an important aspect of socialization. Play in childhood is one early way in which experience of rules is gained. Throughout the life cycle without experience in conduct guided by rules the concept of self cannot develop because it is through rules that voluntary and free selves find characteristic expression of their freedom. In playing in a game or acting in a drama the child learns his part and also learns to assume how others will play theirs. His actions are controlled by his ability to take the part of others who are playing with him. Rules are the means by which we organize the attitudes of those involved in the same process. We 'internalize' social roles through arousing in ourselves the response we arouse in others. The forms of expression used by the self (words, gestures, and so on) are experienced by the actor as they are by his audience. Difficulties in human relationships (i.e. dis-order) originate in communication rather than being merely reflected in it. Thus if new forms of communication cannot be created or if traditional forms cannot be modified so as to adjust to social change it is not possible to reach agreement about united action. When differences between people become so great that symbols no longer possess a common meaning then they turn to leaders who can create new symbols of community. Everyday social difficulties begin in role conflict among many public roles, which constitute community life. Relationships between men depend on the sharing of meanings which are the same both for actor and audience. Symbols of love can be replaced by symbols of hate and individually or in groups people are integrated as much through hatred (of a common enemy) as through love. Social order depends on integrative symbols.

To summarize the principal points discussed above it is worth reiterating that it is impossible to talk about human relationships without some reference to meaning which is usually studied through the interpretation of symbols. Only in this way can meaning be observed. A symbol is a thing regarded by general consent as naturally typifying, representing, or recalling something by pos-session of analogous qualities or by association in fact or thought. It is taken as the conventional sign of some object, idea, or process. It makes little sense to say that symbols are abstractions which have no reality but reflect or point to reality or that they are contained within a self and cannot be observed. Symbols of social order are not private and subjective. They are used because they are public: they represent the thinking or ideas of a community. This is Duncan's (1968:3-8) argument which he prefaces with the obser-vation that American sociologists tend to confuse the symbolic and the subjective. According to this view values are merely the projec-tion of people's desires and feelings. Sociologists are also subjects of a 'trained incapacity' in the use of non-mechanistic models and thus think poorly about communication. A basic proposition is that all we know about the meaning of what happened or is happening in a social relationship is what someone says about its meaning. 'Saying' involves many different kinds of communication. Interpretation of what forces are beyond symbols still have to be interpretations of symbols. If we allow that the manifest content of a dream is not its real meaning we have to show how the real meaning can be reached by using symbols. In saying that there is some reality in relationships 'beyond' symbols we are still bound by symbols in our report of the operations of 'extra-symbolic' phenomena. This is illustrated in our communications about our environment from which we select stimuli which meet the need to have order in our relationships, while symbols of order provide further stimuli in organizing perception and communication. 'Explanations' of social order in purely environmental terms do not take into account its symbolic laws as well as physical and biological laws. Supposing that social systems maintain 'equilibrium' or that people are (potentially) capable of acting according to reason are articles of faith: they cannot be 'proved' or 'demonstrated'. Symbols of authority are needed to maintain order or to 'cure' disorder in its many forms. Health practitioners illustrate this, and some forms of disease may result from social malfunctioning rather than being a characteristic response by the patient. Selves are defined in relation to others: they are bound by symbols the meaning of which in turn depends on reciprocity between actor and audience. Rules are published and have to be clear: they cannot be secret. Their learning occurs in different ways and without them the concepts of self cannot develop. Rules are the means by which the attitudes of people in groups may be organized. Social roles are internalized as the expectations of others are learned. Throughout the life cycle the concept of self cannot develop without experience of conduct guided by rules. Social order depends on integrative symbols. Difficulties in relationships (dis-order) originate in failures in communication.

Communication and Control

Norbert Weiner (1968:18) classed communication and control together. Society, he said, can only be understood through a study of the messages and the communication facilities which belong to it. There are different techniques with which to attack the problems of control and communication: their study is neither new nor trivial. When one person communicates with another he sends a message to him. When he responds he sends a related message which contains information primarily accessible to him and not to the first person. When one person controls the actions of another he sends a message to him (in the imperative mood) and the technique of communication in this case does not differ from that of a message of fact. If control is to be effective the 'controller' must take note of messages from the other person indicating that the order is understood. The commands through which control over the environment is exercised are a kind of information imparted to it. Like any form of information these commands are subject to disorganization in transit: they generally come through in less coherent fashion and certainly not more coherently than they were sent. The implication is that control and communication systems are always attempting to counteract the tendency to distortion of messages, that is the tendency to disorganize and to destroy meaning. (In communication theory these tendencies are known as entropy — the average uncertainty as to what the source of communication will produce next.) The field of study is largely concerned with the limits of communication between individuals. Information is the name for the content of what is exchanged as processes of adjustment facilitate adaptation to the environment. Living effectively involves living with adequate information. Communication and control are essential to the human being's inner life as well as to his social life. This is effectively demonstrated by the results of work on influences affecting formal communication.

Miller (1963:185-86) pointed out that various constraints are found in formal communication and some are inherent in spoken language. He referred to these constraints as contextual and as operating on the sequence of symbols. Grammatical habits (and he implied no judgement of good or bad grammar) are made in the same way as association connections which reflect relatively unstructured verbal habits. In controlled as distinct from free association a person's response is restricted not only by a verbal stimulus but also by specific instructions the sender may give about the message. Referring to experimental findings Miller said that it could be shown that the verbal context influenced the choice of reaction word even when subjects were not explicitly told to choose their responses from a limited set. The detailed research reported has, I believe, the following implications. The words used at any given time determine, to a greater or lesser extent, the words that will be used next. Words do not occur in a random way but follow certain sequences and the context indicates which word may follow which in an utterance. Some contexts place great constraints on the freedom to choose which words will be used. The degree to which freedom is reduced can be determined from knowledge of the relative frequency with which various word sequences occur in a given language. This enables an individual to estimate the information that is provided by the context about the next item. When that item (or bit of information) occurs, some of the information it provides is the same information as that which had already been supplied by the preceding context. The part of the information conveyed by the word that had been available before the word occurred, is, in a sense, redundant. A moderate amount of redundancy in verbal communication is useful as it increases the chances that errors occurring in transmission or reception will be corrected; there would be no need for verbal redundancy as an aid to understanding if errors did not occur, but they occur by accident sometimes, for example because of lack of attention. Excessive redundancy is, of course, wasteful, but this is not to deny that some degree of redundancy, as stated above, is useful.

In the process of development the individual learns to adapt to the physical environment (to obtain what he wants and to avoid what he dislikes) by interpreting as signals the input of information. The process is amplified by the experience of human communication — the use of words instructing, cajoling, persuading, or threatening the individual. A small selected fraction of this input is admitted. But, as Vickers (1972:73-4) puts it: 'even so my intake of experience from then on was to come far more in the symbolic form of words ... and these words were to mould my ways of receiving and interpreting experience so that even the simplest biological facts of life such as the needs for food, activity, repose and sex, were given meanings and values which they could not otherwise have had.' He points out that no communication has any meaning except in conjunction with the setting of the receiving apparatus. Talking and listening set in motion a process which magnifies the individual's experience of relationships but also defines the ways in which the individual *should* experience it (my italics). The language the individual learns contains an implicit order. Nouns provide categories with which to distinguish objects, events, and relationships, adjectives describe their qualities while verbs describe their actions and the individual's reactions. In this way language powerfully conditions the kinds of order which can be distinguished and conceived. It helps the individual to order his experience in his own particular way. An important aspect of learning, often given less importance than learning to manipulate the environment and to conceptualize experience, is how to evaluate action and to assess the truth of propositions. This field of valuation, it is argued, is a field of learning. It is necessary to have standards which are accepted in a social group as the norm, so that people are able to select their responses from a repertory by the use of rules which determine what is suitable to what occasion. The processes involved are complicated but regulation is neither possible nor meaningful except in relation to the norm — the setting which the system tries to maintain. Traditional societies could take their settings for granted. Cultural change, currently, is threatening: its rate may have become disruptive and this may be seen in symptoms of alienation. But political pressures and fears call for rates of change which cannot be attained, and this leads to defensive reactions on the part of groups and individuals. Vickers (1970:178-79) argues that those who fought for *individual* freedom from arbitrary executive power had not experienced the *social* responsibility that success would bring. This is one reason why competing ideologies give rise to considerable public concern. All fields of activity have their own stability to protect and communication (and hence cooperation) depends on shared appreciative systems, ways of valuing, and systematic organization which may have to change considerably before a new equilibrium is approached. Some synthesis, for example between the physical, biological, and social sciences seems to be required. The problem is to achieve control in a multiplicity of conflicting value systems. Such views, controversial as they are, are important both in discussing the context of uncertainty in which social work is carried on, and in looking at the controversies and dilemmas within social work itself.

There seems to be a general and understandable tendency to assume that social life *is* in equilibrium. Sometimes this assumption seems valid: it appears to be confirmed by observation. It also satisfies the need (seen in natural science) to find rational 'explanations'. This tendency may well appear in this book and I make no apology if it does although I do feel it necessary to recognize the more dynamic, interactionist view. The concepts of dynamism, systems, and paradigms are useful and will appear either specifically or as theories. The opposite assumption, that human social life and behaviour are continually in flux is threatening, as was indicated earlier, but seems to be of particular relevance in the study of social work practice, as well as organizations, as it was used by Warham (1977). To be realistic social institutions (and relationships) whether they are a social service, a system of local government, or a profession are best understood as constantly changing. Because such phenomena are dynamic it is not possible to state exactly what they are like. It is an illusion, for example, to see social policy only as making an inroad on a problem. There are dynamic aspects to policy such that it expands a problem, changes it, and generates further problems (Glazer in Weinberger 1974:254). The second point is that as well as perceiving social institutions as processes they are also considered as systems or sets of inter-connected parts. This is helpful in its reminder that the various aspects of social life are not self-contained. Third, Warham used the concept of paradigms as a way of ordering ideas and as an explanation of the ways in which ideas apparently organize themselves.

Because paradigms are a means of ordering ideas and an explanation of how ideas seem to organize themselves, they may take different forms. For example a paradigm of social work may be to take it as a professional occupation. There may be different paradigms of social work in an organizational context. This would be just one mental representation of the thing one is attempting to describe. No one paradigm is ever totally comprehensive, nor can it ever be conclusive since the state of knowledge is always changing. In this sense a paradigm is an achievement in the development of knowledge. Paradigms replace existing ideas and are themselves replaced. An earlier study by Nokes (1967) also placed emphasis on inter-connections in the fields of 'knowledge' and experience. To assume that convictions are one thing and science quite another, he argued, has no cogency in studying social life. Such an assertion invites attempts to dispense altogether with the scientific ethic. The observer necessarily has a unique status in his society and his perceptions and notions of truth are inevitably partial. But it is not a consequence of the sociology of knowledge that one assertion is as good as any other nor that the force with which a view is put forward contributes somehow to its validity. This warning, it seems to me, remains important many years after it was made, since it seems that social scientists may misuse the sociology of knowledge in the way Nokes suggests, particularly in considering different and often conflicting welfare ideologies. It has been argued that to understand procedures in a Social Work Department it is important to pay particular attention to the sets of meanings (referred to as ideologies) which professional social workers themselves assign to their work. Accounts of professional ideologies are multi-dimensional and may be distinguished in terms of the unit of need, the cause of need and the assessor of need (Smith and Harris 1972). Several issues seem to be raised. If professional people use their roles to exert authority and power in certain ways they may be regarded as part of the apparatus of social control. This leads us to consider wider political and social issues again. It seems to me that one of the most important aspects of social change during the twentieth century has been the technological advance of communications which, although it increases the possibility and the scale of conflict and accelerates the tendency, clearly demonstrates the desirability of resolving differences because of the basic desire for unity among human beings. We now have to take up again the question of the dilemmas this raises for members of helping professions and social workers in particular.

7 The Social Worker's Dilemma: Concern for the Individual and for the Welfare of the Community

This chapter deals with the political and wider social implications of the social worker's role. Two social work ideologies are to be examined. They express distinct views of the nature of human beings and their relationship with each other. One ideology takes a personal or individual perspective and works towards social change through reform. It affirms that social and political change is desirable in ameliorating social distress and recognizes that in some circumstances this is urgent. But it seeks to improve conditions by developing responsible, caring services. The other ideology regards this affirmation as failing to deal with basic causes of social distress and as supporting an inadequate social system. This ideology takes a global view and works towards revolutionary change. It is suggested that there is a conflict for social workers inherent in these different ideologies, one of which emphasizes obligations on a personal level while the other calls for more broadly based community action. This chapter therefore relates to the earlier ones about clients and social workers and is based on an analysis of relevant literature. It concludes with arguments for a modified form of the first ideology referred to above.

Social Control: Persuasion and Coercion

Social control was seen earlier to have a central place in sociological analysis. In general it is the means by which social behaviour in groups or society is conditioned or restrained so as to maintain those groups or society. The functionalist approach in sociology emphasizes the consensual nature of social functioning. In this approach social control refers not so much to deliberate influence or coercion but to the fact that each person generally takes into account the expectations that he imputes to others. However, direct enforcement of formal laws is sometimes required. Basically social control, we have seen, takes the following forms.

SOCIALIZATION

As children develop, the family, the education system, and religious institutions teach them the norms of their culture. The standards that are inculcated help to regulate social behaviour within culturally desirable patterns.

DIRECT BEHAVIOUR CONTROL

The formal laws of society define the limits of behaviour and are supported by the power of the police.

RESOCIALIZATION

Social, penal, and medical services are established to help solve social problems and to assist individuals in difficulty.

The alternative approach to that of the functionalists emphasizes that conflict and competition continually lead to social instability and change. Social control is achieved by coercion and the exercise of power by dominant groups in society. Controls affect individual behaviour through the application of sanctions. Valued behaviour is rewarded and negatively valued behaviour is punished. Social control is then seen to be functional for only the dominant groups in society and a consensus of values is ruled out. Social problems are produced because the goals men strive for are not equally available for all.

One of the study probation officers, who completed the postal questionnaire, discussed the probation officer's role conflict as he saw it and the conflict model of society. His comments illustrate a view of social work as currently conservative but potentially a force for change. He agreed with the way the probation officer in the illustration perceived the task. He said that 'the above illustrates the dual nature of probation in that while wishing 'to assist the individual client one must also remember that the community must be protected. This particular case is fairly clear cut and the probation officer is much less likely to experience feelings of conflict or guilt about being an agent of social control.' From his standpoint this respondent said that a Goffmanesque analysis would be useful. The probation officer acted in certain ways 'on stage' in court, playing out his part as servant of the court. 'Thus conflict is rationalized or explained away as one justifies avoidance of confrontation' (with the largely property-owning, middle-class magistracy) 'as being in the client's interest... The issue of social work ideology would need a lengthy essay ... while it is humanitarian it is basically conservative. One would like to see a new ideology with a political base directed towards changes in the community and in the ways in which deviancy is perceived and defined. As social work ideology is basically conservative and designed to assist clients to find their way back to the socially acceptable status quo with the aid of a social worker there is not perhaps much real conflict between the above. The conflict arises with the realization that social work is perhaps a mere palliative – the answers must be sought in the political arena ... one doesn't like court but it must be worse for some clients as whither they go I go too.' This probation officer (CQSW in his early thirties) found it difficult to comment about limits: 'one is not always aware of consciously setting limits ... one may set limits for some clients (in the immature and psychopathic categories) and not for others. Even the limits imposed by the Probation Order are flexible depending on the individual concerned and his difficulties and the probation officer's interpretation of them.' Sustaining supportive relationships are provided for people like those shown in the questionnaire illustration, for people with unsatisfactory socio-sexual relationships and recidivists. It was this officer who said that probation as a punishment would 'suit the middle-class offenders who are used to buying and bribing their way through life and who have consequently lost respect for mankind'. The general purpose of probation was to provide social work 'treatment' for the probationers. Occasionally it was to provide supervision of probationers, i.e. to control or limit probationer's behaviour.

The Conflict Model

Marxist sociology provides the basic theory of conflict and continuous development which is seen as endemic in society (Leonard 1966:24-31). For Marx their economic power gave the wealthy the authoritative control which enabled them to coerce political power

(Marx and Engels 1970:90-1). The classes have different interests at stake which they seek to promote and defend (although the class struggle itself is only one manifestation of change and conflict). Because they occupy different positions in the productive system, the classes come into conflict with each other. The class which owns the means of production is able to secure the surplus product and keep other classes in subordinate positions. The exploited class, however, does not inevitably resist, or even question the ruling class's right to rule.

Class consciousness develops in part because the antagonistic parties engage in struggle, and find themselves lining up with different allies on different sides. They come to know who is friend, and who is enemy, in action. People tend to associate socially with members of their own class which has its own characteristic outlook and sets of ideas about the world. Class is therefore not simply an 'economic phenomenon', but a social one. It permeates all areas of social life. Power, wealth, religious and social prestige, and culturally distinctive ways of life tend to cohere and to form a different nation — a 'culture of class' — for each social class. But the 'weight' of each of these various attributes is not equal, for it was the position of a person in a system of production that was the factor that Marx saw as under-pinning all his other relationships. The 'mode of production' in a society — the way it organizes labour and capital, men and instruments to produce goods — is the foundation or basis on which are built the other major institutions of social life.

Marx did not say that the antagonistic classes had to come into open and direct conflict. They may be objectively in conflict but subjectively lack consciousness. Marx's theory was not simple economic determinism. For the classes the *objective* situation of having a common position in the production system needed complementing by *subjective* class consciousness of their common interests before they could fully become a class. Marx's theory is not an 'objective' theory of class, because for him, a class could never become fully a class without this interplay between their subjective consciousness and their objective life-circumstances which he called a 'dialectical' interplay. Subjective consciousness is not an automatic concomitant of exploitation; it is something that develops and emerges over time. Poor people have been very passive throughout history.

For Marx, the relationship between economic power and political power was clear; the capitalists were not simply an *owning* class; they were a *ruling* class too. Their decisive control over the key type of property (capital) was the basis for control over the society's political life, whether parliamentary democracy existed or not. In the economic sphere they would push production towards its technical limits and were thus agents of economic progress. But when the productive capacity of a state came into contradiction with the owner's interests they would become regressive. They would not give up their wealth and power easily and would have to be removed by revolution (Marx and Engels 1970:103-05).

It has been suggested that the majority of social workers have a consensus view of society, accepting that the norms and values of the capitalist system are acceptable or tolerable with certain modifications. People who are not able to cope within the system have some personal failings and the social worker's role is to help the client to come to terms with *his* problems and become re-integrated in society. It is further suggested that this model of society was strengthened by the psychological ideas that have been incorporated into social work. It has been argued that the conflict model is a more appropriate one. A society which operates for the benefit of the rulers to the detriment of the working class is bound to create problems. Social workers' clients are casualties of a capitalist system which is dominated by profit and property owning rather than the real needs of the people. The solution would be to change the system, but relatively few social workers agree with these ideas. But it seems obvious that the social worker should be a revolutionary (Kincaid 1975:10-11). Halmos (1974) observed that counsellors (and he included caseworkers and psycho-therapists) had become targets for moral and political criticism and condemnation. They were charged with deserting their professional principles of concern because their preoccupation with counselling distracted attention from the situational miseries of their clients. Counselling was a subterfuge and confidence trick to persuade others to seek non-political solutions to their politically inflicted miseries. The implications of the conflict approach for social work are briefly that people in the non-dominant and/or alienated groups who come into conflict with the wider society are termed mal-adjusted, deviant, or abnormal, and therefore the object of social work. Social work is seen as a method by which society can ensure that underprivileged individuals are manipulated and adjust to their social position.

It is necessary to recognize the fundamental difference between the consensus and conflict models. The two positions appear at first to be irreconcilable; both rest on a basic set of assumptions about social relationships and both are thus based on particular 'visions' of society in their extreme versions which have been discussed here. In practice both perspectives provide useful insights into social life and caution students not to decide simply and arbitrarily to emphasize the elements of conflict in society or vice versa. Perhaps the differences have been exaggerated.

The Consensus Model

The consensus approach does not provide a completely satisfactory account of deviance in society. One problem is that a wide range of activities are characterized as deviant and different members of society have different views about what constitutes deviant behaviour. From another point of view society creates deviance by making those rules the infraction of which constitutes deviance and by applying those rules to particular people and labelling them as outsiders. Thus deviance is seen not as a quality of the act the person commits but rather a consequence of the application by others of rules and sanctions to an offender. The deviant is the 'offender'. The deviant is one to whom that label has successfully been applied; 'deviant' behaviour is behaviour that people label 'deviant' (Becker 1963:91). This approach emphasizes the important part played by social reaction to deviant behaviour and raises questions about how it interacts with the deviant's conception of himself. Deviance and conformity both seem to be problematic. The approach does not concern itself so much with the motivation of the offender. It seems to assume that some people who are labelled 'deviant' are so labelled as a result of, to them, quite ordinary activities. Another important contribution of the 'labelling' approach is the way in which it indicates that there is considerable disagreement about who shall be considered deviant. This leads to the notion that instead of assuming that society has a set of shared values, it is safer to assume that there is a plurality of norms and values. Before returning to this point it is necessary to refer to conformity and socialization, as the means by which people learn about values and share some of them thus contributing to social stability. The consensus model however,

does not provide a completely satisfactory account of dev
we have already noted.

The following simple account of socialization does not, of
imply that rules are never broken or that the rules do not cha
is always possible for deviant activities to be stronger than social
control mechanisms. This account cannot be extended too far.
Society is made up of a variety of people engaging in diverse activities which cannot be fitted together by common rules. Most social
activities are governed by rules which are implicit and unstated and
people are often unable to say what the rules they are following
are; the rules of grammar in speech is an example. One reason why
they (or we) do not think of ourselves as following or obeying rules
is because through the process of socialization the rules have become
internalized and made a part of ourselves. From this point of view
conforming conduct is to be understood within the context of
collective life; we learn the rules from others and we share them
with others. It is assumed then that people accept the legitimacy of
the rules and will conform to them unless there is some kind of
pressure on them to deviate. The problem then becomes identifying
the special kinds of motivation which characterize the deviant.
However, this simple assumption that there are situations where
ideas of agreed values, shared norms, and social control mechanisms
apply is open to question; it does not apply well to complex
societies where there are specialized and varied agencies of social
control.

Social control as a process then has to be seen as an independent
variable and not simply as a social reflex action. In attempting to
understand the working of rules in society it cannot be assumed that
they are seen in the same way by everyone. It is necessary to try to
see how they apply to individuals. It cannot be assumed that
common rules or sanctions are applicable to a variety of people
engaging in diverse activities. What is considered to be appropriate
and correct behaviour varies from group to group. This emphasis
on a plurality of norms raises questions about power. Some groups
in society have more power than others. Are they then able to
impose their definitions of rule-breaking on others? Can they effectively make rules for others? If social welfare agencies have social
control functions how are they exercised? To whom are agencies of
social control responsible? These questions will be dealt with now.
First the question of coercion and persuasion as methods of control

will be considered in relation to psychoanalytic theory and then the question of social work and social control.

Two other concepts are usually related to social control. Persuasion and coercion are associated with feelings of powerlessness as the person faces the agencies of modern society — public bodies, business firms, and the mass media for example. Themes such as persuasion, manipulation, and coercion are well represented in modern art and the newspapers. Persuasive and coercive messages are also relayed by individuals but there are difficulties in assessing the effects of mass communication or interpersonal messages. Many of the difficulties are due to different assumptions people make about power and authority relationships, and their legitimacy or otherwise. One individual feels 'coerced' by the system while another regards pressures and strains as an inevitable feature of contemporary life. However it is interesting to question whether people can be compelled by the application of force or psychological pressure to act against their inclinations or their will or their conscience. This issue is highlighted in a dramatic way when we focus attention on phenomena such as 'brainwashing' or torture. What has always interested observers is whether every person has a 'breaking point'. It is a matter of physical endurance or psychic strength that enables some individuals to hold out when subjected to extreme duress. Inevitably such considerations raise questions of moral responsibility, for, when we say a person has been coerced, we assert or imply that there was no choice open to him and thus he was not accountable for his own actions. Not everyone is inclined to accept coercion as a mitigating or extenuating circumstance. For example Szasz (1965:49) accuses lawyers and psychiatrists of diminishing personal responsibility and impairing human dignity through their use of the insanity plea.

There are many ways in which the individual is shaped and moulded by biological, psychological, and social forces. Sometimes, however, the person or those around him may seek to undo the results of prior experience and socialization. The impetus to change the individual may spring from sinister motives or from humanitarian impulses; the effect may be initiated by the person himself, it may occur with his full knowledge and cooperation, or it may be imposed upon him.

What is implied in the two concepts of persuasion and coercion is the conscious application of force or pressure upon an individual and some degree of resistance to this pressure. Some form of communication or interaction between the parties concerned is also taken for granted. For our purposes, we need not assume a radical dichotomy between persuasion and coercion, but rather can consider them to be part of a continuum of influence processes. At present, as we have seen, a satisfactory theoretical framework is lacking and social scientists have to resort to a set of empirical dimensions for categorizing influence processes. A somewhat arbitrary way of circumscribing these processes is based to a large extent on social usage as in the following scheme.

(1) The *amount of pressure* exerted upon the recipient.
(2) The *nature of the agent or agency* exerting the pressure (e.g. its relationship to the recipient; whether its power base is legitimate or legal).
(3) The *nature of the pressure*; whether it is psychological or physical.
(4) The *outcome* or pay-off expected by the pressurizing agent.

Using this set of headings, one may distinguish persuasion from coercion chiefly in terms of the amount and type of pressure being exerted. Thus, persuasion shall be taken to refer to efforts to induce beliefs or actions through arguments, pleading, or urging. Implicit in this statement is the idea that the persuader must rely on moral or psychological pressure or the force of logic to attain his goal. Furthermore, persuasion would seem to be best characterized as a gradual process (rather than an all-or-none event) which can be seen as proceeding through steps or stages; presentation, attention, comprehension, yielding, retention, and, eventually, overt behaviour or attitude change. Finally, the persuader may be seeking behavioural conformity or inner psychological change or both.

Coercion, on the other hand, is used to designate situations where the agent is able, by virtue of his power base, to exercise restraint, force, or physical control over his victim. This implies that the coercive agent is able to do more than just manipulate information; he is in a position to control the environment or total milieu. Moreover, inherent in the notion of coercion is the imputation of corruption or abuse of power and authority. Finally, the expectation is that the person on the receiving end of the coercive pressure will 'give way' or obey the stronger party. The precise dividing line between these two concepts is hazy. There is a very large vocabulary for describing situations of control and influence, and quite often these terms are used interchangeably.

Communication and Values

This leads us to consider language and implicit values and meanings. Szasz suggests that in the social sciences language is not used only descriptively but also promotively, to communicate a moral imperative, i.e. to say not only how things are but also how they ought to be. Looking at the vocabulary used to denote persuasive processes we might order it along a dimension of social acceptability as follows:

> *Education*—persuasion—conversion—seduction—agitation—manipulation—propaganda—indoctrination—subversion—brainwashing—coercion—*torture*.

Taking the ends of the continuum, education is categorized as an acceptable form of influence, while torture is not. While one may not agree with the details of the continuum, the idea that some types of influence are more acceptable than others will probably seem an uncontroversial observation. Whilst accepting that valuation or categorization are fairly universal human tendencies, it is still possible and desirable to become aware of the dimensions and assumptions that underlie our preferences. When we analyse persuasion and coercion, considerations of norms and context are bound to enter into our account in two different ways.

(1) First, the vocabulary we use, which is taken over from the non-technical language of our society, is coloured with moral judgements. To incorporate these words into our speech is to adopt a set of views about right and wrong, good and bad.

(2) Second, to apply this vocabulary we need a set of rules and these rules are bound to reflect the social situation of the user.

The meaning of the words does not exist separately from a social context. Having learned that manipulation or subversion or indoctrination are bad, we then have to acquire the knack of deciding what actions or behaviours belong in these categories. To put it another way, we may all agree that coercion is evil but clash as to whether a particular historical event is or is not coercive (Brown 1963:66-7).

The observations above about persuasion and coercion suggest at least two people in communication — the persuader and the persuaded, or the coercer and the coerced. Another possibility is that a person may try to persuade or coerce him or her self. Learning theorists are interested in self-control achieved through self-reinforcement, delay of gratification, and individuals' personal standards of behaviour (recently discussed, for example, by McLauchlin (1971)). The dynamics of self-persuasion are probably derived from those that govern situations when the influence attempt is initiated from without. The successful persuader generally appeals to his audience's self-interest in an effort to win its attention and cooperation. Getting the audience to begin an internal dialogue may be seen as the first step in a whole chain of internal psychological processes leading to attitudinal or behaviour change. If this analysis is correct then self-persuasion and persuasion by others cannot be distinguished in terms of a passive/active dichotomy. In addition, with self-persuasion, as with other forms of social influence, there is always a possibility that the end result will not be insight, knowledge, or truth, but self-deception or delusion. For instance, it may be convenient for the prejudiced person to persuade himself that members of a minority group are less intelligent or that his neighbourhood is harbouring large numbers of illegal immigrants. Persons with a weight or drink problem frequently convince themselves that they eat or drink very little. Although such attempts at deception may lead to a lack of congruence between beliefs and actual behaviour or social reality which may at times be dysfunctional, there is ample evidence to suggest that it may at the same time help to protect the person from disturbing knowledge about himself. Many such defence mechanisms have been described and studied by psychoanalytic theorists; projection, displacement, denial, rationalization, scapegoating, and repression, to name but a few, all of which serve to ward off or alleviate anxiety. Perhaps what sociologists refer to as 'false consciousness' is a type of self-deception which results in a distorted view of social relations and self interest.

Individual Needs and Wider Community Interests

The tension in social work between concern for individual needs and concern about wider community issues has sometimes been represented as a conflict between sociologist and the caseworker. But this conflict, experienced by individuals as tension within themselves is not confined to social work (Rice 1975). The microist ideology takes an individual perspective and works towards change through reform. The macroist ideology takes the perspective of social or global structure and works towards revolution. The casework perspective focusing on the individual client is said to be inadequate. The social work plan should focus on the family or group. But as the group worker might dismiss individual work the community might decry group work. He broadens the dimension to the local community. But an intervention in one community rebounds on other communities; one is inexorably led to the perspective of society as a whole. Having exposed the limited perspectives of the helping professions some critics conclude their analysis. However, to have a revolution in Britain in the context of an unchanged world would be analogous to continuing casework with a client in an unchanged external situation. To do so deflects effort from larger issues such as the maldistribution of income and social services in the country. This dispute is thus about the level at which social intervention should be made on a spectrum between the micro and the macro. The argument specifically, is about whether social work is treating symptoms or causes.

These issues, however, are not confined to social work. University adult education has been cited as an example. This touches a minority of the population; attempts to further the learning of this minority are sometimes ridiculed. The critic is sure that the effort is wasted, since a few adults encouraged to think more imaginatively can effect insufficient change to justify the educational resources required. As with social work it is alleged that the universities support established institutions and the status quo. The microist-macroist arguments both require acts of faith. The microist may argue that he at least gets on with something practical, while the macroist spends his time despising ad hoc action and espousing theory. It is argued that the microist opts for individual work as a defence against facing and engaging the 'real' issues at the macro level. Busy preoccupation with specific, immediate needs insulates the microist from making the tough analysis of the wider needs on which action is required. By avoiding the wider analysis the microist can deny his responsibility for, and collusion with the system which produces the individual problems he collects. However, the macroist may also be accused of defensiveness; seeing problems in global terms can be a defence against the demands of current individual problems. Also, radical beliefs and progressive views are often conservative in effect; they express an unconscious wish for inaction (Bion 1961:127-28 and 159-60). A Marxist approach to social work practice for example has not yet been formulated in a way that offers new ideas. Marxist social workers, like non-Marxists, try to help individuals to understand their situation in the social structure. Similarly they work with trade unions and seek to initiate collective action with their colleagues. They also share the problem of defining the ultimate aims of social work and they do not explain how the nature of society is to be transformed. Capitalist and communist social systems both have problems resulting from large and complex industrial societies and the relative powerlessness of individuals to influence political and bureaucratic elites.

Returning to the issue of the level of social intervention, experience of this dispute is individual. It consists of conflict at a personal level between specific, immediate demands for action and broader longer terms policies. It is an experience of tension between the ideal and the real, between theory and practice, and between the rights of the individual and the rights of the many. The utopian vision remains elusive. In conclusion Rice (1975) points out that the tension is experienced not only in one's feeling and thinking but also in one's acting. One has duties at both the micro and the macro level. The social worker experiences conflict between his duties as agency professional and as ordinary citizen and such tensions are not easy to handle. There is the responsibility of distinguishing the immoral from the moral compromise and this demands a degree of moral maturity. This is an existential approach which requires rigour and openness. The easier way is to put one's faith in closed ideological blinkers and dodge uncertainty by simply 'knowing', fleeing from the demands of discrimination into arrogant fervour.

Social Workers and Social Action

It has appeared that the weakening of the consensus model and the emergence of the conflict model of society posed dilemmas for social workers in activities related to social control functions. In particular casework came to be seen as a subtle form of brainwashing. Other forms of social work, such as community work, came to be regarded more favourably as it was assumed that in this field social workers were more responsive to community needs. An unduly pessimistic view was taken about supposed threats to the traditions of social work (Munday 1972). It was said that social work students were being exposed to general attacks on traditional beliefs in society. Casework was seen as outmoded and was discredited as a method of dealing with psycho-social problems. Social workers were essentially seen as serving to maintain the capitalist system. The academic material offered to social science and social work students was often depressing and undermined commitment to social work. Social administration exposed the shortcomings of the Welfare State and sociology seemed to teach that the social system was faulty rather than individuals. Social work method, as it took increasing account of sociology was less sure about casework and the trend was more towards militant social action. Psychology, being associated closely with casework, with its concern with individuals and their problems, was highly suspect for that reason. There was a marked decline in social workers' believing that client's problems were clearly intra or inter personal. Sociology teaching on the sociology of education, deviance, and social stratification tended to confirm many students' existing beliefs that the social system was wrong and required radical transformation. The sociology of deviance was particularly challenging to social work students and educators. If society creates deviants for its own purposes social workers, as part of the system of social control, are used to create and amplify deviance rather than try to improve the lot of the deviant.

Deviance and Social Control Agencies

The central place of social control in sociological analysis has been discussed and implications for social work practice have been examined. Two sociological approaches have been distinguished, the functionalist emphasizing consensus in social life and the conflict theory of social change. It has been suggested that most social workers tend to support the existing social order but it does not necessarily follow that the psychological concepts they employ reinforce this ideology. It is not necessarily correct to argue that these social workers fail to see the necessity for social change and reform of the welfare system. Merely to assert that the conflict model is more appropriate for social workers is no more convincing than stating that the opposite view is more appropriate. The handling of deviance in a complex society would seem to be a very complicated area of sociology to which both schools of thought can contribute. How social control operates raises political questions. These certainly have implications for social workers but it is argued that the simple decision to adopt or reject a conflict or consensus model cannot finally dispose of the tensions which inhere in the counsellor's role. Put more strongly one writer has suggested that the personal and political roles of social workers and counsellors are incompatible (Halmos 1974). I believe that this statement goes too far, although it seems realistic to recognize that there is a tension between the political and personal aspects of social work. Halmos' article is helpful in drawing attention to the fact that social workers are not always equally competent or comfortable in their different roles and the article gives clear indications of some of the reasons for this. While it is correct to say that social work performs functions on behalf of the wider social system it is also necessary to recognize that it stands for values and goals which may represent a critique of the system (Heraud 1970:196-99). Revolution is not the only way to achieve change and in human terms it is often a costly way. Change and reform can be achieved by compromise and social work can play a part in achieving this. Certainly the view that social work may be seen as a *totally* political activity is controversial and has been challenged (Lees 1972:96-7). Social workers, it is argued, are often implementing, influencing, and sometimes changing policies that form part of a continuous political process. The special responsibility of social work derives from the nature of the individuals or groups requiring service. In terms of social and political action it would be attractive to offer guidelines but this would be an over-simplification. There is no simple, certain solution to the problems of either the individual or society. But to recognize the political implications of social work underlines an additional area of responsibility.

The paper by Munday seems in some ways to be confused. Although it raised questions about social workers' political commitments and aims they sometimes seemed to be misdirected and sometimes to oversimplify issues. For example, there seemed to be an assumption that Marxists opposed any or all forms of social control and this is not the case. All advanced societies require some form of social control. A second questionable assumption which appears in Munday's paper is that social change initiated by social workers is revolutionary rather than reformist. The wish for change is not necessarily best represented as a threat to the total social system. Quite often the demands for change alluded to are moderate demands about specific social injustices or social problems and they do not necessarily all emanate from political extremists. Another assumption which should be examined is a view which seems to have grown in strength since 1972 when Munday wrote. It is again one which seems to be an oversimplification, namely, that social community action is in total opposition to casework, and that the social worker has to choose between *either* one method *or* the other. There is an alternative perspective which seems more realistic. This is a counter to the view that casework is automatically regarded as politically reactionary and that community action is automatically regarded as subversive and radical. This view, which supports the above argument was put earlier by a senior probation officer, writing in a social work journal, in the following way:

> 'Personal work with the individual is necessary; his problems spring from many causes, some social, some psychological and help for him to live now in this mammon worshipping society is necessary. But alongside this we need . . . to get into social action to try and combat the kind of inequalities and false values that shape the lives of both our clients and ourselves. How is this to be done? Our "sympathy with the one" is not incompatible with "sympathy with the many" but . . . we need to bring some clear thinking to bear on our strategy.'
>
> (Thornborough 1971)

To return to the earlier point about social workers as agents of social control this appears to be an oversimplification because social workers seem increasingly to be expected to exercise control over what to them seem the 'wrong' things, i.e. problems to which a repressive rather than a constructive controlling response is expected. The repressive notion is associated with 'containing' people *irrespective of their needs or aspirations*, for example people living in poor accommodation (as many of the probationers who were interviewed were), or people who seem unable to obtain their rights from Departments of Health and Social Security offices, or people appearing in court on criminal charges but not receiving a custodial sentence. A

number of statutes have contributed to the extension, to an excessive or certainly a marked degree, of social workers' powers and responsibilities. They include the Mental Health Act 1959, the Children
and Young Persons' Acts of 1963 and 1969, the Social Services Act
1970, the Chronically Sick and Disabled Persons Act 1970, and the
Criminal Justice Act of 1972. The recommendations in the Report
of the Advisory Council on the Penal System: Young Adult Offenders 1974, and the White Paper on *Better Services for the Mentally
Ill* all have considerable long-term implications for the social services.
The problem then is not simply that social workers are agents of
social control but the kinds of demands that are made on them and
how decisions are made about *what* values to support and *how* they
are to be supported. One suggestion (Callahan 1972) is that:

> 'in handling the ethical problem of the life sciences, it is quite
> possible that the democratic political method is the best we have
> and all that we should aspire to. It does provide a procedure for
> resolving public disputes and, together with the courts, ways of
> adjudicating conflicting values. If that is the case, then the best
> path to follow would be to attempt to maximize public infor-
> mation and debate, submit vexing issues to the courts and legis-
> lators, and hope for the best.'

Possibly a more arresting answer to the question of who decides and
who ought to decide normative behaviour, is given in the following
quotation:

> 'It is a fact that a few men in the leadership position in the indus-
> trialized nations of the world now have the power to determine
> among themselves, through collaboration or competition, the sur-
> vival or extinction of human civilization ... Given these contem-
> porary facts, it would seem logical that a requirement imposed on
> all power-controlling leaders — and those who aspire to such
> leadership — would be that they accept and use the earliest
> perfected form of psycho-technological, biochemical intervention
> which would assure their positive use of power and reduce or
> block the possibility of their using power destructively ... In
> medicine, physical diseases are controlled through medication.
> Medicines are prescribed by doctors to help the body overcome
> the detrimental effects of bacteria or viruses — or to help the
> organism restore that balance of internal biochemical environ-

ment necessary for health and effectiveness. Medicines are not only used to treat the diseases of individuals, but are also used preventively in the form of vaccines. All medicines are drugs — and all drugs used therapeutically are forms of intervention to influence and control the natural process of disease. Selective and appropriate medication to assure psychological health and moral integrity is now imperative for the survival of human society.'

(Clark 1971)

This view is perturbing since it fails to say how social leaders should carry out the recommendation and it seems unlikely that it would be carried out.

One study (Haurek and Clark 1967) of patterns of interaction of social control agents focused on the integration of the social control system. It located poor integration in control networks related to the ideological split between punitive and welfare orientations. A theory of social control structures was proposed by Stoll (1968) which used a model for the purposes of studying sources of strain in any social control network. These were regarded as the consequence of discrepancies in the ideologies of various social control agents. The model would be used in identifying critical points in the careers of deviants as they are exposed to the ideologies and behaviour of control agents. The ideologies of deviance of control agents shape their modes of treating deviants. The theory, it was claimed, consisted of the sequence of potential agents who manage the deviant. The observation that people judge others partly on the basis of a lay theory of behaviour led theorists such as Mead (1913) and Becker (1953) to develop hypotheses about social control. Such propositions were the basis of Stoll's work. The core concept for the analysis was the social control agents' image of man with respect to their belief about the ability of individuals to control their own destiny. Occupations related to meeting problems of social control were likely to have a formalized ideology of human behaviour on which expression of the occupational role requirements was based. Stated simply the postulate was that theory guided practice. Stoll quoted work in support of this proposition and added that the proposition that causal assumptions would shape social control preferences was part of a more general axiom in sociology that individuals interact with others partly on the basis of expectations as to how people behave. The next postulate was that to the degree that there are contradictions in ideologies of deviance between agents of control and that no institutionalized means for coping with the contradiction exist, there will be strains in the social control network. Third, conflicting ideologies of deviance place the deviant in role strain.

The career of the deviant may be imagined as a progression through a complicated maze with entry and exit points. Agents of social control stand on the paths and assume responsibility for holding or sending on the deviant. These agents would be: (a) agents of detection and surveillance, for example a victim who reports a crime or the policeman who apprehends a suspect; (b) agents of dianosis and disposition who judge the validity of detection agents' assumptions and say how the deviant will be treated; (c) agents of rehabilitation who can assume the individual is deviant and work to return him to a state of taking his place in society in as normal a manner as possible. Two types of discrepancies arise in the control network: (a) lateral discrepancies where more than one agent is present in part of the maze with such agents holding different definitions of the deviant; and (b) longitudinal discrepancies wherever the deviant is exposed to differing definitions of his role as he progresses from one stage to another. One form of lateral discrepancy is in total institutions where custodial and therapeutic staff disagree about the nature of the deviant under treatment. A longitudinal discrepancy occurs when a mentally ill person is diagnosed and referred by a doctor to a restrictive state institution. The number of individuals or roles which meet the three functions in the deviants' career may be one or many. Lawyers, judges, and social workers may be involved in the allocation process. Therapists of various kinds and probation officers serve the rehabilitation process. That numerous individual role players and occupational groups participate in the network suggests the presence of strain in the system. Another distinguishing characteristic of control networks is the degree of consensus about the definition of deviance. The many agents who diagnose and treat physical illness agree that the deviant is not responsible for his disability, and that he is curable and deserves treatment.

A contrast is seen in the ideologies of agents who control crime and contradict one another. The offender, because of his subcultural ideology, denies responsibility. The police define the crime as deliberate defiance of the law. The social worker does not.

The police want to punish the criminal. The social worker wants to treat him while the offender prefers to have no reaction from control agents at all. Role strain appears to be less for the deviant with a physical ailment than it is for some offenders, for example those who come from a subculture which accepts or encourages behaviour involving infringement of the law. This is an over-simplification but norms associated with physical attractiveness are ideals and as Goffman (1968:153) observes almost every-one falls short of them. It would appear to be possible, given the ideologies of different control agents, to predict the way a deviant would be dealt with at any stage in his career. Again by looking at discrepancies in ideologies among control agents it should be possible to locate potential sources of change in the control sys-tem taking into account the interaction between control agents. Does theory guide practice? In applying the model certain em-pirical deviations occur. Is it correct to assume that all occupational groups can be characterized as having a basic ideology? It is not always the case, for example, that there is a single occupational ideology among judges in relation to many kinds of crime. It seems that consensus within an occupation would be least for marginal types of deviance such as mental disorder, sexual offences or ab-normalities, and addictions.

Another reason for lack of consensus in an occupational group as to the nature of deviance would be a function of the occupation itself. Occupational therapists in mental hospitals or prisons will be exposed to conflicting ideologies, for example the custodial versus the therapeutic orientations.

The occupational groups' ideology may prescribe actions not within the agents' opportunities for implementation. In the case of social work excessive bureaucratic demands may obviate the possi-bility of usefully assisting the client. In some cases agencies' demands force social workers to treat the client, contrary to their own convictions, in an impersonal way. It should be noted that the occupations are not closed systems. Particularly at the rehabilitation stage they are often part of a bureaucracy with the occupations forming a status hierarchy. The best theoretical intentions may be led astray in practice whenever the propounded ideology is rhetoric (rather than action), when opportunities to implement theoretical guidelines are not available, or when others involved in managing the deviant must be accommodated. It should be noted too that discrepancies between stated beliefs and practices, if recognized by the deviant may be seen as hypocrisy. In the delinquent's career his perception of social workers, police, and judges as hypocrites nurtures a sense of injustice which further affects his view of delinquent behaviour. A social control agent, a judge, may be swayed by a lawyer's rhetoric in deciding how to sentence a criminal. He may send the man to prison believing that there are facilities for rehabilitation. Strains may then occur. The deviant moves from court to prison only to learn that facilities are not as they were said to be. The judge has placed the criminal in a less rehabilitative situation than say probation might offer. Strains arise when control agents argue about their respective contributions in dealing with a deviant person.

Differences in ideology seem more likely to occur at the rehabilitation stage, since this is the most problematic. They seem least likely at the disposition stage where one agent has the authority to make the final decision. Ideological disagreement at the detection stage has implications for the deviant's entry into the control network. Such disagreements could occur for example between the witness to a crime and the police, or between the family of a mentally ill person and the psychiatrist. The ways in which occupational groups resolve their conflicts have implications for the deviant person's treatment. The most effective changes occur through legislation supported by professional group lobbies. An example is redefinition of sexual offenders so that they are eligible for treatment rather than a custodial sentence. Change sometimes occurs through the adaptations of professional organizations with one another. A compromise ideology may be sought by conflicting agents, or they may just have to agree to disagree. A pluralistic consensus is thus reached based on division of labour, for example between psychiatric nurses and psychologists. The paper by Stoll (1968) is a valuable attempt to integrate knowledge of deviance and social control so as to cut across traditional boundaries. Several advantages may be claimed for this approach. It may be applied to all kinds of deviant behaviour and it provides a dynamic perspective. It provokes questions about the structure and functioning of controls on the system level and also about the effects of the system on individuals.

It has been said that although social workers view social control as an inappropriate function, it can be seen as the *primary* function

of social welfare (Cowger and Atherton 1974).* One is then faced
with the problem of the relationship between the social services and
society. To whom are the providers of social services accountable?
Cowger and Atherton answer that

> 'those who provide social services are accountable to their con-
> stituency — the legislators, the donors and the citizens who
> support agencies and programs, and the consumers who use the
> services. The providers of services are responsible for helping
> people resolve the problems of their lives in ways that permit
> them to get along better in society. This concept is not revol-
> utionary, nor does it need to be. But as soon as one takes this
> position one returns to the original theme: the primary function
> of social welfare is social control. Social workers — and others in
> the helping professions — are free, in most societies at least, to
> define normative behaviour compassionately but are less free to
> espouse values independent of their constituency. The answer
> to the question "Who decides normative behaviour?" is thus
> answered as best it can be within the framework of the constitu-
> ency concerned. Social agencies are funded and chartered to
> achieve certain ends. Social programs are funded and designed
> to attain specific objectives. For example, family agencies are
> expected to strengthen family life. This expectation does not
> impose such a severe limit that the family agency cannot be
> innovative or accepting toward changes that have taken place
> in relations between men and women. However, it is doubtful
> whether a family agency could continue to operate if the staff
> decided that elimination of family life was their mission.'

Cowger and Atherton claim that if the concept of social control
was accepted by social workers as a primary rationale of social
welfare this would lead to better understanding of the aims of
social work:

> 'their constituency would better understand what social workers
> are trying to do. Social control has more honesty and integrity
> than the notion that social services are based on simple altruism

---

*Charles D. Cowger and Charles R. Atherton, 'Social Control: A Rationale for
Social Welfare'. Copyright 1974, National Association of Social Workers, Inc.
Reprinted with permission from *Social Work*, Vol. 19, No. 4 (July 1974),
pp. 456-62.

and goodwill. It is not enough to tell people that social workers' hearts are pure. People are now asking embarrassing questions about the benefits that social services provide and for whom they are provided. No longer are social workers automatically seen as the "good guys in the white hats".

In today's cynical society, altruistic rationales are not marketable. Good intentions are not enough to earn sanction for social welfare programmes. Dependence on altruistic rationales rather than concrete contributions to society may have helped social workers win the sarcastic sobriquets of "do-gooder" and "bleeding heart".

The concept that social control is the primary function of welfare and that social control involves providing constructive services — this is a marketable idea. People can understand being responsible to a constituency. Such a rationale is realistic in the contemporary socio-political arena. Social work could move from idealistic, well-intentioned moralism about the nature of man to rational and pragmatic provision of evidence that social services contribute significantly to society in terms of desired outcomes — for example, less child abuse, fewer family breakdowns, and less class and racial discrimination. Unless the social worker thinks in terms of such specific accomplishments, social work will no longer be sanctioned and funded even at present levels.'

They argue that social and economic situations are constantly changing with new needs continually appearing. If the needs of people adversely affected by change are not met deviance is likely to continue and multiply. Some societies have relied heavily on police power to counter disorder and deviance. Some have relied on social welfare systems although there is not always a firm conviction that this is a satisfactory means of social control in some problem areas, for example drug abuse and juvenile delinquency. They conclude that:

'social workers can contribute significantly to an orderly society by helping to seek and provide remedies or solutions for the dysfunctions in the social and economic system. Their contributions would include helping the poor, minorities, and other disfranchised people participate actively in the social and economic system of the society. This is not to suggest a new thrust for social welfare services. The task of the social services should involve the provision of evidence that the best way to control disorder and deviance in society is by responsive, universal, and flexible social services focused on (1) alleviation of individual problematic behaviour and (2) intervention in the ongoing process of social life. This may be done by direct service to individuals and groups, social change strategies, and planning. As the social services are able to demonstrate that their approach to disorder and deviance is effective, the approach will be more universally sanctioned and provide a viable alternative to the direct behaviour control of police power.'

Although social workers may dislike the idea of making demands on people's behaviour and may not like to think that their work is part of a process to produce social competence for the good of society, when anyone (parent, teacher, doctor, or social worker) sets limits to behaviour according to certain values they are engaging in social control. Psychotherapy is a form of social control in so far as it encourages family members to modify some interactions; when social workers help someone to obtain work or financial assistance their objective is to enable clients to get along better in the social order and they are thus engaging in the process of social control. The problem is not whether social workers are involved in social control as we said earlier but to decide what values to support and how to support them. Considerable deviance by individuals and groups can be tolerated in social systems but various limits have to be defined if society is to survive. Survival depends on a complex system of organization and this demands a degree of conformity in behaviour. Social controls have to operate at some level if certain social values are to be upheld. Social workers are one group among many in society who exercise control functions, but available evidence suggests that they do not accept this role blindly. Provided that social workers are able to maintain vigilance about the demands made of them and what is expected of them, and to use democratic processes to influence and if necessary modify or change these demands they may not be pressured into acting to maintain the status quo. To see social control as *the* primary function of social welfare is to take too restricted a view. The well being and care of individuals, helping them to deal with their needs and difficulties so that they are able to cope more effectively in society, seem to be basic roles but these functions cannot be separated from operating some degree of social control.

We have seen that a number of writers have discussed the question of the social workers' concern for the welfare of the individual and the wellbeing of society or the community. For example it has been argued that when a choice between a society's needs and those of an individual become inevitable for the caseworker he must know which to prefer. This dichotomy between the one and the many in social work was seen to present

> 'so complex a problem that the profession can hardly, so it seems, develop their study of its two roles simultaneously. On the one hand there is the *individual* who, basically, cannot be helped against his real wish ... and on the other hand there is *society*, chiefly embodied in the agency, which is part of the reality of the client's situation even in cases where the issues are mainly psychological.'
>
> (Pollard 1962:8)

This view may be compared with the observations made by Halmos (1965:24-5) that disillusionment with politics was a motive for entering social work and who later doubted if the aims of casework and politics could be combined (Halmos 1978:11-13). I find the argument advanced by Plant originally in 1970 more persuasive: it will be noted that like Pollard he does not regard the dilemma an easy one: 'It will be argued that caseworkers because they are involved in this dual concern need to be very clear about the relationship between the individual and society. The discussion and description of this relationship is, however, far from easy and some of the concepts involved are highly elusive' (Plant 1970:1).

In reviewing the position of social work today it is ironic to recall Halmos's (1965:177-78) view that people became social caseworkers because of disillusionment with politics; they saw casework as non-political but were in fact mistaken about this. While Halmos saw counsellors as the product of a politically disillusioned century he thought that they would eventually desist from saying that political solutions were futile. They would have to become alert to the political avenues of betterment, as soon as they could see that a personal service society would provide more scope for counselling activities. They would not be political cynics or nihilists. Counsellors realized that deficiencies in child care made it imperative to review the social norms of family life, the social and economic circumstances which regulated it, and social institutions which served it. Halmos argued that doing this might eventually lead to a full scale criticism of the social order and structure: 'there are already signs that the initially apolitical counsellor can and will re-awaken his political conscience after a period of counselling work in the field... The withdrawal from politics may lead to a resumption of political activity but this time on a more mature level.' The prophecy turned out to be correct although some might question whether the counselling professionals' re-engagement in the political area has been more 'mature'. But in his last book Halmos (1978:156-59) examined the change in attitudes towards personal and political problems. He set out to justify the view that 'the maintenance of the equilibrium between the personal and the political is fundamental to our social science as well as to the *praxis* of our social life.' He questioned whether it was possible for people concerned with meeting individual needs *and* seeking more widespread alleviation of social distress to combine these two concerns which he saw as divergent. He referred to the 'political offensive against healers, doctors,...caseworkers and others' and said:

> 'From community action H.Q. to senior and faculty common room, the politicizers charge the personalist ideologies with effete indulgence, with dishonest distraction, and last but not least, with being the instruments of reaction. To the personalists, on the other hand, wholesale solutions never amounted to wholesale therapies and in the personalist's heart of hearts the road to nowhere in particular is paved with political intentions.'

Halmos reviewed the ways some revolutionary political thinkers (Paolo Freire and Camillo Torres for example) ventured to personalize the political by stating that true revolutionaries should be motivated by love and appreciate the value of non-directiveness: being a leader involved dialogue and cooperating with others in solving problems rather than instructing them. He was impressed by these proposals for social innovation but regarded it as unlikely that they would be any more acceptable than the arguments of political radicals in their attempts to politicize the personal. For Halmos there is no ecumenical compromise between the faith of the counsellors and the creed of the revolutionaries and no compelling reasons for assuming that there can be. I think it necessary to question the extreme position thus adopted by Halmos who appears to have over-reacted to developments in radical politics from the late

1960s, found (as he commented) particularly in institutions of higher education and in social work radicalism, which threatened the traditionalists and divided the profession, and represented greater impatience with social inequality and political defensiveness or conservatism at local and national levels. As far as social work is concerned there has consequently been a protracted and frustrating debate about the identity of the profession and in what terms its critical state should be considered. The debate has been frustrating and sterile, I think, when ideological positions have not been critically examined and clarified with the result that issues have been exaggerated or distorted or have been introduced into arguments and have then distracted from discussion of fundamental principles. An example is the heated denigration of Freud's thought often regarded as a monolithic and exclusively individualistic system of ideas. Arguments based on these assumptions do not recognize that Freud's thought can be analysed in terms of various models, that it needs to be considered in its social and intellectual context, and that it is more accurately regarded as a set of hypotheses about (family) groups than being *wholly* concerned with the individual psyche. To make these comments is not to suspend critical assessment and thus fail to recognize the theoretical and practical problems and controversies provoked by Freud and his followers. Rather, they ought to stimulate closer consideration of ideological and theoretical perspectives, and investigation of the work done by psychoanalysts since Freud's time. Rogers is one example of a very influential figure whose work has appealed particularly to social workers. A scrutiny of the debate about social work's aims and methods, and an example of the kind of analysis which seems to be productive is to be found in another, recent book. Its authors, Pritchard and Taylor (1978) raise the question whether it is reasonable to argue that social work necessarily has a relationship of continuous tension arising from the conflicting roles of maintaining consensus (and acting as an agent of social control) and on occasions of being involved in conflict and confrontation against authority? I think that it has and that there is a tension which is unavoidable in being a social worker, although some social workers would disagree. It is possible to adopt different stances in looking at the problems involved and it seems to be that most social workers find various ways of dealing with them.

The Continuing Debate

In saying that social workers have emphasized their caring role but
seem to have evaded or played down the issue of control I argue that
this moral dilemma is complex but during the 1970s it steadily came
into greater prominence in public discussion. The debate continues:
this concluding summary aims to take account of some of the complexities that have been discussed already but offers arguments for
reconciling care and control functions in social work, and for seeing
them as complementary. The view which sees social workers princi-
pally as agents of the state who label people as deviants if they are
ill, disabled, or old and consequently non-productive seems to me to
be sinister and misguided. It is a narrow view which does not take
account of the complex nature of social interaction and the
phenomena of deviance. In a society where welfare services were
aimed just at maintaining an economically productive work force
they would be far less important than they are in the welfare state
today. Further, seeing social workers simply as state agents would
appear to ignore the ways the welfare state came into existence. It
has been noted that the welfare state came into existence partly as a
result of the struggle of the working class *against* their exploitation.
This casts doubt on the idea that social welfare is *mainly* a way of
exploiting the working class and ensuring that they remain pro-
ductively servile. It is an oversimplification too, to regard social
workers as having functions similar to those of other state agencies
such as the police or the armed forces. It seems to me more reasonable to compare their roles with those of teachers. This is not
an evasion of the ways in which social workers may be instrumental
in intervening in ways which do involve control — in protecting the
welfare of children, sick or old people and making use of statutory
powers to do this. Nor can the serious implications of the 1959
Mental Health Act for civil liberties be ignored. No other law (except
in very serious emergencies relating to people mentioned above)
places such powerful constraints on the freedom of others and the
social worker shares with patients' relatives and doctors the responsibility for taking such drastic action. Compulsorily admitting a
patient to hospital means being responsible for that individual losing
his personal liberty at least to a large extent. Clearly, as earlier discussion has suggested, such influence or physical coercion conflicts
with an absolute principle of self-determination which social workers

regard as very important. But an *absolute* right to free choice is illusory. As an agent limiting the right to self-determination the social worker is recommending and carrying through compulsory detention procedure because it is required for the patient's own health or safety or for the protection of other people. The argument that our right to self-determination in any social system is absolute is untenable. This view, based on our varied experience of different political and social systems through history, seems to have a fair degree of support in the literature.

If arguments against the conflict view are accepted one is left with an alternative perspective which, it has been pointed out already, has certain deficiencies. Broadly these are that its accounts of deviant behaviour and of social control are incomplete but I do not want to repeat the detailed criticisms. The consensus view sees social work as a benevolent method of social control and this is one of its functions. Its other functions which can complement the control function include the general aims of relieving social distress, and offering material aid and counselling to individuals and families. Another general aim is social reform through pressure on government to implement or change social welfare policy. In discussing the consensus view it is important not to overlook a point made by Cowger and Atherton (1974) which seems to me to be fundamental. Commenting on the way that social workers have tended to view the control function as inappropriate they said that part of the problem lies in the term social control which has become equated with an arbitrary exercise of power by an elitist group. As a sociological term they said that social control 'refers to those processes in a society that support a level of social cohesiveness sufficient for the survival of the society as a recognizable functional unit'. The consensus view then would support these functions of social work within the wider framework of welfare provision, and a cohesive society. In arguing for this view it is essential that social workers continually re-examine their position in relation to the norms or rules governing social life which they are supposed to support (Day 1979). It seems then that an unqualified argument for the consensus view is not satisfactory and among questions it does not resolve (and *neither* of the views I am discussing could resolve them) are how satisfactory or adequate the performance of the care function is and whether control is exercised over the 'right' things and in a 'proper' way. During its history social work has had as one of its central concerns the welfare of individuals and families and, since the family (including the single parent-child unit) is a primary source of socialization social workers' involvement here clearly relates to the socializing function. This is a wide spectrum and one part of it, mental health work, has been mentioned. In that field as well as in the care and control of children and older people the distinctions between voluntary and compulsory intervention are blurred.

The situation is complicated when we consider as an example the social worker's dilemma in helping children in trouble and/or regarded by courts or social agencies as needing care and control. The dilemma needs to be seen against the background of approaches to deviant behaviour. The welfare or treatment approach to deviant behaviour described earlier involves seeing the social unit (the family or other group) as the environment to which the child (or adult) is able to adapt or in which he or she 'fails' to cope or conform. Deviant behaviour is then regarded as a symptom of disorder in the person and his situation which needs attention: this contrasts with deviant behaviour as *freely* chosen. If delinquent behaviour is seen in this way the treatment recommended by the legal institutions of the state (the court for example) will not be based on an idea of retribution and punishment but on rehabilitation of the individual so that he is reinstated in his community. This philosophy has been vigorously attacked, notably by right-wing supporters of 'law and order' who seek wider use of punitive measures. They adhere to the so-called justice model.

'The justice approach explains crime as freely chosen action against the rule of law. The primary purpose ... is to detect wrong doing and to punish the offender so that the public are protected and the rule of law reinstated. It is however, equally important that innocent people shall not be wrongly convicted and the emphasis within the criminal approach is upon the finding of guilt... Once a person has been convicted the justice approach holds that the proper determinants of his sentence will be the need to deter him and others from future offences of this kind and the need to express the vengeance and retribution of society.' (Parsloe 1976)

Parsloe discussed ways 'in which the social worker may ensure that the balance between justice and welfare does not tip too far towards welfare in the juvenile justice and parole systems and so endanger not only the welfare approach but possibly the system itself.' She said that the social worker needed to be aware of the justice approach, and an attitude of mind which would help to overcome human reluctance to control the exercise of one's own discretion. She noted the tendency of the literature to deal largely with voluntary relationships, and argued that confining, structuring, and checking discretion is not the same as abolishing it: it is to prevent it becoming arbitrary and thus to devalue individuals. Clearly social workers wish to express their recognition of the worth of the individual and his particular and unique place in his community: this is a view shared by many other citizens, and of course, it has a long history in its support. The needs and contributions of individuals in an increasingly complex and dangerous world, in which control and all the authoritarian values apparently become more necessary if anarchy and destruction are to be avoided, were assessed in the inaugural series of the BBC Reith Lectures. Bertrand Russell said:

> 'a community needs if it is to prosper, a certain number of individuals who do not wholly conform to the general type. Practically all progress...has depended upon such individuals who have been a decisive factor in the transition from barbarism to civilization. If a community is to make progress, it needs exceptional individuals whose activities though useful are not of a sort that ought to be general. There is always a tendency in highly organized society for the activities of such individuals to be unduly hampered, but, on the other hand, if the community exercises no control, the same kind of individual initiative which may produce a valuable innovator may also produce a criminal. The problem like all those with which we are concerned is one of balance: too little liberty brings stagnation, and too much brings chaos.'
>
> (Russell 1949:37)

Returning now to the other set of problems, namely the adequate performance of the caring function, discussion focuses on the question of resources. This may be related to what has just been said about the welfare model. Facilities may well be inadequate to offer the rehabilitative help which a person seems to need. Social work staff resources may be inadequate to provide intensive help for a family at home. Or, to take a common example, a teenager may be admitted to an adult ward in a psychiatric hospital, because of inadequate specialist facilities for the therapy he requires. The field of mental handicap and psychiatric illness exhibits problems of inadequate resources for care *and* control only too clearly. From the point of view of the conflict model attempts to remedy these material deficiencies, as well as the legal framework, are seen merely as cosmetic measures aimed at concealing unwillingness to take radical remedial action. The consensus theorist is regarded as colluding with these evasions. He would argue that militant action could be counter productive and, while agreeing about the need for change, he would argue that consistent moral pressure and non-violent political action, in conjunction with help for individuals and families, would be preferable on moral grounds. To leave the argument there may first appear to be unsatisfactory and frustrating. I claim that this represents the position in day-to-day practice. These dilemmas *are* frustrating and it is difficult to live with the uncertainties associated with them. If they adopt the modified consensus position which has been advocated here social workers might well be opting for a more difficult and uncomfortable stance than that of the workers whose actions are more militant and overtly divisive. It comes down in the end, not to adopting an allegedly weak and morally ambiguous approach: it is my belief that seeking out personal meanings and attempting continual careful analytical scrutiny of different ideologies or accounts of social reality, and subjecting forms of social intervention to moral evaluation is to *recognize* conflict. Further intellectual recognition and emotional accommodation where it is possible are ways of maintaining an essential honesty in communication about care and control. If there is self-deception and lack of integrity towards others then the social work enterprise becomes intellectually disgusting and morally and politically reprehensible: with greater openness, healthy debate, and compromise the potential strength of consensus is realized.

Appendix

The information about the views of probationers and probation officers was obtained by using a schedule of questions to guide the interviews with probationers and a similar questionnaire to be completed by the probation officers for each client. A different questionnaire was sent by post to thirty probation officers and twenty-six replies were received. The probationers who were asked to help in the study were approached at the time of referral in the first place and then forty probationers who had been on probation for between one year and eighteen months were asked to help.

Topics in the Schedule for Probationers

(1) The charge made against the probationer and whether he regarded it as valid.

(2) Previous charges and their outcome.

(3) Reasons probationer thought the court placed him on probation.

(4) Things he thought he required help with and how much they bothered him.

(5) Whether he thought probation was intended to help him and in what ways.

(6) How he felt about being placed on probation.

(7) His description of his probation officer and his relationship with him.

(8) His ideas about whether his probation officer helped him to make decisions and how: by giving direct advice or by talking things over.

(9) His views on how strict or how easy going he thought the probation officer was, and whether he was friendly.

(10) His views on what in general the purpose of probation was.

Topics in the Schedule for Probation Officers

The subjects of the questions to the probationers were raised with the probation officers in a different form, e.g. they were asked why the probationer thought he placed on probation, and whether he thought it was intended to help him and so on. The probationer officers were also asked for their own views, e.g. whether they had influenced the probationer and in what ways, whether they thought themselves strict or easy going, and for their views on the purpose of probation. Further they were asked how they differentiated among probationers in order to give appropriate help (the 'typology' used is indicated in the text). In addition they were asked about their experience since training, the form of their training, and their age group.

The Postal Questionnaire

The imaginary case history which was used is given in Chapter Three, which describes the probation officers' orientations. In addition to questions about this case history the officers were asked about the following subjects.

(1) Their views on the purpose of probation.
(2) Whether they perceived a conflict between their court duties and professional social work ideology.
(3) If they saw a conflict and if so how they dealt with it; (a) for themselves; and (b) with their clients if they were asked about it.
(4) Like the other probation officers they were asked about their age brackets, experience, and form of training.

Other Methods of Obtaining Information

It was particularly helpful to have less formal conversations with probation officers in the different offices. This happened quite frequently, for example, when probationers failed to come to see their probation officer and/or for their interviews about the project. In a similar way probationers expressed interest in the project, and talked informally about their experience of the penal system and the police as well as probation itself. Some men for example, while agreeing with the rehabilitative ideal, said that in their own cases they would have preferred punishments in the form of a fine instead of having the extended obligation entailed in probation. This comment was made only by two men but illustrates something of the value of these less formal aspects of the meetings. The other case material, suitably disguised, was obtained through direct requests to Social Service Departments, with the explanations of its use as illustration.

References

Abraham, J.H. (1977) *The Origins and Growth of Sociology.* Harmondsworth: Penguin.

Allport, G.W. (1969) *Pattern and Growth in Personality.* New York: Holt, Rinehart and Winston.

Apter, D. (ed.) (1964) *Ideology and Discontent.* New York: Free Press.

Arblaster, A. (1974) *Academic Freedom.* Harmondsworth: Penguin.

Aron, R. (1968) *Main Currents in Sociological Thought.* Vol. 1. Harmondsworth: Penguin.

Bailey, R. and Brake, M. (1975) *Radical Social Work.* London: Edward Arnold.

Bandura, A. and Walters, R.H. (1963) *Social Learning and Personality Development.* New York: Holt, Rinehart and Winston. Quoted in D. Jehu (1967) *Learning Theory and Social Work.* London: Routledge and Kegan Paul.

Barker, E.N. (1975) Communicating and Attaining Knowledge in Psychology. In H. Brown and R. Stevens (eds) (1975) *Social Behaviour and Experience.* London: Hodder and Stoughton.

Barker, R. (1963) On the Nature of the Environment. *Journal of Social Issues* **19** (4).

Becker, H.S. (1953) Becoming a Marihuana User. *American Journal of Sociology* **59**:577-602.

—— (1963) *Outsiders: Studies in the Sociology of Deviance.* Glencoe: Free Press.

—— (ed.) (1964) *The Other Side: Perspectives on Deviance.* Glencoe: Free Press.

Berger, P.L. (1966) *Invitation to Sociology.* Harmondsworth: Penguin.

—— (1967) *The Social Reality of Religion.* London: Faber & Faber.

——— (1971) *A Rumour of Angels*. Harmondsworth: Penguin.

Berger, P.L., Berger, B., and Kellner, H. (1974) *The Homeless Mind*. Harmondworth: Penguin.

Berne, E. (1968) *Games People Play*. Harmondsworth: Penguin.

Bion, W.R. (1961) *Experiences in Groups*. London: Tavistock Publications.

Blackburn, R. (ed.) (1976) *Ideology in Social Science*. Glasgow: Fontana — Collins.

Blau, P. and Scott, W. (1963) *Formal Organizations*. London: Routledge and Kegan Paul.

Bloom, M. (1975) *The Paradox of Helping*. New York: John Wiley and Sons.

Bolton, C. and Kammeyer, K. (1968) The Decision to Use a Family Agency. *The Family Co-ordinator* 17:52.

Bottomore, T.B. and Rubel, M. (1963) *Karl Marx: Selected Writings in Sociology and Social Philosophy*. Harmondsworth: Penguin.

Brenton, M. (1978) Worker Participation and the Social Service Agency. *British Journal of Social Work* 3 (2):209-27.

British Association of Social Workers (1973) *The Inalienable Element in Social Work*. Discussion Paper No. 3. London.

Brown, J.A.C. (1963) *Techniques of Persuasion*. Harmondsworth: Penguin.

Brown, R.G.S. (1975) *The Management of Welfare*. Glasgow: Fontana — Collins.

Brown, R. and Ford, M. (1961) Address in American English. *Journal of Abnormal and Social Psychology* 62:375-85.

Brown, R. and Gilman, A. (1960) The Pronouns of Power and Solidarity. In P.P. Giglioli (ed.) (1972) *Language and Social Context*. Harmondsworth: Penguin.

Butrym, Z. (1968) *Medical Social Work in Action*. London: Bell.

Callahan, D. (1972) Normative Ethics and Public Morality in the Life Sciences. *Humanist* 32:5.

Casement, P.J. (1970) The Setting of Limits: A Belief in Growth. In B. Butler (ed.) *The Voice of the Social Worker*. London: Bookstall Publications.

Cicourel, A.V. (1964) *Method and Measurement in Sociology*. London: Collier Macmillan.

Clark, K. (1971) The Pathos of Power: a Psychological Perspective. *American Psychologist* 26:1056-057.

Cloward, A. and Ohlin, L. (1960) *Delinquency and Opportunity*.

Glencoe: Free Press.

Coates, K. and Silburn, R. (1970) *Poverty: The Forgotten Englishmen*. Harmondsworth: Penguin.

Cohen, A. (1971) Consumer View: Retarded Mothers and the Social Services. *Social Work Today* 1 (12).

Cohen, A.K. (1955) *Delinquent Boys*. Glencoe: Free Press.

—— (1966) *Deviance and Control*. Englewood Cliffs, New Jersey: Prentice Hall.

Cowger, C.D. and Atherton, C.R. (1974) Social Control: a Rationale for Social Welfare. *Social Work* 19: 456-62.

Davison, E. (1965) *Social Casework*. London: Bailliere, Tindall and Cox.

Dawtry, F. (1957) Whither Probation? *British Journal of Delinquency* 8:180-87.

Day, P.R. (1966) The Influence of the Academic Setting on Social Work Students' Learning. *Social Work* 23 (4).

—— (1968) Communication and Social Work Roles. *Case Conference* 15 (6).

—— (1970) Communication in Social Work. Thesis for the degree of Master of Philosophy. Nottingham: The University. Unpublished.

—— (1972) Aspects of Learning and Probation Treatment. *Probation* 18 (1).

—— (1976) Probation and the Concept of Social Learning. *Social Work Today* 8 (12).

—— (1979) Care and Control: A Social Work Dilemma. *Social Policy and Administration* 13 (3).

Day, P.R. and Eyden, J. (1973) Perspectives on Privacy. *Social Work Today* 4 (7).

Day, P.R., Rhodes, V., and Truefitt, T. (1968) Priorities and an Area Team. *Social Work Today* 10 (7).

Duncan, H. *Symbols in Society*. New York: Oxford University Press.

Durkheim, E. (1897) What Is a Social Fact? In H. Brown and R. Stevens (eds) (1975) *Social Behaviour and Experience*. London: Hodder and Stoughton.

Edwards, B.H. (1975) Changes and Differences in the Educational Attitudes of College of Education Students. Thesis for the degree of Doctor of Philosophy. Nottingham: The University. Unpublished.

Erikson, E. (1965) *Childhood and Society*. Harmondsworth: Penguin.

Etzioni, A. (1964) *Modern Organizations*. Englewood Cliffs, New Jersey: Prentice Hall.

—— (ed.) (1969) *The Semi-Professions and Their Organization: Teachers, Nurses and Social Workers*. New York: Free Press.

Finlayson, D.S. and Cohen, L. (1967) The Teacher's Role: a Comparative Study of the Conceptions of College of Education Students and Head Teachers. *British Journal of Educational Psychology* 37:22-31.

Fitzjohn, J. (1974) An Interactionist View of the Social Work Interview. *British Journal of Social Work* 4 (4).

Folkard, M.S., Lyon, K., Carver, M., and O'Leary, E. (1967) *Probation Research: A Preliminary Report*. Home Office. London: HMSO.

Folkard, M.S., Fowles, A.J., McWilliams, B.C., McWilliams, W., Smith, D.D., Smith, D.E., and Walmsley, G.R. (1974) *IMPACT: Intensive Matched Probation and After Care Treatment*. Home Office Research Studies Vol. 1. London: HMSO.

Folkard, M.S., Smith, D.E. and Smith, D.D. (1976) *IMPACT*. Home Office Research Studies Vol. 2. London: HMSO.

Foren, R. and Bailey, R. (1968) *Authority in Social Casework*. Oxford: Pergamon Press.

Fortes, M. and Evans Pritchard, E.E. (1940) *African Political Systems*. Oxford: Oxford University Press.

Fowler, D. (1975) Ends and Means. In H. Jones (ed.) (1975) *Towards a New Social Work*. London: Routledge and Kegan Paul.

French, J.R.P. and Raven, B. (1959) in *Studies of Social Power*. Ann Arbor: University of Michigan; Institute for Social Research.

Geertz, C. (1964) Ideology as a Cultural System. In D. Apter (ed.) *Ideology and Discontent*. New York: Free Press.

Glastonbury, B. (1975) The Social Worker: 'Cannon Fodder' in the Age of Admin.? *Social Work Today* 6 (10).

Glastonbury, B., Burdett, M. and Austen, R. (1973) Community Perceptions and the Personal Social Services. *Policy and Politics* 1 (3):194.

Glazer, N. (1974) The Limits of Social Policy. In P. Weinberger (ed.) (1974) *Perspectives on Social Welfare*. New York: Macmillan.

Goffman, E. (1968) *Stigma*. Harmondsworth: Penguin.

—— (1969) *The Presentation of Self in Everyday Life*. Harmondsworth: Penguin.

Goldstein, H. (1973) *Social Work Practice: A Unitary Approach*.

Columbia: University of South Carolina Press.

Gould, T. and Kenyon, J. (eds) (1972) *Stories from the Dole Queue*. London: Temple Smith.

Gouldner, A. (1954) *Patterns of Industrial Bureaucracy*. New York: Free Press.

Gravett, S.M. (1973) *Consumer Research Survey*. Chester: Cheshire County Council, Social Services Department.

Haines, J. (1975) *Skills and Methods in Social Work*. London: Constable.

Hall, A.S. (1974) *The Point of Entry*. London: Allen and Unwin.

Halmos, P. (1965) *The Faith of the Counsellors*. London: Constable.

—— (1974) The Personal and the Political. *British Journal of Guidance and Counselling* 2 (2).

—— (1978) *The Personal and the Political*. London: Hutchinson.

Handler, J.F. (1968) The Coercive Children's Officer. *New Society*, 3rd October:485-87.

—— (1973) *The Coercive Social Worker*. Chicago: Rand McNally.

Hardiker, P. (1977) Social Work Ideologies in the Probation Service. *British Journal of Social Work* 7 (2):131-54.

Hart, J. (1977) The Caseworker in the Organization. *Social Work Today* 8 (41).

Haurek, E.W. and Clark, J.P. (1967) Variants of Integration of Social Control Agencies. *Social Problems* 15:46-60.

Hayakawa, S.I. (1968) *Language in Thought and Action*. London: Allen and Unwin.

Heraud, B. (1970) *Sociology and Social Work*. Oxford: Pergamon Press.

Home Office (1962) *Report of the Departmental Committee on the Probation Service*. Cmnd. 1650 (Morison Report). London: HMSO.

Horowitz, I. and Liebowitz, M. (1968) Social Deviance and Political Marginality: Towards a Redefinition of the Relation between Sociology and Politics. *Social Problems* 15 (3):280.

Howe, D. (1979) Agency Function and Social Work Principles. *British Journal of Social Work* 9 (1):29-45.

Hugman, B. (1977) *Act Natural*. London: Bedford Square Press.

Irvine, E. (1956) Transference and Reality in the Casework Relationship. *British Journal of Psychiatric Social Work* 3 (4).

Israel, J. (1972) Stipulations and Construction in the Social Sciences. In J. Israel and H. Tajfel (eds) (1972) *The Context of*

Social Psychology: A Critical Assessment. London: Academic Press.

Jahoda, M. (1959) Conformity and Independence — a Psychological Analysis. *Human Relations* 12:99-120.

Jehu, D. (1967) *Learning Theory and Social Work.* London: Routledge and Kegan Paul.

Johnson, T.J. (1972) *Professions and Power.* London: Macmillan.

Jordan, W. (1970) *Client-Worker Transactions.* London: Routledge and Kegan Paul.

Kincaid, J.C. (1975) *Poverty and Equality in Britain.* Harmondsworth: Penguin.

Kluckjohn, C. and Murray, H. (1953) Personality Formation: the Determinants. In C. Kluckholn, H. Murray, and D. Schneider (eds) *Personality in Nature, Society and Culture.* New York: Alfred Knopf.

Kogan, L.S., Hunt, J.M., and Bartelme, P.F. (1953) *A Follow-Up Study of the Results of Social Casework.* New York: Family Service Association of America.

Kuhn, M (1962) The Interview and the Professional Relationship. In A.M. Rose (ed.) (1962) *Human Behaviour and Social Processes.* London: Routledge and Kegan Paul.

Laing, R.D. (1971) *The Politics of the Family.* London: Tavistock Publications.

Land, H. (1969) *Large Families in London.* London: Bell.

Leavitt, H.J. (1951) Some Effects of Certain Communication Patterns on Group Performance. *Journal of Abnormal and Social Psychology* 46:38-50.

Lees, R. (1972) *Politics and Social Work.* London: Routledge and Kegan Paul.

Leonard, P. (1965) Social Control, Class Values and Social Work Practice. *Social Work* 22 (4).

—— (1966) *Sociology in Social Work.* London: Routledge and Kegan Paul.

Lipset, S.M. (1963) Working-Class Authoritarianism. In S.M. Lipset (ed.) *Political Man: The Social Bases of Politics.* New York: Anchor Books.

London, P. (1969) *Behaviour Control.* New York: Harper and Row.

Luckmann, B. (1970) The Small Life Worlds of Modern Man. *Social Research* 37:580-96.

Lutz, W.A. (1964) Marital Incompatibility. In N.A. Cohen (ed.)

(1964) *Social Work and Social Problems*. New York: National Association of Social Workers.

Lyman, S.M. and Scott, M.B. (1970) *A Sociology of the Absurd*. New York: Appleton, Century Crofts.

Lynch, B. (1976) The Probation Officer as Employee. *Probation Journal* 23 (2).

McBroom, E. Socialization and Social Casework. In R.W. Roberts and R.H. Nee (eds) (1970) *Theories of Social Casework*. Chicago: University of Chicago Press.

McCall, G.J. and Simmons, J.L. (1966) *Identities and Interactions*. New York: Free Press.

McDermot, F. (ed.) (1975)   *Self Determination in Social Work*. London: Routledge and Kegan Paul.

McEachern, A.W. (ed.) (1961) *Views of Authority: Probationers and Probation Officers*. Los Angeles: Youth Studies Centre, University of Southern California.

McGuire, W.J. (1973) Persuasion Resistance and Attitude Change. In I. de Sola Pool *et al. Handbook of Communications*. Chicago: Rand McNally.

McKay, A., Goldberg, E.M., and Fruin, D.F. (1973) Consumers and a Social Services Department. *Social Work Today* 14 (16):486-91.

McLauchlin, B. (1971) *Learning and Social Behaviour*. New York: Free Press.

Marsden, D. (1969) *Mothers Alone: Poverty and the Fatherless Family*. Harmondsworth: Allen Lane.

Marshall, T.H. (1972) Value Problems of Welfare Capitalism. *Journal of Social Policy* 1 (1):18-32.

Marx, K. and Engels, F. (introduced by A.J.P. Taylor) (1970) *The Communist Manifesto*. Harmondsworth: Penguin.

Mayer, J.E. and Timms, N. (1970) *The Client Speaks*. London: Routledge and Kegan Paul.

Mead, G.H. (1913) The Psychology of Punitive Justice. *American Journal of Sociology* 23:577-602.

—— (1935) *Mind, Self and Society*. Edited by C.W. Morris. Chicago: University Press.

—— (1964) *On Social Psychology*. Edited by A. Strauss. Chicago: University Press.

Merton, R. (1968) *Social Theory and Social Structure*. Glencoe: Free Press.

Miller, G.A. (1963) *Language and Communication*. New York:

McGraw Hill.

Miller, J.D.B. (1965) *The Nature of Politics*. Harmondsworth: Penguin.

Moffett, J. (1972) *Concepts in Casework Treatment*. London: Routledge and Kegan Paul.

Munday, B. (1972) What Is Happening to Social Work Students? *Social Work Today* 3 (6).

Nisbet, R.A. (1967) *The Sociological Tradition*. London: Heinemann.

Nokes, P. (1967) *The Professional Task in Welfare Practice*. London: Routledge and Kegan Paul.

Parad, H.J. and Miller, R. (1963) *Ego-Oriented Casework*. New York: Family Service Association of America.

Parry, N., Rustin, M., and Satyamurti, C. (1979) *Social Work, Welfare and the State*. London: Edward Arnold.

Parsloe, P. (1976) Social Work and the Justice Model. *British Journal of Social Work* 6 (1):71-89.

Payne, M. (1979) *Power, Authority and Responsibility in Social Services*. London: Macmillan.

Pearce, I. (1976) Differing Perceptions of Interview Behaviour and the Nature of Delinquency. *Social Work Today* 7 (8):246-48.

Pearson, G. (1973) Social Work as the Privatized Solution of Public Ills. *British Journal of Social Work* 3 (2):209-27.

—— (1975) The Politics of Uncertainty: A Study in the Socialization of the Social Worker. In H. Jones (ed.) (1975) *Towards a New Social Work*. London: Routledge and Kegan Paul.

Perlman, H.H. (1968) *Persona. Social Role and Personality*. University of Press.

Phillipson, M. (1971) *Sociological Aspects of Crime and Delinquency*. London: Routledge and Kegan Paul.

Plant, R. (1970) *Social and Moral Theory in Social Casework*. London: Routledge and Kegan Paul.

Pollard, B. (1962) *Social Casework for the State*. London: Pall Mall Press.

Poulantzas, N. (1976) The Problem of the Capitalist State. In R. Blackburn (ed.) (1976) *Ideology in Social Science*. Glasgow: Fontana — Collins.

Pritchard, C. and Taylor, R. (1978) *Social Work: Reform or Revolution?* London: Routledge and Kegan Paul.

Rabinowitz, W. and Rosenbaum, I. (1960) Teaching Experience and

Teachers' Attitudes. *Elementary School Journal* 60:313-19.

Rees, S. (1973) Clients' Perspectives on Social Work Services. Unpublished paper. Aberdeen: The University.

—— (1978) *Social Work Face to Face*. London: Edward Arnold.

Reid, J.W. and Epstein, L. (1972) *Task Centred Casework*. New York: Columbia University Press.

Reid, W. and Shapiro, B. (1969) Client Reactions to Advice. *Social Service Review* 43 (2).

Rice, D. (1975) Of Microists and Macroists. *Social Work Today* 6 (16).

Roberts, R. and Nee, R. (eds) (1970) *Theories of Social Casework*. Chicago: Chicago University Press.

Rogowski, S. (1977) Consensus or Conflict? *Social Work Today* 8 (23).

Rose, A. (ed.) *Human Behaviour and Social Processes: An Interactionist Approach*. London: Routledge and Kegan Paul.

Ross, E. (1969) *Social Control*. Cleveland: Press of Case Western Reserve University. (First published in 1901.)

Rowbottom, R., Hey, A., and Billis, D. (1974) *Social Services Departments: Developing Patterns of Work and Organization*. London: Heinemann.

Russell, B. (1949) *Authority and the Individual*. The Reith Lectures 1948-49. London: Allen and Unwin.

Rycroft, C. (1972) *A Critical Dictionary of Psycho-analysis*. Harmondsworth: Penguin.

Sainsbury, E. (1975) *Social Work with Families*. London: Routledge and Kegan Paul.

Salzberger-Wittenberg, I. (1970) *Psycho-analytic Insight and Relationships*. London: Routledge and Kegan Paul.

Satyamurti, C. (1979) Care and Control in Local Authority Social Work. In N. Parry, M. Rustin and C. Satyamurti (eds) (1979) *Social Work, Welfare and the State*. London: Edward Arnold.

Saville, J. (1975) The Welfare State: An Historical Approach. In E. Butterworth and R. Holman (1975) *Social Welfare in Modern Britain*. Glasgow: Fontana — Collins.

Scheff, T.J. (1969) Negotiating Reality: Notes on Power in the Assessment of Responsibility. *Journal of Social Problems* 16 (1).

Schultz, D. (1971) Psychology: a World with Man Left Out. *Journal of the Theory of Social Behaviour* 1 (2).

Schumacher, E.F. (1977) *A Guide for the Perplexed*. London: Sphere Books.

Scott, R.A. (1969) Professional Employees in a Bureaucratic Structure. In A. Etzioni (ed.) (1969) *The Semi Professions and Their Organization*. New York: Free Press.

Shaw, I. (1976) Consumer Opinion and Social Policy: A Research Review. *Journal of Social Policy* 5 (1).

Simpkin, M. (1979) *Trapped within Welfare: Surviving Social Work*. London: Macmillan.

Smith, D. (1965) Front Line Organization of the State Mental Hospital. *Administrative Science Quarterly* 10:381-99.

Smith, G. (1970) *Social Work and the Sociology of Organizations*. London: Routledge and Kegan Paul.

—— (1977) The Place of Professional Ideology in the Analysis of Social Policy: Some Theoretical Conclusions from a Pilot Study of the Children's Panels. *Sociology Review* 25 (4):843-65.

Smith, G. and Harris, R. (1972) Ideologies of Need and the Organization of Social Work Departments. *British Journal of Social Work* 2 (1).

Stalley, R.F. Determinism and the Principle of Client Self-Determination. In F.E. McDermott (ed.) (1975) *Self-Determination in Social Work*. London: Routledge and Kegan Paul.

Stoll, C.S. (1968) Images of Man and Social Control. *Social Forces* 47 (2).

Szasz, T. (1965) *Psychiatric Justice*. London: Collier-Macmillan.

—— (1970) *Ideology and Insanity*. Harmondsworth: Penguin.

Thibaut, J.W. and Kelly, H.H. (1959) *The Social Psychology of Groups*. New York: Wiley.

Thornborough, P. (1971) Integration not Dichotomy. *Social Work Today* 2 (12).

Timms, N. (1962) The Public and the Social Worker. *Social Work* 19 (1).

—— (1964) *Social Casework*. London: Routledge and Kegan Paul.

Towle, C. (1957) *Common Human Needs*. New York: National Association of Social Workers.

Turner, R.H. (1962) Role Taking: Process versus Conformity. In A.M. Rose (ed.) (1962) *Human Behaviour and Social Processes*. London: Routledge and Kegan Paul.

Tutt, N. (1979) The Nature and Scope of Control. *Social Work Today* **10** (30).

Vickers, G. (1970) *Value Systems and Social Processes*. Harmondsworth: Penguin.

—— (1972) *Freedom in a Rocking Boat*. Harmondsworth: Penguin.

Voelcker, P.M. (1960) Juvenile Courts: The Parents' Point of View. *British Journal of Criminology* **1** (2).

Warham, J. (1977) *An Open Case*. London: Routledge and Kegan Paul.

Weiner, N. (1968) *The Human Use of Human Beings*. London: Sphere Books.

Wolfgang, M., Savitz, L., and Johnston, N. (eds) (1962) *The Sociology of Crime and Delinquency*. New York: John Wiley.

Wright, B.D. and Tuska, S.A. (1968) From Dream to Life in the Psychology of Becoming a Teacher. *School Review* **76**:253-93.

Younghusband, E. (1978) *Social Work in Britain 1950-78*. Two Volumes. London: Allen and Unwin.

Zijderweld, A.C. (1974) *The Abstract Society*. Harmondsworth: Penguin.

Name Index

Subject Index